Aid and Influence

'This powerful critique of aid by a distinguished practitioner cannot be brushed aside. As Browne argues, doubling aid without radical redesign is unlikely to deliver accelerated development. He offers an attractive recipe for reform.'
PAUL COLLIER, PROFESSOR OF ECONOMICS, OXFORD UNIVERSITY

'Stephen Browne provides a radical and original take on a familiar subject, with careful analysis and drawing on a wealth of personal experience ... Readable stuff, destined to make those in the aid business think harder.'
SIR RICHARD JOLLY, INSTITUTE OF DEVELOPMENT STUDIES, SUSSEX

'This book is badly needed. It answers the question on everyone's mind: why has aid often failed to trigger successful development?'
KISHORE MAHBUBANI, DEAN OF LEE KUAN YEW SCHOOL OF PUBLIC POLICY, SINGAPORE

'Stephen Browne takes us back to the early days of development aid, through its evolution into partnership, to the present day ... The book reads very well, is snappy and sharp, and is backed up with real life examples.'
KUNDA DIXIT, EDITOR-IN-CHIEF, *NEPALI TIMES*

'Stephen Browne takes [the aid] story, tests it against many countries and periods and discovers the wide prevalence of aid and influence ... This book deserves a wide readership among students of aid relationships and decision-makers.'
JUST FAALAND, FORMER DIRECTOR, CHRISTIAN MICHELSEN INSTITUTE, NORWAY

'The developing countries – particularly those in Africa – deserve a better deal, not as the passive recipients of aid, but as active participants in a fairer global economy. This book contains some important proposals on how a new deal could be struck, which is beneficial to both South and North.'
DONALD KABERUKA, PRESIDENT OF THE AFRICAN DEVELOPMENT BANK

Aid and Influence

Do Donors Help or Hinder?

Stephen Browne

London • Sterling, VA

First published by Earthscan in the UK and USA in 2006

Reprinted 2007

The views in this book are the author's own and do not necessarily represent those of the United Nations or its governing bodies.

ISBN-10: 1-84407-202-9   paperback
ISBN-13: 978-1-84407-202-6 paperback
ISBN-10: 1-84407-201-0   hardback
ISBN-13: 978-1-84407-201-9 hardback

Typesetting by MapSet Ltd, Gateshead, UK
Printed and bound in the UK by TJ International Ltd, Padstow, Cornwall
Cover design by Yvonne Booth

For a full list of publications please contact:

Earthscan
8–12 Camden High Street
London, NW1 0JH, UK
Tel: +44 (0)20 7387 8558
Fax: +44 (0)20 7387 8998
Email: earthinfo@earthscan.co.uk
Web: **www.earthscan.co.uk**

22883 Quicksilver Drive, Sterling, VA 20166-2012, USA

Earthscan is an imprint of James and James (Science Publishers) Ltd and publishes in association with the International Institute for Environment and Development

A catalogue record for this book is available from the British Library

Library of Congress Cataloging-in-Publication Data:
Browne, Stephen.
 Aid and influence : do donors help or hinder? / Stephen Browne.
   p. cm.
 ISBN-13: 978-1-84407-202-6 (pbk.)
 ISBN-10: 1-84407-202-9 (pbk.)
 ISBN-13: 978-1-84407-201-9 (hardback)
 ISBN-10: 1-84407-201-0 (hardback)
 1. Economic assistance—Political aspects. I. Title.
 HC60.B7338 2006
 327.1'11—dc22

                                                              2006005899

The paper used for this book is FSC-certified and totally chlorine-free. FSC (the Forest Stewardship Council) is an international network to promote responsible management of the world's forests.

Mixed Sources
Product group from well-managed forests and other controlled sources
www.fsc.org Cert no. SGS-COC-2482
© 1996 Forest Stewardship Council
FSC

To Frédérique, Malika, Olivia, Nolan,
Andrew and Mungo

And in fond memory of Hans Singer

Contents

List of Boxes, Figures and Tables

BOXES

FIGURES

TABLES

List of Acronyms and Abbreviations

ACP	African, Caribbean and Pacific
AFESD	Arab Fund for Economic and Social Development
AGFUND	Arab Gulf Programme for United Nations Development Organizations
AMF	Arab Monetary Fund
ASEAN	Association of Southeast Asian Nations
BADEA	Arab Bank for Economic Development in Africa
CAR	Central African Republic
CARE	Center for American Relief in Europe
CFC	chloro-fluorocarbon
CP	civil and political
DAC	Development Assistance Committee
DfID	Department for International Development
DOM/TOMs	départements et térritoires d'outre-mer
EPTA	Expanded Programme of Technical Assistance
ESC	economic, social and cultural
FAA	Foreign Assistance Act
FAO	Food and Agriculture Organization
FTA	free-trade agreement
GATT	General Agreement on Trade and Tariffs
GAVI	Global Alliance for Vaccines and Immunization
GDP	gross domestic product
GFATM	Global Fund for AIDS, Tuberculosis and Malaria
GNI	gross national income
GNP	gross national product
GPG	global public good
HDI	human development index
HIPC	heavily-indebted poor country
HIPCI	Heavily-Indebted Poor Countries Initiative
IBRD	International Bank for Reconstruction and Development
ICAO	International Civil Aviation Organization
ICOR	incremental capital-output ratio
IDA	International Development Association
IDB	Islamic Development Bank
IDCA	International Development Cooperation Agency
IFAD	International Fund for Agricultural Development
ILO	International Labour Organization

IMF	International Monetary Fund
IMR	infant mortality rate
I-PRSP	interim poverty reduction strategy paper
IRO	International Refugee Organization
ITU	International Telecommunication Union
KOICA	Korea International Cooperation Agency
LDC	least developed country
LICUS	low-income countries under stress
MCA	Millennium Challenge Account
MDG	Millennium Development Goal
MEPI	Middle East Partnership Initiative
MFA	ministry of foreign affairs
MTEF	medium-term expenditure framework
NAM	non-aligned movement
NIMBY	not in my back-yard
NLD	National League for Democracy
OA	official assistance
ODA	official development assistance
ODI	Overseas Development Institute
OECD	Organisation for Economic Co-operation and Development
OEEC	Organisation for European Economic Co-operation
OFID	OPEC Fund for International Development
OPEC	Organization of Petroleum Exporting Countries
OXFAM	Oxford Committee for Famine Relief
PEMFAR	public expenditure management and accountability review
PEPFAR	President's Emergency Plan for AIDS Relief
PIU	project implementation unit
PRIDE	poverty reduction in difficult environments
PRSP	Poverty Reduction Strategy Paper
SADC	South Africa Development Community
SAPRIN	Structural Adjustment Participatory Review International Network
SLORC	State Law and Order Restoration Council
SPDC	State Peace and Development Council
SUNFED	Special United Nations Fund for Economic Development
SWAP	sector-wide approach
TA	technical assistance
UAE	United Arab Emirates
UNCDF	United Nations Capital Development Fund
UNCTAD	United Nations Conference on Trade and Development
UNDP	United Nations Development Programme
UNEP	United Nations Environment Programme
UNESCO	United Nations Educational, Scientific and Cultural Organization
UNFPA	United Nations Population Fund
UNHCR	United Nations High Commission for Refugees

UNICEF	United Nations International Children's Emergency Fund (now United Nations Children's Fund)
UNMISET	United Nations Mission of Support in East Timor
UNRRA	United Nations Relief and Rehabilitation Administration
UNTAC	United Nations Transitional Authority for Cambodia
UNTAET	United Nations Transitional Administration in East Timor
UPU	Universal Postal Union
USAID	United States Agency for International Development
WHO	World Health Organization
WTO	World Trade Organization

Preface: An Aid Memoir

We learn most from what we do. Or, as John Locke put it, there is no knowledge beyond experience. Most of what I know about aid comes from my tours of duty for the UN to different parts of the developing world. The experience has been fascinating and enriching. It has taken me to countries of widely different income status; to newly-emerging and newly-deteriorating states; to post- and pre-conflict situations.

The practice of aid-giving always looked troublesome to me. Officially, aid was not generous enough, but at ground level it often seemed too generous. And not just wrongly sized, but wrongly wrought too. How sincere was donorship? Indeed, how sincere were we, the agency personnel, about fighting poverty? We came over as self-righteous, and disappointed in our counterparts. But what gave us that prerogative?

My start was in Thailand. Looking back, I realize how well it was doing, even then. If you had to pick a model developing country, this could be close. Despite halting progress towards open democracy, but because of a remarkable degree of institutional continuity and national self-confidence, it was already cantering ahead into middle-income status. Aid was not a very big part of the development equation, and already in the early 1980s, its visibility was declining. Thailand's canny and diminishing utilization of aid carried some of the first important lessons for what I was to observe later.

I was a young economist in Bangkok – my first adventure in the tropics. I worked in one of the UN's regional commissions, originally set up in the late 1940s to serve as a cooperative forum for the expanding number of independent Asian countries. The analytical work in the secretariat was interesting, although I never discovered how useful it was for the countries of Asia and the Pacific. I was also struck by the degree to which the small number of richer member countries dominated the forums of the commission. They included the former colonial powers – Japan, US, UK, France, Netherlands and the USSR – which had all become important donors to the region and to the commission itself. Their voices were often heard above those of the Asian countries. So while the developing countries had lots they could have agreed on among themselves, much of it critical of rich-country trade policies and Cold War politics, none of this came out in the resolutions, which were mostly anodyne. The donors dominated.

My next stop was Mogadishu, capital of the former state of Somalia. The contrast couldn't have been greater. The president, Siad Barre, was one of those despots who have held Africa back. He claimed to practise a brand of 'scientific socialism', but his agenda did not apparently include education, health, infrastructure and the other virtues of development, in spite of the fact that Somalia received more aid per head than almost any other country in the world at the time. We donors played an uneven role. When I was there, in the mid-1980s, school enrolment and literacy were falling steadily. UNICEF was the main reason there was any primary education to speak of. But there was also a huge project funded by a bilateral donor to support the National University, where the courses were all in a European language, taught by professors from the donor country on six-month tours. There was a willing rotation, because the salaries were much higher than at home.

In Somalia, I also witnessed some of aid's famous discombobulations. I remember a donors' meeting with the national range agency, at which several of us discovered that we had each appointed the same civil servant as our national project director, to whom we were each paying a full salary.

It was an unseemly juxtaposition of substantial aid and no development. Donor interest in Somalia was sustained by the ideological balancing act of the Cold War. It had been in the Soviet sphere, but after the Soviet-supported Ethiopian army attacked it in 1977, it ran to the willing arms of the West. In 1989, after I had left, the country disintegrated and it became even more of a humanitarian basket-case. Relief has continued, but during the 1990s, Somalia's strategic significance declined to zero and the donors mostly turned their backs (as we shall see in Chapter 5). Today, there is a revival of interest in the country because of its potential to become a new international terrorist haven.

I also spent time in Ukraine, and that experience is reflected in the book too. I was part of the first eager wave of foreign missions to the country in 1992, but although we tried to exert our influence, I think we all felt by the end of our assignments that we hadn't really made much beneficial difference. Ukraine was one of the largest countries to come to independence, and it did so with virtually no experience of the outside world from which it had been previously cut off. Its banks hadn't even handled foreign currency. For Ukrainians to extricate themselves from three generations of isolating communism was unlikely to occur within a few years. It meant changing mindsets, and as Chapter 3 describes it, while most of the Soviet republics were ready to accede to regional statehood, there was limited interest in markets and democracy, which seemed to be delivering steady impoverishment. Humanitarian aid did help sustain people during this transitional nightmare, but technical assistance was mostly premature and thus unproductive.

In Rwanda, the story of the 1994 genocide was mingled with the role of the powerful countries and their agencies which, as everyone now admits, was mostly an ignominious one. Chapter 5 talks of the 'awful probability of complicity or oblivion' and probably both. When I arrived there in 1998, most of the UN was still held in low regard by the government. I was supposed to straddle the humanitarian and development mandates of the UN at a time when all aid was steadily diminishing. There were, besides, nagging questions of probity all across the aid picture. I also saw at first hand another lingering post-colonial feature of donor influence – linguistic rivalry. Africa is still made up of anglophone and francophone (and lusophone) spheres, and Rwanda was switching. The consequences for donor allegiance were surprising and carried substantial financial and political consequences.

I later came across the same rivalry again in Timor-Leste, as donors vied with each other over the predominant language of the justice sector. It was just one of the dilemmas facing the government in their dialogue with partners. The prime minister, Mari Alkatiri, appears in Chapter 1 with his remarks about sovereignty. Timor will be an interesting test case of donor sincerity when it comes to country ownership.

In June 2005, I was on an aid mission in Mongolia. The President, Nambaryn Enkhbayar, told us rather candidly: 'per capita aid is very high, but results are very low!', and that is a fitting summary of what many people in the aid business have known for some time. Yet, we have all toiled uncomplainingly. Part of the explanation is that we have not attached adequate concern to aid effectiveness. But that's really not the whole story. Aid is a vehicle for so much else, besides development.

Acknowledgements

Many people have inspired me over the years, and thus contributed in some way to the contents of the book. They are too numerous to name here, but I acknowledge them nonetheless in silent salute. Here, I shall only mention those who have made comments on what they read in draft.

The writing of this book began in New York and ended in Bangkok. The first chapter to be written was the one on conditionality (Chapter 4) and it was the subject of a brief seminar in UNDP in late 2004. Several colleagues commented on the earlier draft, and when it came to be re-written for the book, it benefited from the valuable advice of Peter Uvin and Santosh Mehrotra.

Chapter 5 was the other one that was extensively discussed and annotated by reviewers. My main debts are to Kunda Dixit, Richard Horsey, Morten Pedersen and Charles Petrie. Useful comments were also received from David Abbott, Serdar Bayriyev, Francesco Galtieri, Olaf Juergensen, Muttukrishna Sarvananthan, Mark Suzman and Nescha Teckle.

Chapter 7 benefited enormously from research by Daniel Hanspach, Daniel Kirkwood, Krystyna Peczek and Haibing Zhang. Chapter 8 has drawn on the useful insights of Aidan Cox and Philip Courtnadge.

Others who have contributed thoughts and comments on content and style include Bob Griffin, Cherie Hart, Roger Riddell and Leelananda de Silva.

All the above are to be thanked for improving the text, but not blamed for the remaining inadequacies.

A special acknowledgement goes to Doungkamon Vongin, who looked for sources in places I had not even imagined and toiled away to turn numbers into figures and graphs. Many thanks also to Pramaporn Mongkolthavorn who helped to compensate for my imperfect word-processing skills.

The book is dedicated to the gang at home who extended support in each of their own splendid and inimitable ways.

1

The Great Mismatch

It is hard to argue that donor countries 'know best' in relation to political issues and it is even more difficult to argue that they are in a position to judge issues in which economic considerations are deeply entangled with social forces and political motivations.
JUST FAALAND, 1981

National ownership must mean that from time to time national decisions will be made that are at variance with donor priorities or established practice. We should always be willing to listen to advice, and draw on the knowledge and experience at the disposal of donors, but we should also take responsibility for our national policies...achieve our own successes and make our own mistakes.
MELES ZENAWI, PRIME MINISTER OF ETHIOPIA, 2005

Celebrated Norwegian economist Just Faaland wrote a book 25 years ago with two collaborators about aid during the early years of Bangladesh.[1] When I first read it, the story sounded familiar. I had not actually served in that country, but I had worked in, and on, many other developing countries of varying status in different regions of the South. Their experience was similar: in various ways, donors link aid to their own ends. I decided then that the story – from which this book takes its title – deserved a wider airing. It's an appropriate place to start.

THE BIRTH OF BANGLADESH

East Pakistan was the more populous half of the new Muslim state carved out of British India at independence in 1947. Separated by 1600 kilometres across the shoulders of India, the two Pakistans maintained a precarious union until a violent separation in 1971. Divorced from the main institutions of central governance, the new country of Bangladesh faced a challenging future. Its dense population was crowded into a highly fertile river delta prone to devastating floods that frequently inundated one-fifth of the country. It was heavily dependent on a single commodity, jute. Its financial condition was parlous and it could not pay for the food and oil that it urgently needed.

More keenly than any newly independent country before it, Bangladesh knew that it needed aid. But it had no inkling of the complications that were to follow.

Relief assistance came first. Bangladesh's initial donors were the United Nations, the Soviet Union and India, which provided mostly humanitarian aid. India alone provided nearly one million tons of food aid. However, when Bangladesh began to face the need for longer-term development assistance, obstacles appeared.

First there was politics. Some countries stayed aloof. While the secession had been actively supported by India and the Soviet Union, it had been opposed by the United States, which had allied itself closely to (West) Pakistan. China, newly-designated as a veto-wielding permanent member of the Security Council (replacing Taiwan) and in a territorial dispute with India, also kept its distance.

Bangladesh could have benefited from assistance from all sources, but its allegiance was sought to one of the two ideological camps dividing the aid world. Its socialist-leaning government recognized an affinity with the Soviet bloc but also felt that it had much to gain from links with the West. The choice was between an aid consortium of western donors, or more ad hoc assistance from the Soviet bloc. In the event, at the first aid meeting in Dacca in March 1973, the proceedings were dominated by the West. And the reason was soon evident.

Banking considerations were uppermost. Rather than focusing on the country's development needs, the western donors urged the government to accept liability for a share of the debts contracted by Pakistan prior to 1971. The new government did not accede immediately to these demands, but it was forced onto the back foot. In addition to the huge development challenges to its viability, Bangladesh was about to start life as an impoverished debtor of the West. The following year the first full aid consortium was organized, not in Dacca as the government had wanted, but in Paris, and not chaired by the government but by the World Bank. (Potential donors from the socialist bloc attended this first meeting, but never returned to the subsequent consortia.)

Next were the donors' own aid concerns. They were not standing back and waiting to be asked for support. They would market it themselves and follow through with an active 'after-sales' service hedged with conditions. There appeared to be limited faith in the capacity of those governing the new country either to choose the kind of aid they needed or – once it had arrived – to administer it. With aid came a large implantation of western development personnel, mostly with sound technical and financial management skills, but knowing rather less about the more subtle political and social context of the country.

Thus an inverted supply–demand relationship developed, and Bangladesh was soon trying to accommodate the numerous – and sometimes conflicting – demands of donors: they specified the precise nature of the aid, the choice of supplier, the preferred domestic partner, the need for appropriate counterpart resources, even – perhaps especially – the 'correct' policies for running the country. Beyond the more technocratic considerations – often stemming from

---

BOX 1.1 AID AND INFLUENCE IN BANGLADESH

However unjustified, it often seemed to be assumed by economists, bankers and other experts from abroad that those responsible for directing the economy were unaware of what was needed...

...donors did not hesitate to impose detailed conditions...they wished to ensure that their aid would be effective and were generally distrustful of the readiness and ability of Bangladesh to ensure this unless donors stipulated explicit conditions in an effort to enforce compliance.

The relationships that had to be established were not just those between aid-givers and the recipient. A number of special interests had to be accommodated. Sometimes these related to suppliers in the donor countries, anxious to create conditions conducive to the sale of their products or expertise by political as well as commercial intervention.

If it is right for donor countries to assume a collective obligation for helping those in need, should there not also be meetings resembling those held by consortia to review the progress of individual donors in meeting the requirements of the less developed countries?

Source: Faaland et al (1981)

---

standard development blueprints conjured by donor agencies – what was not taken into account was the readiness and the capacities of the country to absorb this aid.

WRONG ANTECEDENTS?

Another source of inspiration was an article that I had encountered for a UNDP policy journal about 'correcting the precedents' of aid (Morgan, 2002). The author pointed out that international technical assistance had a long pedigree, but that it changed markedly in 1950, my starting year for development assistance. Aid took on the trappings of patronage for the first time, against several historical precedents that followed a very different pattern.

For example, back in the early 18th century, when Peter the Great started the modernization of Russia, he turned to the outside for assistance, inviting the best engineers, shipbuilders, architects and craftsmen in from Europe. Hundreds of Russians were also sent to Europe for an education and to learn new skills.

Japan opened to the outside world in the mid-19th century, and sought to catch up with the West. It called for external assistance. More than 3000 foreign experts were brought in with a range of skills. Japanese were sent abroad to study in growing numbers.

In the last century, the Iran of Reza Shah built infrastructure – including the Trans-Iranian railway – with foreign help since it lacked its own skilled manpower. He made a point of hiring these experts on an individual basis and under Iranian control, since he did not want to be subjected to foreign influence.

There is also an important historical example from China. Soon after its establishment at the end of the First World War, the League of Nations received a request for help with its modernization through the provision of capital and skills. In the ambiance of contemporary international relations, the deal required careful negotiation. The League was at pains to adhere to its neutrality and to demonstrate that the missions were purely technical in character. But by the early 1930s, the first foreign experts (in health and hygiene) were in the field. In 1933, a 'technical representative', acting as a resident development ambassador of the League, was appointed and by 1941 the League had provided China with 30 experts (Rist, 1997). This was probably the first example of multilateral assistance to the South.

In all these instances of countries seeking to modernize, they decided on their best course of action and purchased overseas the skills that they lacked. Where additional capital was also needed, they borrowed on commercial terms, abroad if necessary. The client country paid and the jobs got done the way the client wanted. These were examples of how technical and capital assistance from abroad helped drive development. It was market rules: supply responding to demand.

Now contrast this with aid in the form we know it. Aid has always been pre-financed, meaning that it is offered and fully financed in advance by the donor, either as a grant or a subsidized loan. And it mostly consists of transfers from public sectors in the North to the public sectors of the South. From these conditions has flowed the whole complexion of aid that, as this book will set out to demonstrate, has been a creature of rich-country governments.

Pre-financing

The notion of aid as pre-financed patronage is so ingrained that it is rarely questioned. Over the years, the word 'cooperation' has crept into the development lexicon, but aid, or development assistance, has generally connoted a richer party helping a poorer party as part of a 'from–to' relationship.

If the notion was based on the assumption that the newly independent developing countries could not afford to do what Russia, Japan, Iran, China, Argentina and others had done prior to the aid era – buy or borrow what they needed from outside – then the assumption was false. Most developing countries were adequately solvent at the time of their independence to have afforded to procure assistance. Part of the proof is the fact that, as dependent states, they had not been kept afloat on the patronage of the colonial powers but were – for the most part – economically viable. Given the precipitous nature of its birth, Bangladesh was one of the exceptions.

As dependencies, their external markets were closely meshed with those of the metropolitan powers. What they needed at independence was the continuation of favoured market access, and a fair trading and financial system to compensate for falling commodity prices. In other words, then as now, they needed trade, in preference to aid, and fairer global rules. But this was not to be.

Pre-financed aid was difficult to refuse when it was offered – although some developing countries, like Sri Lanka (which first benefited handsomely from rising export prices), still needed some persuading. In this book, we seek to discover the extent to which even technical assistance, although pre-financed, has in reality been un-free, because of the connections and agendas that have trailed it. The most eloquent manifestation of the problems of prepaid assistance is the constant exhortation heard in aid circles about the need for 'country ownership'. The Nehrus, Sukarnos, Titos and other leaders at the first Bandung conference of newly independent countries (1955) would be dismayed to look down today and find that ownership is even an issue. Pre-financing substantially undermined it.

Loans

And of course, most aid was on loan – for infrastructure, but also for technical assistance, critical commodities and even food aid. With lending has come added perils. In addition to buying many unsuitable things and tying up additional domestic resources, donor-driven loan projects often fall short of those much-vaunted rates of return, adding to general indebtedness. Right up to today most recipients have never been able to repay their aid debts in full. On the contrary, overall indebtedness has steadily worsened and most of the poorest developing countries are financially in a much more precarious state than when they started out at independence.

Bureaucracy

Unlike in those earlier historical instances, aid was founded on transfers between governments. But as a child of bureaucracy, it took on other attributes. Bureaucracy breeds procedure and formality. As Morgan (2002) puts it, aid 'was now to be managed as a public sector activity in accordance with the government regulations and procedures of each supplying country. Technical assistance activities were to be bureaucratically structured and controlled as part of a process of change'. This author knows at first hand that bureaucrats are not adept at devising simple procedures. And multilateral bankers are scarcely any better. From the beginnings of aid, recipient countries have faced the costly administrative need to accommodate the innumerable and separate requirements for aid design, approval and reporting of individual donor sources. Donors are today belatedly striving to 'simplify and harmonize' their procedures for the benefit of recipients. Juggling multiple procedures was and is the reverse of logic: donors should have been responding to the respective requirements of the recipients. Harmonization has become another mantra like country ownership.

There are also rigidities in bureaucratic working practices that are ill-suited to supporting development processes. The new development specialists co-opted the project – a device from the engineering field – as their primary instrument for administering aid. The project conveniently divides aid into time- and money-bound fragments and is geared to short-term 'results'. For capital funding of infrastructure and other tangible assets, projects have obvious relevance. But technical assistance also wholeheartedly bought into projectization, because of the many advantages that it seemed to offer to aid administrators. Projects are an appropriate channel for public funds approved in annual tranches and intended to deliver visible short-term returns. The performance of aid agency staff is also measured by their effectiveness in moving money. In reality, however, the complexities of the development process do not lend themselves to quick-time inputs and outputs, which are more suited to limited technocratic challenges. Development is about lengthy, localized, idiosyncratic change. It is engendered within a subtle context alien to project rhythms and often resistant to outside interventions, however well meant. From the beginning, the project fixation within bureaucracies distracted agencies from all-important institutional issues, the critical signifi-cance of which has only recently surfaced in aid discussions.

Mighty agencies

From publicly administered aid arose numerous well-financed development agencies, which took on lives of their own – in fact, if any has ever closed down, it has usually been resurrected under a new acronym. There are now 80 of them administering 35,000 separate projects. In addition to their complex proce-dures and working practices, aid agencies develop their own agendas, which serve the interests of their paymasters in ministries of finance and parliaments. Each bilateral donor has at least one agency to administer its aid programmes and they have assumed growing sophistication. The most refined examples, however, are the secretariats of the multilateral World Bank and International Monetary Fund (IMF) in Washington. Their own agendas have attracted labels like the 'Washington Consensus', which, as we note in Chapter 4, have some standard attributes. Donors have become used to propagating their develop-ment formulae, limiting the space for developing country government strategies and reinforcing the North-to-South direction of the aid relationship.

These agendas were subject first to the scrutiny of the providers of funds. Understandably, therefore, they followed donor preferences before develop-ment needs. This made the development agencies answerable upwards to fund providers, rather than downwards to the recipients. Programmes devised in the northern capitals needed to be 'rolled out', discussed with and sold to developing country representatives. Hence the frequent exhortations in the aid lingo about 'buy-in'. Aid has inverted the market. It is supply, which is guaran-teed, looking to match demand, which is not.

Tying

Answering upwards rather than downwards also meant the need for aid agencies to show value for money to paymasters in tangible ways. This 'value' to the domestic economy tends to take precedence over broader notions of development effectiveness in the economies that aid is intended to support. With aid tied to its sources, it finances the capital and consumer goods and the range of training and consultancy services available from the aid giver. The costs of tying are high, not just because of monopolistic costing, but more especially because lack of choice obliges the recipient country to accept goods and services that may not be appropriate to their needs.

AID DOES NOT MATCH NEED

So aid does not go where development demand would naturally draw it, because there is not a market-style expression of that demand. Rather, its size and direction is subjectively determined by donors.

There are various ways in which this incompatibility can be shown:

- *Aid is not correlated with human development.* If aid per capita is plotted against the human development indices (HDI) for a large sample of developing countries[2] – as proxies for levels of development – a matching relationship would be shown as a backward sloping line: the lower the index, the higher the aid. However, for all three years shown below (1980, 1990 and 2000) the relationship appears to be entirely random (see Figures 1.1, 1.2 and 1.3). The country with the lowest HDI rank, Niger, receives less aid per capita than any of the high human development Baltic states (Estonia, Latvia and Lithuania). Among those in the low human development range, Djibouti receives four times as much aid per head as Haiti or Ethiopia.
- *Aid is not correlated with country income levels.* The low-income countries (GDP per head of less than US$735) account for three-quarters of people living in poverty, but receive only 40 per cent of aid. Sub-Saharan Africa, with the largest number of low-income countries and where poverty is most widespread, receives only one-third of total aid.
- *Aid is volatile.* Aggregate data over time also reveal the fickleness of aid. As illustrated by Figure 3.1 in Chapter 3 (page 34), official development assistance (ODA) rose quite steadily for 4 decades after 1950, but began to fall away sharply after 1992. The decline was not in response to donor perceptions of reduced need for development assistance – in fact, the decade of the 1990s was an especially difficult one for many countries – but in large part because the geopolitical rationale related to the Cold War, which had been a dominant donor motivation for aid, had suddenly been removed. Almost perversely, the 1990s saw a distinct switch in the direction of (reduced) aid away from Africa and towards Europe, as the donors

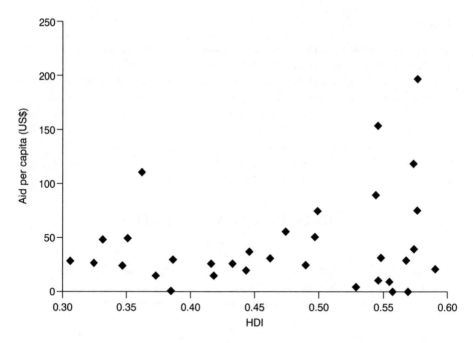

Figure 1.1 *HDI and aid per capita, 1980*

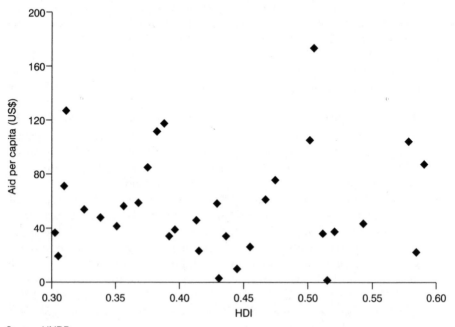

Figure 1.2 *HDI and aid per capita, 1990*

sought to build influence with Eastern Europe and the newly independent states of the former Soviet Union (White, 2002), responding to what I have described elsewhere as a 'post-wall' rationale (Browne, 1999).

- *Aid depends on donor concerns of affordability.* The donors were also preoccupied during the 1990s with their fiscal health. Japan was entering a period of protracted economic crisis that caused it to cut its aid sharply from mid-decade. In Europe, Finland, Italy and Sweden were running the largest deficits and made the sharpest cutbacks, while Ireland and Norway had smaller deficits and maintained their aid levels (Hjertholm and White, 2000).

- *Aid follows the non-developmental objectives of donors.* As we shall see in the chapters that follow, aid is a means of influence that may be related to factors of commercial, geopolitical, strategic/security or historical importance to donors. To take just the last factor, for example, patterns of aid allocation are still skewed by former colonial ties. For all the talk of supporting democracy and economic openness, the former colonial powers still give about twice as much aid to their former colonies that are not democratic or that have relatively closed economies, than they give to democratic and open non-colonies (Rogerson, 2005).

Once it is understood that the objectives of donors are not solely – or even mainly – developmental, the measurement of aid effectiveness becomes a largely vain pursuit. Indeed, where aid is allocated mainly for the 'wrong' purposes, it may be better to hope for failure!

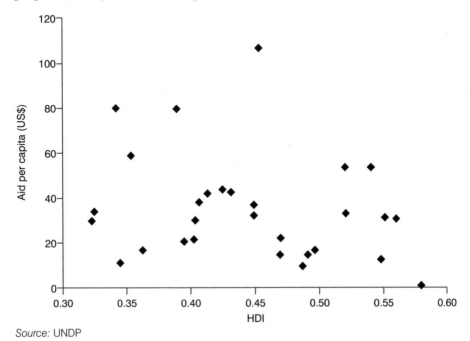

Source: UNDP

Figure 1.3 *HDI and aid per capita, 2000*

THE ARGUMENT

The basic thesis of this book is straightforward. Development is essentially a domestic matter. History – which this book draws on liberally – provides ample evidence that development progress depends critically on the way governments manage. The developing countries that are now emerging into middle- and upper-income status have mostly managed well. They have used the resources at their disposal to development ends and they have acted as facilitators of enterprise and progress. The developing countries that still languish have suffered from poor and inappropriate management. At worst, they have been at the mercy of cynical regimes of despoilers, not developers. Many have also suffered the disadvantages of challenging geography, limited resource endowment and natural disaster.

Developing countries need resources to develop, and development is favoured by a propitious external environment. Unfortunately, the rich countries that have much to offer have often not provided what developing countries have needed most. Much aid has been inappropriate, the global economy has been unevenly weighted, and the global public goods of greatest universal benefit have not been sufficiently forthcoming.

Here we mainly concentrate on aid itself, or official development assistance to give it its full title (see Box 1.2). We find that aid has offered externally grafted solutions, and, in many cases, has actually undermined the capacity of the recipients to direct their own affairs. Not all assistance has been wasted. Far from it. There are many well-chronicled successes. But if you look more closely, these successes have generally occurred where the developing countries and their institutions have remained in control. As a general rule, the well-managed developing countries that have performed best in reducing poverty and meeting human goals are those that have learnt soonest to reduce their dependence on aid: up front are the Asian tigers – Singapore, Taiwan and South Korea – then Brazil, Chile, Costa Rica, South Africa, and next come the emerging donors such as Malaysia and Thailand.

The less aid you have, the better you do? The aid lobby claims the opposite, and exhorts a doubling and tripling of aid. But if it is aid on the old terms, it will not bring progress. Saying that, the world is richer than ever and implying that development can simply be purchased with more of the same resources is a monumental deception. It ignores the primordial need for countries to foster their own capacity to develop.

In the following chapters we set out to reveal exactly why and where aid has failed to foster that capacity. In Chapter 2, we show how aid failed from the outset to compensate for chronically unfavourable trading conditions for the developing countries and how it was allocated on the basis of the geopolitical and commercial concerns of donors. Chapter 3 tells how donors conceived a succession of blueprints for development, reflecting an evolving understanding of how development was supposed to occur. In Chapter 4, we critique the use of conditionality in policy-based aid lending. Conditionality is intended to make money talk, but inhospitable environments have often rendered it dumbly impotent when trying to influence reform. Many of the poorest countries have proved to be unsuitable candidates for banking strictures and yet they bear the main financial onus for poor donor judgement.

Chapter 5 looks at the record of aid in fragile and poorly performing states and finds that, for reasons that are largely subjective to donors, the wrong aid has often been provided in the wrong circumstances. We make a plea for continuing engagement, but on the right terms. Chapter 6 is about assistance from the largest donor, the United States, which uses aid as a proxy for what many are describing as a new form of imperialism. US aid is largely interest-driven, but even those interests are often unfulfilled. Chapter 7 reviews the 'donors from the South', including China, India and the richer Arab States, and finds that aid from these sources is also mainly a vehicle of influence, and that it may act as a counterweight to rich-country aid.

We conclude in Chapter 8 that aid has been a poor match for development needs, for the reasons outlined above, but that the shortcomings of aid can also be a guide to reform. Some basic principles must be restored and respected. To truly qualify as donors, the rich countries should dismantle the obstacles that they have put in the way of development in the form of trade and agricultural protectionism. They should fund more of the global public goods that are needed to underpin development progress, including keeping the peace, developing vaccines and cleaning the environment. But above all, history should be rolled back. A market should be reinstated. Developing countries should become the active consumers of aid rather than the passive recipients. More ways should be found to put purchasing power into the hands of the developing countries and encourage them to choose their sources. It would revolutionize the development business, but only because that business has been run so inefficiently for so long.

I have compared aid with a latter-day 'imperialism'. Is this an exaggeration? Can aid really be imposed, and can donors enforce their changes on recipients? The following two stories show that they try. The rest of the book says that influence doesn't stick.

The aid coordinator of a newly-independent Eastern European country – starting with a clean aid slate – was holding a meeting in his office with a large visiting delegation from a development bank, which had come to negotiate the first-ever technical assistance loan. This meant borrowing money for the services of external experts identified by the donor. At the end of the meeting the aid coordinator asked the head of the delegation how his mission was being financed. 'By your country' came back the reply. After the meeting, he understood the implications of the deal and refused to sign the loan agreement. A few weeks later he was removed from his post by the prime minister. The loan was later signed without him and the bank's missions continued to arrive with growing frequency. The author was a witness to that meeting, which took place in Ukraine in the early 1990s. It could also have been in Bangladesh or in one of many other recipient countries encouraged to anticipate the benefits of aid.

BOX 1.2 DEVELOPMENT AID DEFINED

'*Official*': in this book, aid is used synonymously with 'official development assistance' (ODA), and broadly follows the definition established by the Organisation for Economic Co-operation and Development (OECD) in the late 1960s. 'Official' flows are those of which the sources are the governments and official agencies of donor countries. They are distinguishable from private flows, which include long- or short-term commercial loans (whether or not guaranteed by an official agency), private trade credits, direct investment and investments in bonds and other securities. They include official contributions to private voluntary agencies engaged in development, but they exclude the resources that these same agencies raise from private sources. There is also a difference between ODA and OA (official assistance), the latter being aid provided to non-qualifying countries – mainly middle-income and countries in transition.

'*Recipients*': aid comprises resources that are channelled to developing countries, either directly or through the intermediary of a multilateral institution or private voluntary organization. Aid is not confined to resources allocated to independent countries, however. In the case of France, for example, aid statistics include the substantial transfers to its remaining colonies and dependent territories ('départements et térritoires d'outre-mer', the so-called DOM/TOMs) although the figures are listed separately. In 2003, there were 150 ODA-eligible countries and territories according to the OECD, also referred to as Part I countries. A further 36 – including more advanced countries and some of the former Soviet republics – are called Part II countries, eligible for 'official aid' (source: http://www.oecd.org/dataoecd/35/9/2488552.pdf).

'*Development*': aid is 'developmental', but that term is rather imprecise. ODA actually includes resources provided to developing countries for relief, emergency and humanitarian (including refugee) purposes. In practice, the distinctions between development and relief aid are often unclear. However, using their own definitions, donors appropriate resources for development and for relief separately, in the latter case usually setting aside a reserve to be drawn down as needs demand. When there are major emergencies, special pledging conferences may be called to raise supplementary relief resources. This book deals mainly with ODA for non-relief purposes.

'*Non-military*': formally speaking, ODA excludes all assistance of a military nature, but here also there are margins of ambiguity. For example, donors use ODA to support paramilitary and police forces, for which the rationale is presumably that the training can be turned to useful civilian applications. For the most part, however, assistance directed to military recipients is excluded from classification as aid, even though development assistance appropriations are sometimes tied closely to the provision of military assistance.

'*Concessional*': the terms of aid are concessional, meaning that aid is provided either as grants in funds or in kind, or as loans at costs low enough to be discounted to values that are small in comparison with the total original disbursement. Loans are determined by the OECD to be concessional, and therefore eligible as ODA, if they have a 'grant equivalent' value equal to a minimum of 25 per cent. (A full commercial loan has a grant equivalent of 0 per cent, and a grant 100 per cent. The exact grant equivalent of a loan can be calculated using a formula. A qualifying concessional loan has a low interest rate (for example, 5 per cent or less), a relatively long maturity (for example, 15 years) and also an initial grace period during which no repayments are made).

'*Aid*': aid is usually defined to include those forms of assistance that can be financially valued – capital, goods (food and commodities) or services (technical cooperation) purchased with aid funds. Reckoning aid in these terms leaves out of account other implicit transfers that may be significant but that do not lend themselves easily to measurement. One important example is price subsidization: essential goods sold by developed countries to developing countries at prices below world market levels, or purchases of exports from developing countries at higher than prevailing levels.

'*Overheads*': not all of the resources reported as aid are available for delivery to developing country recipients. A proportion is absorbed by the general administrative budgets of aid agencies, while intrinsic to every aid project there are costs of management and execution. There is a wide variation in the proportion of project budgets taken up by administrative costs. In the case of International Development Association (IDA) credits, there is an annual 'commitment' fee on the undisbursed portion and a 'service' charge of 0.75 per cent on disbursements. At the other end of the scale, complex projects may absorb high proportions of their overall values in costs of execution.

Much more recently, during the writing of this book, one of the countries visited by the author was Timor-Leste, a small new state (established in 2001) in East Asia, which – like Bangladesh – came to independence through violent separation. It was another clean slate case and it had no debts to inherit. It has the potential good fortune of energy deposits offshore worth US$20 billion (from which Australia – one of Timor's principal donors – has so far mainly benefited after redrawing the legal international boundaries in its favour). During our mission we had the opportunity to meet the prime minister for a discussion on capacity development. He impressed us with a bold statement about ownership. Furthermore, he intended to use the royalties from oil and gas to avoid taking development loans and running up external debts. We complimented him on his boldness and asked if he thought the country could remain loan- and debt-free. 'We expect to have a fight on our hands', he said. Timor's own struggle against donor influence was already under way.

2

Aid Origins

More than half the people of the world are living in conditions approaching misery. Their food is inadequate. They are victims of disease. Their economic life is primitive and stagnant. Their poverty is a handicap and a threat both to them and to more prosperous areas. For the first time in history, humanity possesses the knowledge and skill to relieve the suffering of these people.
US PRESIDENT HARRY TRUMAN, 1949

Aid began with those heady words from a former US President. It was a statement of pure altruism and it was made in the certain belief that the rich countries could help the people of the poor countries to overcome their disadvantage. Truman would surely be despondent if he knew that today, very similar statements are still being made by world leaders.

Where did we go wrong? Or more realistically, why were Truman's assumptions to be proved wrong over the next half-century? In this chapter, we look at the beginnings of aid and the debates that surrounded its birth. From the early stages, it was evident that aid was to be a form of patronage serving the political and commercial interests of its donors.

THE INSTITUTIONAL BEGINNINGS

Charity began at home. Development assistance as we know it can be dated from 1950, but it was preceded by a phase of aided reconstruction, mainly in the richer countries.

The post-war relief and reconstruction gave birth to several new organizations, which became some of the key founding aid institutions. The world's first international aid agency, the United Nations Relief and Rehabilitation Administration (UNRRA), had been created by the Allied powers at the end of 1943 and was mandated to respond to the ravages of war in Europe and the resettlement of six million of its displaced people. Headed by a former mayor of New York,[1] UNRRA had successfully accomplished its mandate by 1949. There were private charities at work also, including the Oxford Committee for Famine Relief (OXFAM), assisting refugees from Greece, and the Center for American Relief in Europe (CARE).[2]

The International Bank for Reconstruction and Development (IBRD) was set up by the UN Monetary and Financial Conference at Bretton Woods (New Hampshire) in 1944 and began operations in 1946, concentrating during its first few years on lending for the reconstruction of war-affected economies, mainly in Europe. With the Marshall Plan, the US established its own major reconstruction programme for Europe in 1948. The Plan ran for 4 years, disbursing some US$13 billion (90 per cent in grant form) for the benefit of western European countries, equivalent to about 1 per cent of the American economy – generous by any past or present standards. In today's money, Marshall funds were equivalent to more than US$70 per year for every person in western Europe.

The results were palpable, for Marshall aid helped to restore economic health to Europe within a few years. By 1950, the level of industrial production in Europe was 25 per cent higher than it had been before the war. Agricultural production was growing rapidly again and Europe's trade deficit shrank from US$8.5 billion in 1947 to US$1 billion in 1950 (OECD, 1978). For the next 25 years, the western economies were to enjoy a period of unprecedented expansion.

Reconstruction was the goal and UNRRA, IBRD and the Marshall Plan – all substantially backed by US funds – were successful in their primary objective of restoring vibrancy to America's major trading partners. Japan, which was not part of the Marshall Plan, also received generous assistance from the US, amounting to over US$1.5 billion from 1947 to 1950 (Ferguson, 2004).

These early institutions of multilateral assistance were the foundations of the new aid infrastructure. UNRRA was succeeded by the International Refugee Organization (IRO; later the UN High Commission for Refugees – UNHCR) and some of its functions were also assumed by the UN International Children's Emergency Fund, as UNICEF was then known. Both these UNRRA offspring were to become the core of world-wide humanitarian efforts. The Marshall Plan was administered by an agency that the Europeans had set up for themselves in 1948, the Organisation for European Economic Co-operation (OEEC). The OEEC later welcomed other non-European members into what effectively became the club of rich western countries, the Organisation for Economic Co-operation and Development. Within the OECD, the Development Assistance Committee (DAC) became active in monitoring aid flows and harmonizing donor policies.

Besides IRO/UNHCR and UNICEF, several other UN specialized agencies were created during the 1940s: the Food and Agriculture Organization (FAO), and International Civil Aviation Organization (ICAO) in 1945, the UN Educational, Scientific and Cultural Organization (UNESCO) in 1946, and the World Health Organization (WHO) in 1948. The UN system also inducted several regulatory organizations created much earlier: the International Telecommunication Union (ITU) from 1865, the Universal Postal Union (UPU) from 1875 and the International Labour Office (ILO) created by the Treaty of Versailles in 1919.

MULTILATERAL AID

With European reconstruction largely accomplished, 1950 was effectively year zero for official development assistance (see Box 1.2). In January 1949, President Truman laid the foundations with 'point four' of his inaugural address. He anticipated that financial assistance 'should foster capital investment in areas needing development' and he foresaw that technical assistance 'should make available to peace-loving peoples the benefits of our sum of technical knowledge in order to help them realize their aspirations for a better life'. He combined enlightened self-interest: 'experience shows that our commerce with other countries expands as they progress industrially and economically' with a recognition of the importance of multilateralism: 'a cooperative enterprise in which all nations work together through the United Nations and its specialized agencies whenever practicable'.

Capital assistance through the multilateral system began with the World Bank's first development loan to a developing country (Colombia) in 1950. In the same year, as Truman had anticipated, technical assistance (TA) also started up, initially under multilateral UN auspices. The donors made pledges of US$20 million – equivalent to about US$150 million in contemporary terms – to the UN's Expanded Programme of Technical Assistance (EPTA). These funds were to be made available to the UN specialized agencies to enable them to provide free technical services to developing countries.

But while Truman's speech read like its first blueprint, the start of development aid was heavily laboured and followed a tortuous debate about the wisdom of international charity. Although the Marshall Plan paid huge dividends in Europe, subsequent proposals for 'massive transfers' to the developing world were mistrusted. The uncertainties of the developing world could not guarantee returns to justify the means. Certainly, in the 1940s, there was no stomach for an untried global welfare scheme.

Yet, there was a very legitimate concern after the war that the newly independent countries of the South would be seriously disadvantaged by international trade conditions. Some of the strongest early proponents of aid founded their case not on a humanitarian rationale, but on the need for some form of compensation for low commodity prices.

Trade was perceived then as critical to economic growth and thus fundamental to development progress. But the terms of trade were determinant. If the prices of primary commodities exported by the developing countries were more volatile, or moved consistently less favourably than the prices of the manufactured goods that they needed to import, the primary exporters would be progressively penalized.

The perception by some economists of a chronic tendency for the terms of trade of developing countries to decline (for example, Singer, 1982) was brought into the debate on the construction of the new international financial structures. The Bretton Woods conference led to the creation of a mechanism for capital transfers (the World Bank) and for temporary financial compensation (the International Monetary Fund). It also considered proposals for a commodity-based currency unit, a buffer stock scheme and a code of trading. The first two of these proposals would have provided some safeguards for commodity exporters, but only the third survived to become the basis for the General Agreement on Trade and Tariffs (GATT),[3] which during its first few decades was limited in membership, mainly to the richer countries.

Individual commodity funds and buffer stock proposals were revived later under UN auspices, but they were also limited in scope. There were objections of principle and practice. The rich countries would never have endorsed intervention in international markets on the requisite scale (notwithstanding their widespread propensity for trade protectionism), and the proposals would have been extremely costly in the long term. Also, the arguments for compensation were temporarily weakened by the rapid appreciation of commodity prices during the Korean War in the early 1950s.

Bretton Woods was predicated on more limited financial intervention. Where payments imbalances arose (for example, as a result of deteriorating terms of trade), temporary compensation was available through short-term borrowing from the IMF, the original objective of which was to redistribute from surplus to deficit countries. Alternatively, countries could seek longer term solutions by borrowing from the World Bank or the capital markets to purchase essential imports.

The aid proponents continued to argue in favour of grant funding, as an alternative to attempting to render the trading system more equitable, or to running up developing country debt. For the conservatively-inclined administrations in the rich countries, however, aid – unlike loans – provided no performance guarantees. Granting funds was like international welfare. Aid could be justified for humanitarian purposes, but for development, it could only bring temporary relief, and did not put the receiving country under any necessary pressure to redress the causes of the imbalances. Aid could encourage permanent and growing dependence. More appropriate banking solutions could be orchestrated through the Bretton Woods institutions, which the rich countries largely financed and which they effectively controlled through a weighted voting system. The proposal for a Special United Nations Fund for Economic Development (SUNFED), put forward in 1949, made no headway against the opposition of the donors. It was not until 1960 that the first multilateral concessional fund – the euphemistically named International Development Association – was established, not within the UN but at the World Bank.[4]

Unfortunately, the trade pessimists were right, an issue to which the next chapter returns.[5] The biases against the poorer countries, recognized half a century ago, never went away. Failure to address these chronic weaknesses in the original design of the multilateral system, compounded by systematic trade protectionism by the richer countries, effectively knocked a huge hole in the foundations of development assistance. Adverse trading conditions – and as a partial consequence, chronic indebtedness – have held back development progress in many of the poorest developing countries throughout the aid era.

BILATERAL AID

Although there were historical precedents for bilateral aid,[6] the Marshall Plan made it the first model for large-scale assistance. It was generous, timely and immediately successful. But the circumstances were unique. Marshall aid was channelled to formerly strong, well-resourced and institutionally mature economies needing to rebuild. They lacked the one thing that Marshall provided – cheap capital – and they were quickly restored to a path of self-sustaining growth, without the chronic trade penalties suffered by the poorer countries.

Marshall was a model, however, for the geopolitical biases that were to drive most bilateral aid for the next 40 years. When Marshall had made his proposal to Europe in 1947, he had not excluded assistance to Eastern bloc countries, leaving the onus on the Soviet Union to decide whether to accept. When they declined, as expected, the precedent was set for the ensuing ideological rivalry in aid.

The independence movement vastly expanded the theatre of cold warfare. When the Philippines and Lebanon gained independence in 1946, there were just 74 independent countries, North and South. By the time of the first Afro-Asian Conference in Bandung, Indonesia in 1955, there were 13 more independent countries in the South. More than 40 were added in the 1960s (see Box 2.1). Soviet assistance began in earnest, with Nikita Khruschev proclaiming in 1956 that the developing countries 'need not go begging to their former oppressors' but could obtain aid 'free from any political or military obligations'. The Soviet Union signed a series of 'economic cooperation agreements' with its recipients, the first of these included Mongolia, North Korea, Turkey, India and Afghanistan. By 1960, there were 18 such agreements. Soviet aid was less generous than US assistance. In the late 1950s it was running at an annual average value of about US$450 million, about one-quarter of the US figure. But the terms were often harder and entailed repayments both in currency and in kind from some recipients (Browne, 1990).

In the early years, US and Soviet aid was concentrated on developing countries that surrounded the Soviet Union, ramped up by the conflict on the Korean peninsula. Later, the geographic reach expanded, setting up East–West rivalries in all regions. Some newly independent countries, such as Sri Lanka, proclaimed their non-alignment. They were initially resistant to bilateral aid (De Silva, 1984) but relented after the collapse of commodity prices following the Korean War. For others, such as India, non-alignment was interpreted as openness to aid from both East and West. Egypt in the 1950s and Somalia in the 1970s, switched their aid allegiances from one bloc to the other.

Independence encouraged other bilateral donors to build aid programmes in the 1950s as a sequel to their colonial obligations. France founded its aid programme on support for its expatriate population in the ex-colonies. Since it maintained large numbers of public service officials and experts after independence, decolonization was largely a book-keeping exercise as far as resource

BOX 2.1 THE CHRONOLOGY OF INDEPENDENCE

Most of the aid-receiving countries became independent or self-governing after 1946, with the independence movement concentrated on Africa, Asia and the Pacific. In Asia, only Iran, Nepal and Thailand, and in Africa, Ethiopia and Egypt, were independent by the close of the Second World War. Except for some smaller Caribbean dependencies, the countries of the Americas had gained their independence much earlier. In the Middle-East, most countries became independent during the first half of the century. A few developing countries became independent of others during this period: Bhutan from India in 1949, Namibia from South Africa in 1990, Eritrea from Ethiopia in 1993 and Timor-Leste from Indonesia in 2001 (these countries are not included below). Much more recently, the break up of the Soviet Union led to the renewed independence of the 3 Baltic states and 11 former republics since 1989.

1946	Philippines (*us*), Lebanon** (*fr*)
1947	India (*uk*), Pakistan (*uk*), French Guiana (*fr*), Guadeloupe (*fr*), Martinique (*fr*), Reunion (*fr*)
1948	Sri Lanka (originally Ceylon) (*uk*), Burma (*uk*)
1949	Indonesia (*nl*)
1951	Libya (*it*), Netherlands Antilles (*nl*), Surinam (*nl*)
1952	Puerto Rico* (*us*)
1956	Gambia (*uk*), Morocco (*fr*), Tunisia (*fr*), Sudan (*uk*)
1957	Malaysia (Malaya) (*uk*), Ghana (Gold Coast) (*uk*)
1958	Guinea (*fr*)
1960	Benin (Dahomey) (*fr*), Burkina Faso (Upper Volta) (*fr*), Cameroon (*fr*), Central African Republic (*fr*), Chad (*fr*), Congo-Brazzaville (*fr*), Congo-Kinshasa (*be*), Cyprus (*uk*), Gabon (*fr*), Ivory Coast (*fr*), Madagascar (*fr*), Mali (*fr*), Niger (*fr*), Nigeria (*uk*), Senegal (*fr*), Somalia** (*uk*/*it*), Togo (Togoland) (*fr*)
1961	Mauritania (*fr*), Sierra Leone (*uk*)
1962	Algeria (*fr*), Burundi (*be*), Jamaica (*uk*), Rwanda (*be*), Samoa (*nz*), Trinidad and Tobago (*uk*), Uganda (*uk*)
1963	Kenya (*uk*)
1964	Malawi (*uk*), Zambia (*uk*)
1965	Cook Islands* (*nz*), Singapore (*uk*), Maldives (*uk*)
1966	Barbados (uk), Botswana (*uk*), Guyana (*uk*), Lesotho (*uk*)
1967	Yemen (South Yemen) (*uk*)
1968	Mauritius (*fr*), Nauru (*au*/*nz*/*uk*), Swaziland (*uk*), Equatorial Guinea (*sp*)
1970	Fiji (*uk*), Tonga (*uk*)
1971	Bangladesh***
1974	Grenada (*uk*), Guinea-Bissau (*pt*), Malta (*uk*), Niue* (*nz*)

1975	Angola (*pt*), Cape Verde (*pt*), Comoros (*fr*), Mozambique (*pt*), Papua New Guinea (*au*), Sao Tome (*pt*)
1976	Seychelles (*uk*)
1977	Djibouti (*fr*)
1978	Solomon Islands (*uk*), Tuvalu (*uk*), Dominica (*uk*)
1979	Kiribati (uk), Vanuatu (*fr/uk*)
1980	Zimbabwe (Rhodesia) (*uk*)
1981	Belize (*uk*), Antigua and Barbuda (*uk*)
1983	Brunei (*uk*)
1986	Micronesia** (*us*), Marshall Islands** (*us*)
1989	Estonia (*ru*), Latvia (*ru*), Lithuania (*ru*)
1991	Armenia (*ru*), Azerbaijan (*ru*), Belarus (*ru*), Georgia (*ru*), Kazakstan (*ru*), Kyrgyzstan (*ru*), Moldova (*ru*), Tajikistan (*ru*), Turkmenistan (*ru*), Ukraine (*ru*), Uzbekistan (*ru*)
1994	Palau** (*us*)

Key (countries from which independent): USA = us, UK = uk, France = fr, Belgium = be, Netherlands = nl, Italy = it, Portugal = pt, Australia = au, Spain = sp, Russia = ru *self-governing ** previously under UN mandate *** formerly East Pakistan

transfers were concerned. French aid became more broad based as the expatriates returned home, but it has always included assistance to its dependencies (départements et térritoires d'outre-mer). Britain leaned more to a policy of graduation, seeking to prepare its colonies for a status after independence, which would have enabled them to meet their own capital needs from borrowing.[7]

Other bilateral donors had none of the same post-colonial motivations for providing aid. The programmes of Canada, the Netherlands and the Nordic countries (which came to be known as the 'like-minded' donors) were motivated by a more developmental vocation, although their aid was an obvious adjunct to foreign policy, linked to the desire to build political bridges to developing countries.

Thus there were mixed motivations for bilateral aid, but in one way or another, it has always been a vector of influence. Political considerations have been predominant for all donors. In some cases, these were overlaid by colonial tradition and the continuity of past relationships. During the Cold War, geopolitics had a major influence on aid destinations.

The composition of aid has been heavily influenced by commercial motives, ensuring that substantial proportions of bilateral aid resources were disbursed in donor countries. True altruism was mainly confined to short-term relief assistance, but even humanitarian aid has not been immune from politics.

'There has been one constant in the history of aid', said a major study recently, 'namely that the development objectives of aid programmes have been distorted by the use of aid for donor commercial and political advantage' (Hjertholm and White, 2000).

To understand these biases better, it is necessary to review the evolution of the aid agenda.

3

Evolving Development Fashions

For decades, the development community has intervened in poor countries with little understanding of the political and institutional landscape, and with scant regard for the impact of their actions on local political relationships and incentives...Donors have consistently been unrealistic about the capacity required to manage complex processes of change, and have virtually ignored the need to build a social and political consensus for such change. They have expected poor countries to put in place a range of 'best practice' institutions, which are far more sophisticated than those present in OECD countries at a similar stage of their economic development. And they have assumed that creating those institutions involves little more than the supply of material resources and technical assistance. CENTRE FOR THE FUTURE STATE,
INSTITUTE OF DEVELOPMENT STUDIES, 2005

Too much aid in the past was badly used, often because it was driven by the priorities and preferences of donors rather than of poor people and poor countries.
UK DEPARTMENT FOR INTERNATIONAL DEVELOPMENT, 2005

Japan does not have military powers. Our means are diplomatic communication and overseas development aid. To get appreciation of Japan's position it is natural we resort to those two major tools. I think there is nothing wrong with that.
MASEYUKI KOMATSU, HEAD OF JAPAN'S FISHERY AGENCY, 2001

Ideological rivalry was the principal driving force behind the growth and geographical orientation of aid during the four decades of the Cold War. We have also seen that the nature and content of aid were largely determined by the donors, through their bilateral and multilateral aid agencies. Development paradigms evolved and were refined according to changing agency perceptions of how development worked. These doctrines influenced the nature of aid.

Very broadly, the history of Western-inspired development doctrine can be divided into three phases. In the first phase, roughly spanning the 1950s, 1960s and part of the 1970s, development was conceived as a do-as-we-did process. Because developed countries were considered to have advanced through sufficient capital, export earnings and skills, these were specifically what aid should provide: investible funds, balance of payments support and technical assistance.

In a second phase – the 1970s and 1980s – development was still implicitly equated with economic growth. But the impact of aid on growth was already being seriously questioned. Even more importantly, the merits of growth itself were in doubt. This was the era of basic needs and bottom-up paradigms, but also the sustainability of development and the natural resources that supported it.

By the 1990s, thinking had evolved again. The long-standing ideological debate between East and West was considered to have been resolved in favour of neo-liberal market democracy. Donors now latched on to a new 'institutional' agenda of good governance and respect for human rights: do-as-we-say.

However, as this and the chapter following make plain, these successive development fashions have not followed an evolution of the way development actually works, but of how it is perceived to work.

PHASE I: AID AS GAP-FILLING

In spite of contrasted East–West ideologies, there was initially a degree of convergence over development paradigms. Most of the post-war world was Keynesian. The British economist, also a leading architect of the Bretton Woods institutions, was closely identified with theories that linked economic growth to capital investment. Growth theory, little used in economic analysis before the war, became the essence of development studies. Indeed, the terms 'development' and 'economic growth' were essentially synonymous.[1] Reconstruction under Marshall, with its focus on restoring dynamism to the economies in Europe, clearly perceived capital as the ingredient of progress. Early development doctrine built on that experience.

At the heart of the theory was the 'incremental capital-output ratio' (ICOR), considered to be a stable function over time, which assumed that increases in capital investment led directly to output growth.[2] Several economists in the 1950s and early 1960s (Kuznets, 1954; Rostow, 1956; Rosenstein-Rodan, 1961) considered that the capital-oriented development experience of the industrial countries could be directly transplanted to the developing world. With the neo-classical theorists, the argument ran that the returns on capital would be higher in the developing world where capital was scarcer relative to other factors of production, particularly labour.

The influence of these theories – built around the so-called Harrod-Domar model – could also be seen in the first national plans of the developing countries (De Silva, 1984) and 'public investment plans' still form the centrepieces of some World Bank Consultative Group meetings. The role of aid was to bridge the domestic resource gaps of the developing countries by raising the rates of productive investment. A seminal work from this era by Rostow came closest to defining a development model (Rostow, 1960). In the stages of economic growth, the first condition for 'take-off' was a rise in the investment rate, which could be achieved through an exogenous injection of capital.

A further refinement of Rostow was developed in 1966 by Chenery and Strout, outlining the role for aid more comprehensively (Chenery and Strout, 1966). It was another stages-of-development approach, also known as the two-gap model: during the first two stages of economic development, aid was required to bridge the difference between capital investment needs and domestic savings (the internal gap), and to finance the necessary increase in imports (the external gap).

Much of the essence of these theories is lost in paraphrase. There were other critical aspects of these and other theories, but they were accorded limited attention during the early stages of development assistance. Rostow's third condition had been the emergence of a political, social and institutional framework that facilitated ongoing expansion. Chenery and Strout also laid stress on the importance of technical assistance and the development of skills as an essential accompaniment to capital and as fundamental to absorptive capacity. This was the third gap.

Aid from the Soviet bloc carried many of the same prerogatives and it came in similar wrappers. Socialist principles, handed down from the commanding heights of heavy industry, had served Soviet economic advance well. They also emphasized capital investment, as manifested in the vast Soviet industrial and infrastructure projects that began to appear in the developing countries. The Soviet Union also developed elaborate trade and barter schemes to provide essential imports – often on quite unfavourable terms – to its developing country allies. Training was tied in with these aid programmes, including lengthy study-tours and scholarship schemes. Russian became a second language among the elite classes of Cuba, Mongolia and Vietnam.

Gap 1: Aid as capital

The role of aid in investment has been exhaustively investigated through project evaluations. For the most part, these project evaluations have shown positive outcomes. For example, the World Bank reported average rates of return of over 10 per cent on its capital projects during the 1960s and 1970s in every major region and almost every sector. More recent assessments have determined higher average rates of return.[3] The results from other development banks have been similar.

These positive results would be sufficient evidence of the effectiveness of capital assistance if they were accompanied by proof that such aid had also had beneficial consequences for macro-economic growth. However, empirical studies reach a very mixed conclusion. Already in the 1970s, studies showed a negative correlation between aid and domestic savings (Griffin and Enos,

1970; Weisskopf, 1972). More recently, research has shown that there has been a very uncertain correlation between aid and growth.[4] In some countries, a poor correlation can be explained by the fact that capital aid has replaced, rather than supplemented, the domestic savings or the private foreign capital that might have funded the investments. For example, the World Bank and the IMF advanced 22 separate loans to Pakistan between 1970 and 1997 that were tied to reductions in the primary budget deficit, yet they failed to close the gap (Mallaby, 2004). Continuing aid can discourage savings. Thus, the overall (macro-economic) effects of incoming flows are increased consumption, not increased investment.

This conclusion cannot be generalized because the circumstances of each developing country have been very different. The amounts of investible funds within aid programmes varied enormously from recipient country to recipient country. In some, the inflows were large relative to GNP, in others quite small. High inflows went to countries with consistently high savings rates and higher investment rates (Malaysia, South Korea). These countries – showing a high correlation of aid to investment – have needed capital aid least, but have put it to the most productive use. High investible inflows of aid funds have also gone to countries with low domestic savings rates, in which investment and savings have remained at chronically depressed levels. These were the countries – showing a low correlation of aid to investment – that might have needed capital aid most, but have used it least well.

Although there are many variants of these relationships, it is tempting to concur with some critics that capital aid has gone either to countries that do not need it or to those that cannot use it. The 'displacement theorists' conclude that in the neediest countries aid has been diverted to other than productive uses and has removed the incentive for recipient governments to improve fiscal and monetary discipline, and to raise public and private savings performance.

Private capital

The effects of aid are mitigated by private capital. After 1970, private flows to developing countries increased substantially. (By the end of the 1990s, they exceeded aid by between four and five times.)

The rise in private lending to developing countries during the 1970s can be explained in large part as a balance of payments need. In 1973 and again in 1979, the substantial rises in the price of OPEC oil left the oil-importing countries with substantial new requirements for capital that, in the absence of adequate official capital, could only be met from the large surpluses of the high-income, oil-exporting countries. The monetary recycling occurred in one of two ways. First, the Organization of Petroleum Exporting Countries (OPEC) – mainly the Arab states and Iran – became important sources of augmented official aid (see Chapter 7). Second, recycling occurred through the intermediary of Western commercial banks where a major portion of the 'petrodollars' was deposited. These deposits augmented the rapidly rising liquidity of the euromarkets, and banks responded to the capital needs of developing countries with large new lending operations. Between 1972 and

1976, the total value of private bank lending to developing countries more than doubled in real terms.

But the substitution of aid by private capital was reversible. The oil shocks were followed by a global liquidity crisis, with higher interest rates and stagnation in the developed countries at the end of the 1970s. Those countries that had adjusted their economies during the decade and retained an export earning capacity were able to surmount their indebtedness. But the serious debt problems from which many developing countries are suffering originated during this period. For the poorest among them – mainly in Sub-Saharan Africa – the responsibilities of creditor have shifted steadily from private to official (bilateral and multilateral) lenders.

External capital – whether from official or private sources – has been an essential component for development but not a sufficient one. In open, well-managed economies that have given priority to export expansion, external capital has been productively used, and private capital and foreign investment have come to replace aid (in the form of capital from official sources). Flows of external private capital, however, are potentially volatile. Sound macro-economic management and a well-regulated financial sector are necessary to promote confidence in the host economies and minimize the risk of capital flight.

In more stagnant and closed economies, capital aid has been a poor primer of investment. It has been less productively used and has tended to dampen domestic savings and investment efforts. The difficulties of such economies in meeting their balance of payments requirements have been compounded by poor export performance and by an adverse global economic environment in which terms of trade deteriorated sharply (especially for oil-importers), global growth declined and the costs of capital rose. The gap-filling needs of many of these economies have been met by both private and official capital, but borrowing has led directly to intractable debt burdens.

In sum, there has been an uncertain correlation between the provision of capital aid and development progress. The uneven performance of developing countries in the use of official and private finance can be explained by the strengths and weaknesses of domestic policies and institutions, the degree of openness of the economies (and the varying impact of global economic conditions).

Gap 2: Aid for imports

Another traditional justification for aid was as a temporary expedient for developing countries to fill an external payments gap and sustain imports. Aid has indeed been essential to countries subject to sudden external shocks – such as a collapse of export prices – or crisis needs, for example food shortages following poor harvests. But over the longer term, development assistance would have served developing countries best by stimulating trade expansion and facilitating their capacity to export. In this respect, aid in its different forms, and the policies followed by the donors have been unhelpful at best, and, at worst, have proved an impediment to trade expansion. Commodity and food aid has been used as a long-term substitute for trade; the tying of aid has distorted trading conditions and terms; and the protectionist policies of the donor countries have annulled some of the potential benefits of aid by putting up barriers to exports from the developing countries.

Commodity and food aid

The Marshall Plan established the pattern of commodity aid and was the inspiration for the US Food for Peace programme enacted by Public Law 480. Food aid from the major grain exporters – which is channelled either bilaterally or multilaterally (for example, through the UN's World Food Programme) – became a widespread form of external gap-filling, constituting some 10 per cent of total aid value overall, and much more in the instance of some individual donors. A major reason for the popularity of long-term food aid with some donors is that it allows the major food producing donors to dispose of substantial quantities of surplus produce (which in the case of the European Union have been accumulated as a result of overproduction stimulated by farm subsidies). In times of humanitarian crisis, food aid has been of critical importance, for example during emergencies in eastern and southern Africa since the 1970s. But as a developmental resource, the utility of food aid has been questionable (Raffer and Singer, 1996).

Where food aid directly replaces commercial imports and where it reaches those who are too poor to buy food, it can free domestic resources for other purposes. Food aid is often monetized from local sales and the proceeds used to finance development projects. 'Micro' gains from the provision of food aid can usually be demonstrated, although there are also documented misuses of food aid due to the difficulty of effective targeting of needy recipients. But, as with capital assistance, food aid – particularly where it has been provided over a long and continuing period – has tended to have deleterious 'macro' consequences. Food aid dependence has depressed domestic food prices and inhibited efforts to stimulate domestic food production in some countries (Schultz, 1960).

Protectionism

The post-war period has been one of unfair trade. Developing countries sought to protect their own fledgling manufacturing and processing sectors, but had to face a hostile protectionist environment in developed country markets, particularly for certain commodities in whose production they have the greatest comparative advantage: agricultural commodities in raw and processed form, garments and other non-technological consumer goods. Under multilateral auspices, there have been many initiatives to achieve fairer trading conditions, but the results have been mixed. Attempts by the UN (notably the United Nations Conference on Trade and Development – UNCTAD) and the European Union to try to compensate for market forces and build commodity protection agreements, or provide compensatory funds, have been expensive and unsustainable, since they only address one side of the transaction (supply) in the face of declining or weak demand.

Eight rounds of global trade negotiations under GATT, leading to the creation of the World Trade Organization (WTO), have encouraged freer trade, although a high degree of protectionism by the richer countries – and some of the poorer – still persists in agricultural and textiles trade. By most estimates, the costs to the developing countries of unequal access to markets are substantially larger than the value of net aid transfers, prompting the conclusion that developing countries would be better off with less aid, but fairer trading rules.

Aid as donor export support

The commercial motivation for bilateral aid has always been strong and an important proportion of capital assistance – about one-third for donors overall, substantially higher for some of them individually – is tied to the purchase of goods and services in the respective donor countries. It can be applied as a more general support mechanism, or as a specific subsidy, when it can take the form of a 'mixed credit' (in which aid is associated with a trade loan). For some donors – such as the US and UK – the returns via the multilateral banks were much higher. In the late 1980s, Nicholas Brady, the US Treasury Secretary, remarked with satisfaction that 'for every dollar provided to these (multilateral) banks, the US economy gets back US$9 in US procurements'.[5]

Aid tying is motivated by a belief that aid can act as an economic stimulant in the home country and circumvent export competition, but there is no solid basis for believing that either objective is actually achieved. Subsidies in whatever form tend to inhibit, more than they foster, competition. For recipient countries, tied aid constitutes a net gain in terms of resource transfers, but it distorts trade. Analysis shows that tying reduces the value of the aid by 15 per cent or more through rent-related cost increases of the goods and services procured.[6] There are also various indirect costs of tied aid for recipients. Goods and services provided may be of low priority, excessively capital-intensive and otherwise technologically incompatible. Aid tying also creates dependency on continuing imports from the donor country.

In sum, a combination of aid and the protectionist stances of the donor countries inhibited and distorted trade for developing countries, rather than assisting in the creation of export capacity. Again, the fundamental question is whether the recipient countries would have been better off without long-term food and commodity assistance and tied aid. While the transfers of resources would have been substantially less, developing countries would have been subject to fewer commercial pressures and distortions.

Gap 3: Aid as technical assistance

While a major role of aid was to serve the ends of economic growth through support to investment, it was recognized that the capacity to absorb capital was constrained by low skill levels, as well as weak management and organizational capacities. The emergence of a political, social and institutional frame-work that facilitated ongoing expansion was also a condition for 'take-off'.

During this first phase, technical assistance (TA) programmes focused on training and human resource development as a means to close this perceived gap. TA was heavily weighted by donor interest and composition. All bilateral and multilateral TA was funded by donors and a major part of the funds were spent on donor goods and services.[7] Associated with capital assistance, TA provided pre-investment and feasibility studies and supplied specialist advice to those sectoral ministries (industry, agriculture, education, health and so on) in which individual donors had a particular interest, and where they had specific expertise to offer.

Institution building has been more graft than craft. Donors established autonomous management units to run 'their' projects, without careful consid-eration of how these offices would be integrated into existing administrative structures, once the projects ended. On a larger scale, donors created or supported whole new organizations of doubtful use or legitimacy, which were not willingly sustained by the recipient country.

The problems of TA approaches ran deep, and they derived then – as they do now – from assumptions that there was indeed a skills 'gap' requiring to be bridged. TA mainly consisted of a transference of knowledge from expert practitioner to 'counterpart'. The expert was there to accurately diagnose the knowledge hiatus and vest the counterpart with the necessary skills. TA, born out of Western rationality, was a process that has been described as 'techno-hubris' (Morgan, 2002). Like implants of capital, skills were packaged and purveyed in definable units ('projects') for the benefit of counterparts in need of capability upgrades. But because TA was largely a response to donor-contrived definitions of need, it mostly did not stick.

Transferring skills from person to person through training was, in any case, not an effective vector of change if the complexities of the institutional and societal context were not taken into account. The strengthening of capacity – personal and organizational – has to adjust to the subtle norms and rules of conduct that guide individual and collective behaviour. Where training was superficial and disembodied, TA contributed little to local capacity develop-ment and helped to accelerate the permanent exodus of personnel from the recipient countries. Far from building capacity, TA often undermined it.

As a gap-filler, therefore, TA had very uneven success in fostering the processes and the institutions needed to underpin and, more importantly, sustain beneficial change. As a UNDP analysis of African aid concluded a few years ago, 'almost everybody acknowledges the ineffectiveness of technical cooperation in what is or should be its major objective: achievement of greater self-reliance in the recipient countries by building institutions and strengthen-ing local capacities' (Berg et al, 1993).

To sum up the first phase of aid's history, the first three decades were inspired by a model of development, refined by western academics, that envis-aged a threefold gap-filling role for donors. Filling the savings gap saw a concentration of support for state-led investment from both Western and

Eastern donors. Central planning was in vogue in most of the developing world and donors helped to draw up and finance investment plans. Aid also financed the external gap by providing imports – usually through loans. To close the skills gap, technical assistance provided pre-investment and feasibility studies – many packaged with donor-financed capital projects – and supplied specialist advice to sectoral ministries (industry, agriculture, education, health and so on).

On all three counts, however, the evidence that aid made any sustainable impact in closing these gaps is ambiguous.

PHASE II: THE QUALITY OF GROWTH

Basic needs

Phase I had stressed the importance of economic growth, but the quest for growth through aid was elusive. Was it also an illusion? By the 1970s, economists were discovering that more did not necessarily mean better. The evidence of faster-growing countries like Brazil showed that the benefits of growth could not be relied on to 'trickle down' to the poor. Where there were very marked income inequalities, high growth simply did not translate into higher incomes for all.[8] But much more than mathematical tautology was at play. Aided development was building enclaves of modernization within developing economies with limited benefits for the majority of the population.

These concerns prompted the search for a new development paradigm and led to the 'basic needs approach', first publicly enunciated by the President of the World Bank at a speech in 1972.[9] Developing countries and their sponsors needed to pay much closer attention to the well-being of individuals in terms of their need for food, health, education, shelter and clothing. This focus on the ends of development rather than the means anticipated by nearly two decades the work of the UNDP on human development indicators (which highlighted the more subjective concerns of meeting needs) and the Millennium Development Goals enshrined by the international community a decade after that (2000).

Much of the intellectual work on basic needs was done in the UK (at the Institute of Development Studies, Brighton) and in Switzerland by the International Labour Office in Geneva (ILO, 1977). The ILO then set out to develop national strategies on basic needs in several countries. The World Bank, meanwhile, was examining a form of economic expansion that it dubbed 'redistribution with growth' (Chenery et al, 1974).

Carrying capacity and the global view

The 1970s were also preoccupied with sustainability and the possibility that growth targets would exhaust available resources. In 1972, the UN sponsored a conference in Stockholm on the 'human environment', which examined the quality of human life and the natural resources that support it. There was growing concern – again mainly emanating from the rich countries – about the 'carrying capacity' of the natural world. Many developing countries were sceptical about participating, since they saw the conference as providing a rationale for dampening their growth aspirations. After the conference, notwithstanding the establishment of the UN Environment Programme (UNEP), interest in environmental concerns diminished within the international community – North and South. Many in the developing countries continued to see a trade-off between environment and economics. And environmental dangers were perceived to be mainly local: if it was 'not in my back-yard' (NIMBY), it wasn't a global concern. But when in the 1980s, more reliable scientific evidence linked 'local' environmental degradation to global meteorological changes, and as the signs of global warming began to appear, environmental management concerns rose up the agenda again. The importance of global action by the rich countries to help the development cause was becoming apparent.

A second global preoccupation was with the number of people. Population was the divisor in any calculations of carrying capacity and the large and rapidly growing populations in the South were widely considered by the donors to be a danger to development prospects. The now rich countries had not experienced population growth on a similar scale during their own development. Such growth overturned traditional resource balance calculations and led many development specialists to advocate reductions in population growth. A belief that spending on population control methods would significantly reduce population growth goaded the donors to give more generously to the UN Population Fund (UNFPA), which they had set up in 1967, and other international non-governmental organizations committed to birth control.[10]

Structural adjustment

But the bankers were also on the march. The surplus global savings balance of the 1970s – accumulated in part by the huge increase in unspendable export earnings by OPEC – had stimulated substantial lending to developing countries. By the turn of the new decade, the unfamiliar phenomenon of 'stagflation' was assailing the developed countries and the costs of borrowing had mounted rapidly. The South was heavily in debt and in 1982, Mexico came close to defaulting. After several decades of aid, most of the developing countries were as far away as ever from closing their external and domestic financing gaps. The banking system accommodated partially. The most exposed commercial banks absorbed some of the losses through bad-debt provisions, and limited grant aid was diverted to provide for official debt restructuring.

The Bretton Woods financial mechanisms, originally established to regulate global imbalances, took none of the hits,[11] but responded with more short-term lending. By mid-decade the flow of funds had turned around so that the developing countries as a whole became net creditors of the World

Bank and IMF. These costs of financial dependence were attributed by World Bank economists at the time to policy failure on the part of the borrowers.[12] To the uncertainties of trade, and the burden of debt in the developing world, had been added the necessity for comprehensive structural adjustment, essentially a set of policy measures designed to close the internal and external resource gaps.

With the World Bank's first 'structural adjustment loan' in 1980 (to Colombia), a new aid phase of macro-economic governance began, in which the policy choices for the poorer developing countries were increasingly prescribed by Washington. They began to depend ever more heavily on loans from the World Bank and IMF, to which their indebtedness grew. Banking prerogatives sought to establish and maintain the solvency of the lenders. Up front, the IMF was concerned with short-term balancing of external resources and a closing of the domestic resource gap. On its heels, the World Bank sought to put in place the structural reforms necessary to sustain these results. Some of the Western bilateral donors also began to align themselves with the emerging neo-liberal prescriptions that characterized Bretton Woods conditionality (see Box 4.1), incorporating these policy conditions into their own aid strategies, and further infringing the economic independence of the developing countries.

As we see in the next chapter, however, stability and adjustment paid meagre dividends and often resulted in less growth and more poverty. As Hjertholm and White (2000) put it: 'the increase in adjustment lending was not a response to a "development crisis". In general, there was no such crisis... Rather it was a response to balance-of-payments and debt problems'.

The 1980s was a defining decade for aid and development. The serious economic setbacks in Latin America were not being effectively addressed by the structural adjustment programmes that had been pioneered there. In Africa too, structural adjustment was failing.[13] Worse, famines were recurring in some of the most generously-aided countries and were in all cases attributable to factors of human origin that official aid was seemingly unable to influence. In humanitarian crises, private charitable organizations were more agile than government and multilateral agencies in mobilizing and delivering aid.[14] Their role as agents of development and relief assistance grew visibly during the decade, supplementing, and in some cases supplanting, governments and official agencies. South Asia was also continuing to stagnate. And yet, at the same time in East Asia, the 'Tiger' economies were bounding ahead along high-growth paths, but with diminishing development assistance.

Aid was clearly in crisis. 'Does aid work?' asked one exhaustive study in 1986. Yes, but only partially, was the response (Cassen et al, 1986). As the decade wore on, the prescriptions were wearing out, and the effectiveness of the traditional aid institutions was in question. Aid's influence over development appeared limited: where aid was needed, it wasn't working; where development was working, aid wasn't needed.

PHASE III: POST-WALL GOOD GOVERNANCE

With the reunification of Berlin and the disintegration of the last modern empire in 1989–91, the political and economic vulnerabilities of communism were exposed. While the change in the Soviet Union was not a simple triumph of capitalism over communism,[15] the world had crossed a threshold that spread far beyond European politics.

The importance of geopolitical motivation in aid was very well demonstrated in the 1990s. Without the Cold War, aid fell sharply after 1992. Donors turned inwards, some invoking domestic budget pressures. Germany was accommodating the huge expense of absorbing its eastern wing, and other European countries were adjusting to the single currency (which required limits to be set on domestic deficits). Japan and the US also claimed fiscal straitening, and aid fatigue affected almost all donors as doubts grew over its effectiveness. After 1992, a high-water mark, total OECD aid declined over the next 10 years. Between 1992 and 2000, aid fell by 10 per cent and the DAC donors' contribution in 2000 was only 0.22 per cent of their collective gross national income (GNI) – the lowest ever (see Figure 3.1).

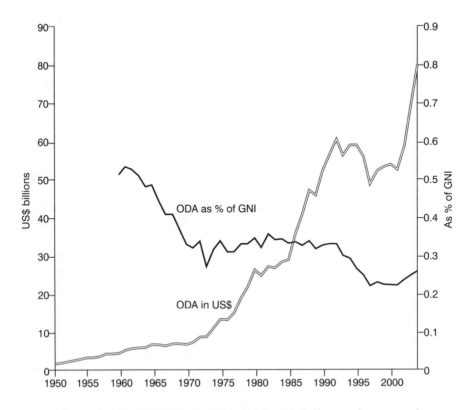

Figure 3.1 *Total OECD/DAC ODA in US dollars and expressed as a percentage of GNI, 1950–2004*

There was also a significant change of direction. In Sub-Saharan Africa, facing the sternest development challenges, there was a decline of 40 per cent over the decade. Individual countries were affected very differently, but there were some big losers. Mozambique saw a flight of donors just as it struggled to recover from protracted civil conflict. (They later returned after a humanitarian crisis.) Asia, India and Pakistan – harbouring an estimated 30 per cent of the world's poorest – lost out in the redistribution, and in Central America, donors reduced their support for El Salvador, even as it was beginning to enjoy a period of stability. In each case, these countries were victims of post-wall realignments. Aid was effectively switched from Africa to Eastern Europe and Central Asia, as former donors became growing recipients. According to the OECD, Europe and the former Soviet Republics were receiving 20 per cent of all official concessional finance (a slightly broader definition than official development assistance) by 1996, compared with virtually nothing in 1989 (Browne, 1999).

Some Western donors made a complete about-face. The US had actively supported military dictatorship on its own doorstep in Brazil and Chile in the 1970s, and the UK was complicit in abetting the autocratic regimes of Commonwealth countries like Ghana, Nigeria and Pakistan. Now these two donors were the most strident in favouring disarmament and democracy. The end of history was proclaimed and the neo-liberal consensus, which had begun to feature in 1980s aid, was now extolled with even greater confidence.

But the new aid programmes aimed at Eastern Europe and the former Soviet Union demonstrated the historically familiar and maladroit determination by Western donors to influence development with limited reference to local political and historical realities. The first mistake was to pretend that every part of the former Soviet empire was ripe for similar donor-inspired remedies. Even among the so-called 'Visegrad' countries (Poland, Hungary, Czech Republic and Slovakia), there was a variable uptake of shock therapy. In the former Soviet Union, which had experienced collectivism for a whole generation longer, the disastrous transition ('more shock than therapy') should have signalled to eager Western partners (including the author in Ukraine at the time) that change was going to be much more protracted. Donors saw a triple transition to statehood, market and democracy. But rapid change on this scale was unprecedented, and was unlikely given the weak commitment of the new countries to the second and third of these revolutions. The backdrop to radical change was economic dislocation that – as in almost every humanitarian disaster – was the root cause of considerable hardship. The economies of most of the 12 former republics shrank alarmingly by up to 50 per cent in the first years of independence and did not begin to grow again until the end of the decade. It was inconceivable to alter hearts and mind-sets in a climate of survival.[16] But the donors tried nevertheless.

In tandem with humanitarian assistance, donors sought to expand their markets across this frontier through hastily extended commercial trade credits to the new countries. One result was a surge in external indebtedness that most of these countries had never experienced. These loans, which could not be categorized as aid, were not supplemented by capital assistance on any significant scale.

Most real 'aid' was in the form of technical assistance, which assumed its familiar guises of policy advice, organizational reform and training, nearly all of it unsolicited.[17] Even by past standards, there had never before been such a concerted campaign of 'make-them-like-us'. But the learning curve was steepest in the donor camp, as development experts discovered the complications of reconstructing whole societies. Reports and analysis proliferated, and they were mainly in English. Ten years on, the verdict of an East European observer on TA from the West was of 'inappropriate development concepts and incentives, lack of downward accountability and transparency in processes and reporting, hidden strategic agendas, inhibitory procedures and rules... undermining of local capacities' (Cukrowski, 2002). It all sounded ominously familiar.

Yet, quite outside the official donor pool, there were examples of success. Arguably the most effective catalyst of sponsored change in the former Soviet Union was from a non-traditional source. The Soros Foundation created national cells and gave them budgets to distribute among fledgling non-governmental organizations. George Soros's private wealth did more than any other organization to foster the germination of a civil society, and it was done flexibly without the leaden panoply of bureaucratic procedures and upward accountability mechanisms. Funding decisions were taken locally and by locals. It was a blatant form of aid as influence, but it stuck because it responded to a need.

This Eastern campaign helped to inspire a new donor paradigm both for the new and the traditional aid recipients. 'Good governance' became the watchword of the decade. The call for better governance was a donor reaction to concerns of at least three kinds: the relative ineffectiveness of aid; frustrations with the lack of commitment by many developing countries to reform processes; and endemic corruption.

Governance considerations became closely linked by donors to their aid programmes in all regions. The World Bank began to define governance as part of its conditionality process as early as 1989. The United States Agency for International Development (USAID) added governance to its global agenda in 1990. But the problem was to define governance in a manner in which it could be comparatively defined and assessed. What criteria would determine how well a country was governed? How would 'progress' be measured?

The World Bank's initial definitions of good governance were an extension of its structural adjustment advocacy, and were based on public sector management, accountability, legal frameworks, information and transparency (World Bank, 1992). Later, the definition was refined to include the following six dimensions (Kaufmann et al, 2005):

1   *Voice and accountability* – the extent to which citizens are able to participate in the selection of government.
2   *Political stability and absence of violence.*

3   *Government effectiveness* – perceptions of the ability of the government to produce and implement good policies.
4   *Regulatory quality* – the incidence of market-unfriendly policies.
5   *Rule of law* – the extent to which agents have confidence in and abide by the rules of society.
6   *Control of corruption* – perceptions of corruption in both business and politics.

The Bank has developed indicators for each of these six governance dimensions for all countries. The indicators are percentile rankings based on composite measurements determined by some eight or more northern-based sources (for example, Economist Intelligence Unit, World Economic Forum, Freedom House, Columbia University). The Bank itself acknowledges the perils of these indicators, all of which show wide margins of potential interpretative error. The indicators are also subject to rapid change, especially measures of 'political stability'.

Some donors specify their focus as 'democratic governance', thus explicitly incorporating a political dimension into the concept. The Bank's charter formally prohibits it from taking political considerations into account in its lending operations,[18] although the US has often exerted its predominant influence to prevent the Bank from lending to countries not to its liking on political grounds, including at different times, Cuba, Iran and Vietnam. Where the Bank lends, it has found it difficult to factor considerations of government legitimacy into its lending criteria, adopting a more technocratic 'policy' approach. As a result, in its lending operations, 'the approaches used to strengthen good governance in developing countries remained strikingly similar to those used to promote economic reform' (Santiso, 2001).

Economic rationalists are better able to deal with policies than politics. Yet politics has an important – but uncertain – bearing on policy and governance. There is no automatic correlation between democracy[19] and good governance. A fully-fledged democracy is a better guarantee of individual rights and freedoms, but does not vouchsafe development progress. 'Statistical studies find that neither authoritarianism nor democracy is a factor in determining either the rate of economic growth or how it is distributed', was the verdict of UNDP (2002).

India is one of the oldest and largest democracies, but until the 1990s, successive governments made virtually no impact on widespread poverty. When the revolution in economic reform took place from 1991, precipitated by the country's parlous financial state, these concerns were sufficient to override popular vocal objections to the discomfort of the reforms. Another large Asian democracy, Bangladesh, has also had mixed success. It has enjoyed buoyant growth in recent years and an improvement in human development indicators (including female education). But its vibrant political rivalries have detracted from consistency in policies, and attempts at reform have usually been met by vehement, and often violent, opposition. The country consistently languishes at the bottom of the ranks of Transparency International's

Corruption Perceptions Index.[20]

In Latin America, where democracy has made significant advances over the past two decades, the region is nevertheless confronting growing social and economic problems. The belief in democracy is waning, particularly where large inequalities persist. A recent UN survey found that:

> *a large proportion of Latin Americans rank development above democracy and would withdraw their support for a democratic government if it proved incapable of resolving their economic problems; 'non-democrats' generally belong to less well-educated groups, whose socialization mainly took place during periods of authoritarianism and who have low expectations of social mobility and a deep distrust of democratic institutions and politicians; and although 'democrats' are to be found among the various social groups, citizens tend to support democracy more in countries with lower levels of inequality.* (UNDP, 2004)

Looking at East Asia, it is tempting to believe in the superiority of authoritarianism. China and Vietnam have recorded marked development progress for some 20 years. The 'liberal' autocratic regimes of Lee Kwan-Yu (1959–1990) in Singapore and Park Jung Hee of South Korea (1961–1979) curtailed many individual freedoms but also presided over a spectacular transformation of their countries, driven by high growth and poverty eradication. The rights to freedom were circumscribed, but the rights to development were respected.

But it is just as likely that autocracies will also be malevolent. One of the most notorious examples was Mobuto Sese Seko in Zaire, assisted into power by the American CIA in 1965 and who ruled unopposed for the next 32 years. He did very little to promote development and diverted generous amounts of Western aid to shoring up his political survival and contributing to his personal enrichment. A succession of cynical military rulers have contrived to keep Nigeria in poverty over three decades, culminating in the regime of Sani Abacha who presided over a corrupt rent-seeking administration for five years until his death in 1998.

The application of good governance criteria to aid allocation has been fraught with ambiguity. In the 1990s, aid became an adjunct of foreign policy for most donors as the bilateral agencies were even more closely aligned with foreign ministries. But, as we saw, democracy and governance do not enjoy a linear relationship, sometimes travelling in opposite directions. China is undemocratic but well-governed in the sense of delivering development.[21] Thus, although it has come in for much criticism because of its human rights record, China received generous amounts of aid during the 1990s.[22]

Undemocratic regimes and dictatorships may hinder development progress, or they may not. There are also democracies that have been inclusive and transparent (like Bolivia), but that have failed to prevent continuing impoverishment. Others have been more successful. A democratic governance paradigm is misleading for several reasons. For one thing, democracy is diffi-cult to define. It has been simplistically equated with the holding of national elections. Between 1974 and 1999, multiparty elections were introduced for the first time in 113 countries. But although the practice has become much more widespread, elections do not, of themselves, assure legitimation of a regime or prevent the emergence of dictatorship. The claim is always made that bad leaders can be voted out of office. But history shows that bad leaders can also be voted in, and that they can manipulate electoral systems to ensure their re-election. Another problem is that different facets of democratic gover-nance are poorly correlated. There can be effective government – in the administrative sense – without the legitimation of democracy. This case can be made for many socialist countries. Also, there are no simple paths of evolution towards democratic governance. Countries move into and out of democracy and authoritarianism.[23]

Because agendas cannot be formulaic and one-sized, and there are no simple normative checklists to describe the situation in any one country, the problem confronting donors is how to 'score' governance: what relative weights are to be given to different aspects of democratic governance, such as government effectiveness, inclusiveness, human rights and transparency? In reality, practice prevails over principle, and it is the political and commercial expediencies of donors that determine these weightings.

There are at least two other problems. While aid has purportedly flowed increasingly to support more democracy and better governance, there is little evidence to show that it has had a positive influence. Fundamental and sustain-able changes in institutions and policies are rather impervious to outside influence. Results have tended to undermine the whole rationale for large-scale, policy-based lending by the multilateral banks. Aid may, in fact, even have a perverse effect. This debate over the efficacy of aid conditionality merits its own chapter, coming next.

The second difficulty has been civil conflict. Although there has been a significant fall in the number of civil wars during the 1990s in every region except Africa, there are still one billion people living today in low-income countries 'that have been unable to adopt and sustain policies and institutions conducive to development' (Collier et al, 2003). These countries pose a special challenge for donors. How can good governance be built on the back of no governance? These 'failing states' are the subject of Chapter 5.

CONCLUSION

The development agenda began with a belief in the power of money and skills, the two types of resource that the richer countries – following Truman's origi-nal exhortation – were considered to have in abundance. Gap-filling was the early 'input' model of development (Phase I). As analysis became more sophis-ticated, so did the complexity and diversity of the paradigms. Growth was not enough, it was important to look at its quality and its results. This could have been termed the 'output' model. Latterly, there has been greater convergence around what might be described as an agenda of development management and 'outcomes'.

These changing agendas – largely reflecting Northern perceptions of the South – and following an evolution in the understanding of the development process, have been incorporated into the many country programmes that individual donors roll out to recipient countries for validation. Each gains acceptance by recipients, because each is a framework for new patronage. But as realistic blueprints for change, these agenda-based programmes have failed more than they have succeeded. Empirical evidence shows a poor correlation between aid application and development outcomes. Few donor programmes actually achieve their declared development objectives. Although carefully crafted with fixed time periods and resource envelopes, they fail to reach their declared goals and are continually rephased into new cycles of assistance.

These agendas have failed to stick in large part because they have reflected the changing perceptions of donors, rather than the more constant realities of recipients, and they are simply unfeasible. The successive prescriptions of change and reform would require capacities for adaptation, which it is unrealistic to expect in most countries. Furthermore, change requires complex processes of building 'social and political consensus' (see Box 3.1).

Most recipient countries have never had control over the content and uses of aid. Rather than responding to needs that recipient countries have identified for themselves, aid – through the development agendas that have driven it – has sought to shape those needs for itself. In doing so, donors have exerted control over the direction of development in recipient countries, by diverting and tying up matching domestic resources of counterpart staff and counterpart funds.

Of course, while in the aggregate, sustainable development outcomes that can be attributed to aid have been meagre compared with the sum of over one trillion dollars expended (just for ODA), not all aid has been wasted. But where it has been productive, it is in countries with the capacity and the confidence to chart their own development courses. These countries – including in particular those in East Asia – have demonstrated that development progress has been correlated with a capacity to gradually eschew aid and influence, rather than attempt to absorb it.

For the majority of recipient countries, and in particular those that have received substantial levels of aid but continue to languish, aid has proved to be notably unproductive. The question then is: why do the donors – periodically claiming budget stringencies and public disinterest as aid constraints – persist with aid? One explanation follows from the logic of aid as a means of influence. Donor countries stay engaged with developing countries that they mostly choose on historical, political, commercial and (more recently) security grounds. Their tenacity applies to the weaker as much as to the stronger performers. As Fukuyama puts it, donors will not abandon the 'hapless' countries because they 'don't like to give up the influence and power over client countries that dependence brings' (Fukuyama, 2004).

Box 3.1 The limitation of donorship

'For decades, the development community has intervened in poor countries with little understanding of the political and institutional landscape, and with scant regard for the impact of their actions on local political relationships and incentives. If that sounds harsh, consider the record.

In quick succession, donors have advocated state-led development, then marketization and the retrenchment of government from core functions, followed by democratization, decentralization, the establishment of autonomous agencies, the creation of public–private partnerships, and civil society participation in the delivery of core services. All this has been imposed on poor countries, with weak institutions, many of them still in the process of basic state building, and in the context of a rapidly changing global environment.

Donors have consistently been unrealistic about the capacity required to manage complex processes of change, and have virtually ignored the need to build a social and political consensus for such change. They have expected poor countries to put in place a range of "best practice" institutions, which are far more sophisticated than those present in OECD countries at a similar stage of their economic development. And they have assumed that creating those institutions involves little more than the supply of material resources and technical assistance. In the latest "big push" for achieving the Millennium Development Goals, poor countries are expected, as a matter of priority, to promote: the rule of law (through properly resourced, adequately staffed legislatures, judiciaries and executives); political and social rights; accountable and efficient public administration; sound economic policies; corruption-free delivery of public services; and "support" for civil society.

Why this lack of realism?... In part... because realism is inconvenient. It does not support the next ambitious "big push" initiative. It underlines the need for policy and institution building to be driven by a local political process, which takes time and is beyond the control of donors. But a second, less obvious reason for lack of realism is a failure of imagination. The development community finds it difficult to conceive of legitimate public authority in developing countries except in terms of models that have worked relatively well in developed countries.'

Source: Centre for the Future State (2005) *Signposts to More Effective States: Responding to Governance Challenges in Developing Countries*, Institute of Development Studies, Brighton, Sussex

---

Aid ineffectiveness is also a spur for donors to go on spending. It was poor aid performance that encouraged donors to attach more incentives and conditions to their aid programmes. However, as the next chapter makes clear, conditionality has had a limited impact.

4

Influence Through Conditionality

The more active the donors become, the more they get drawn into the murky and, often, perverse rules of the game that they wish to change. In the end, their activism may help neither the integrity of the democratic process nor the substance of the reform measures that the national institutions are encouraged to implement.   DEVENDRA RAJ PANDAY,
                    FORMER FINANCE MINISTER OF NEPAL, 2005

The International Financial Institutions have radically overestimated their own power in attempting to induce reform in very poor policy environments. They have, in effect, ignored domestic politics.   PAUL COLLIER,
              FORMER WORLD BANK DIRECTOR OF RESEARCH, 1999

In the last chapter we reviewed the evolution of development agendas over more than half a century. These agendas have been donor-inspired and donor-funded, but they have also carried costs for recipients in the form of sets of conditions that they are required to fulfil.

These conditions had their origin in the conservative banking orthodoxies under which capital assistance was first started. Lending was as much concerned with the solvency of the client as with the developmental impact of the loan. Conditionality was first institutionalized by the IMF in the 1950s, but the World Bank also introduced conditions into its own lending programmes and these have become progressively more far-reaching. Bilateral aid has carried its own sets of conditions, usually of a more practical nature, from procurement constraints to project management arrangements. Latterly, as multilateral banks and bilateral donors have sought greater convergence in their aid agendas, there has also been a growing donor consensus around the conditions required of recipients.

Evidence, however, points to the relative ineffectiveness of conditionality. Rather than following donor prescriptions, developing countries have usually found their own paths to policy reform and adjustment. To the extent that this is true, much policy-based aid will have been wasted.

THE IMPORTANCE OF THE POLICY ENVIRONMENT

In 1998, the World Bank brought out an influential research report: *Assessing Aid: What Works, What Doesn't, and Why*. To these three questions, the report posited one broad answer: aid has a positive impact on growth and poverty reduction in countries with 'good' policies, and therefore 'policy-based aid should be provided to nurture policy reform in credible reformers'. The arguments of the report were used by donors as a rationale for more country selectivity in aid allocations. But it also made a significant contribution to the debate on aid effectiveness by highlighting the central importance of the policy environment.

The report also begged other critical questions, however. To what extent had aid led to policy reform, reflected in improved development performance? Was aid only effective in 'credible reforming' countries, or could it make a difference in the non-performers?

Aid effectiveness has traditionally been based on evaluations of project performance. Agency evaluations of projects have tended to be upbeat. The proportion of 'effective' projects – measured in terms of their own intrinsic objectives – is overwhelmingly the majority, and the proportion has been rising over time, giving the complacent impression of development success. But many of these successful projects have been in countries that have been least successful in terms of overall development performance, typically measured in terms of economic growth and poverty reduction. The inconsistency between project results and development performance has been described as the 'micro–macro paradox' (Mosley, 1987; Kanbur, 2003). Partly, the contrast is due to a failure to scale up and replicate projects. Partly, it is because project design has paid too little attention to sustainable capacity development. But mainly, macro success or failure is the result of the policy environment rather than the summation of micro development initiatives. The problem is that, where policy-based aid has been applied, the policy environment in recipient countries, and wider reform processes in general, have proved to be relatively impervious to outside influence.

These are also the findings of the authors of that same World Bank report in their subsequent research (Burnside and Dollar, 2000). In fact, they found no effect of aid on policy. Other analysis has determined that even where aid has been policy-oriented, incorporating specific conditionalities, the correlation has been weak. Kanbur (2003), formerly with the World Bank, calls the Burnside and Dollar findings 'an indictment of policy conditionality'. Morrissey (1998), basing his findings on extensive research, is equally categoric: 'conditionality emerges as at least ineffective and at worst counterproductive as a lever of policy reform'.[1] The title of a study by Killick (1997) is explicit: *Donors as Paper Tigers: Why Aid With Strings Attached Won't Work*.

THE LIMITS OF CONDITIONALITY

These are sobering conclusions, and they are supported by the high priests of conditionality themselves – the staff of the International Monetary Fund. It is instructive to examine that experience.

The IMF introduced conditionality in the 1950s at the behest of the Fund's major shareholders, formally incorporating the practice into its Articles of Agreement in 1969. In 1979, the IMF drew up a set of guidelines, which were to prevail for more than two decades. Conditionality consisted of a set of ex-ante prescriptions of policy associated with a programme of assistance. The logic of conditionality was that it sought to render a client country more likely to overcome its external financial imbalances and therefore ensure that it was able to reimburse the support received. In conservative banking traditions, subsequent tranches of financial support were contingent on compliance with the original conditions.

IMF conditionality traditionally focused on fiscal, monetary and exchange rate policies and was typically demand-constraining. From the 1980s, however, the scope of conditionality expanded considerably, reaching into more fundamental structural concerns and encompassing public sector reform. The number of conditions also increased markedly. Whereas in the 1970s and 1980s the average number had been mostly in single digits, they reached a peak during the Asian crisis of the late 1990s, when the IMF programme for Thailand incorporated 73 structural conditions, for Korea, 94 and for Indonesia, 140 (Buira, 2003)!

Increasing the number of conditions was intended to expand the scope of the policy reform sought by the IMF. However, as the number increased, the rate of compliance declined. If compliance is defined as disbursement of more than 75 per cent of a programme, then the rate fell from over 50 per cent in the early 1980s, to below 30 per cent in the 1990s. With larger numbers of conditions, the proclivity for failure increases, but we can conclude from this record that the harder the effort at policy reform by the IMF, the smaller the success. These were also the conclusions of the IMF itself. In its study on conditionality (IMF, 2001), the IMF found that it had been imposing conditionality 'on policies that were unlikely to be delivered, calling into question the realism of program design'. Unfortunately, these revelations from the global banking specialists came too late for the borrowers and did not relieve them of the obligations to repay.

The World Bank has been the other major exponent of conditionality, starting with its structural adjustment programmes in the 1980s and leading up to the PRSPs from 1999. The Bank has also been candidly critical of its own programmes. A former senior adviser stated in a recent book that 'the hopes for adjustment with growth did not work out. There was too little adjustment, too little growth, and too little scrutiny of the results of adjustment lending' (Easterly, 2002). In reaction to these negative findings, both the IMF and the World Bank are re-examining their approaches to conditionality.

BOX 4.1 THE TENETS OF POLICY REFORM: WASHINGTON CONSENSUS AND STRUCTURAL ADJUSTMENT

Policy reform in the 1980s emanated from the international financing institutions and was in essence mainly economic, at least at first. The IMF put pressure on its borrowers to take short-term measures to close their external and domestic resource gaps. Devaluation of the currency was a standard measure, as were the cutting of public expenditure and divestment of state assets. The World Bank followed up by advocating measures to sustain the gains: tax reform to raise domestic revenues, more privatization and deregulation, downsizing the civil service, a shift of resources to encourage export capacity, and so on. The human consequences were often painful, however. Inflation was stimulated by devaluation and new taxes on consumption, social services were cut and public service jobs were lost. The time-scale of the measures was rarely sufficient to effect restructuring. And there were contradictions. More trade liberalization through lower import tariffs reduced state revenues.

The phrase 'Washington Consensus' was first coined by John Williamson in 1990 to describe the economic policies being pursued by the Bretton Woods institutions during the 1980s. His full list included:

- fiscal discipline;
- public expenditure reform;
- tax reform to broaden the tax base;
- interest rate liberalization;
- a competitive exchange rate;
- trade liberalization;
- liberalization of inflows of foreign direct investment;
- privatization;
- deregulation (to abolish barriers to entry and exit);
- secure property rights.

The last of these heralded a second generation of policy reform programmes, during the good governance era, when the financial institutions began to give more importance to broader non-economic issues. These included the development of new public institutions and the abolition of others, measures against corruption, environmental management, even democracy and gender equality. However well-intended, policy conditionality had become an attempt at engineering on a wholly different scale. The appearance of the poverty reduction strategy papers (PRSPs) in 1999, from the same source, represented a continuing expansion in the scope of conditionality.

Source: Williamson (1990)

In September 2002 the IMF approved new guidelines on conditionality, which stress more country ownership and fewer conditions. The Bank has also been engaged in its own comprehensive review.

Meanwhile, what has been going wrong and why? There are broadly two sets of problems with the use of ex-ante conditionality for the provision of aid: it may not work in practice, and it may not be right in principle. Let us look at these in turn.

WRONG IN PRACTICE

There are several reasons why conditionality has worked poorly. The first is donor inconsistency. Even the IMF and World Bank, which have tried to work together more closely as conditionality has come to feature more strongly in their programmes, have not always achieved complementarity. During the financial crisis in East Asia in the late 1990s, there was considerable disagreement among donors about the nature and severity of the conditions being prescribed by the IMF. Some of the doubters came from the World Bank. Its former chief economist devoted a considerable part of a recent book to his criticism of IMF programmes during the 1990s and earlier, which he often saw as wrongly conceived and executed (Stiglitz, 2002).

The picture is all the more confusing when there are several bilateral donors providing assistance, but making different demands on recipients according to their particular interests and agendas. These donor inconsistencies are further illustrations of the role of aid as influence.

Donor conditions also change over time, following the evolution of the prevailing development wisdom. For example, for much of aid's history, the paradigm has centred on making the public sector more efficient. More recently, with the ascendancy of a stronger pro-market ideology, more emphasis is being placed on the privatization of functions and services for which the state was previously responsible (Hall and de la Motte, 2004). But donors have moved at different speeds and advocated different models. They include both fast-track exponents and gradualists, often reflecting their own experiences and interests. This leads to the conflicting prescriptions referred to above. In the largest privatization movement in history – following the break-up of the Soviet Union – there were almost as many models as development partners, from shock-therapy to gradualism. The results were predictable. Each newly independent country eventually found its own way, but not before substantial time and resources had been wasted – not to mention the inevitable policy back-tracking.[2] Today, in Eastern Europe and elsewhere, some donors have also become strong exponents of involving private enterprise through 'public–private partnerships', but the range of permutations is baffling.

Second, conditionalities do not work because their implementation is not feasible, for political and other reasons. Conditionalities – like the agendas they are attached to – are usually thought up by agency personnel far removed from the programme countries and from local political realities. In the early 1980s, when the author was in Thailand, the prime minister resigned because he was not willing to take the political risk of raising the price of utilities, as exhorted by the country's dominant donor at the time. As a result, the reform programme was abandoned, an all too typical baby-and-bathwater story. Thailand, however, subsequently followed a successful development progression, with steadily diminishing amounts of conditional aid. Aid history is replete with stories of the politically destabilizing consequences of conditionality, but not usually with such salutary consequences. The political infeasibility of conditionalities has led to the abandonment of many aid programmes, and has given reform a bad name – the exact opposite of the intended outcome.

Perhaps fortunately, however, non-compliance does not always lead to the abandonment of programmes – only the abandonment of the conditions. This is because of pressures to get aid disbursed. Two World Bank examples from Africa are illustrative. In Ghana, in the early 1990s, the democratic government abrogated the budgetary conditionality of its structural adjustment loan with the World Bank when it granted substantial pay increases to its civil servants in advance of national elections. The World Bank duly suspended the next tranche of the loan, which was financing a significant part of the country's import bill. But the Bank immediately came under enormous pressure from private sector contractors and some of the bilateral donors to release the tranche rather than dishonour some key import contracts and risk precipitating an economic crisis (Kanbur, 2000). The Bank relented.

Easterly (2002) cites another example, from Kenya, to illustrate how the momentum of aid delivery can override conditionality. Between 1979 and 1996, the World Bank and IMF provided Kenya with 19 adjustment loans, which included conditions to improve the efficiency of state enterprises, including, in particular, Kenya Railways. The loans were mostly disbursed. But by the end of the 1990s, the World Bank was still alluding to the poor performance of Kenya Railways. The pressures to pursue programmes in Kenya came not just from the importance of maintaining an aid relationship with a significant client, but also from the need of the Bank staff to keep disbursements flowing, as a measure of their own individual success and that of their departments.

Third, however, even where conditions can be made to stick – especially in the case of poorer, weaker economies, in which the donors have few mitigating interests of a strategic or commercial nature – the impact may have little to do with the intended objectives. Money is fungible. Aid to governments, however assiduously it is circumscribed, inevitably frees up public money for other uses. Aid destined to support the social sectors, for example, may facilitate increases in defence spending.[3] External aid for infrastructure may reduce the commitment of domestic funding to the transport sector, and so on. Fungibility has been described by Stiglitz (2002) as the simplest reason for the failure of conditionality.

It is partly because of these leakages that conditionality has been broadened in its scope. It found its most comprehensive expression in the structural adjustment programmes led by the World Bank in the 1980s and 1990s. But where those programmes were implemented, they also mostly failed to achieve their objectives, even leading to perverse results. One reason has been the incompatibility of banking concerns with development interests. IMF and

World Bank programmes have tended to stress short-term fiscal and monetary goals, intended to close the primary fiscal gap and reduce external payments imbalances as an enhancement of creditworthiness. But economic balancing often does not serve longer-term development interests well. A comprehensive analysis (Mosley et al, 1991; see also Cornea et al, 1987) of World Bank policy-based lending in the 1980s concluded that:

> *living standards of the poor have evidently fallen in many developing countries, including those which have undergone structural adjustment. This appears to be partly in response to cuts in public expenditure, for which the Bank and the Fund bear responsibility, and partly due to the impact of price reforms advocated by the Bank.*

In many countries, structural adjustment – and accompanying sector reform programmes – went much deeper than resource balancing, seeking to promote freer internal markets for goods, services and manpower, as well as encouraging more openness in foreign trade (see Box 4.1). The record of the 1990s was intensively reviewed by the World Bank, in collaboration with a group of civil society organizations, as part of the Structural Adjustment Participatory Review International Network (SAPRIN), set up in 1997. In its 2002 review of findings – from which the World Bank has increasingly distanced itself – SAPRIN found four ways in which structural adjustment contributed to, rather than alleviated, poverty:

> *The first is through the demise of domestic manufacturing sectors and the loss of gainful employment by laid-off workers and small producers due to the nature of trade and financial-sector reforms. The second relates to the contribution that agricultural, trade and mining reforms have made to the declining viability and incomes of small farms and poor rural communities, as well as to declining food security, particularly in rural areas. Third, the retrenchment of workers through privatizations and budget cuts, in conjunction with labor-market flexibilization measures, has resulted in less secure employment, lower wages, fewer benefits and an erosion of workers' rights and bargaining power. Finally, poverty has been increased through privatization programs, the application of user fees, budget cuts and other adjustment measures that have reduced the role of the state in providing or guaranteeing affordable access to essential quality services.*[4]

WRONG IN PRINCIPLE

Conditionality is also wrong in principle because it contains some inherent contradictions. Overarching its many agendas and interests, the development community seeks in programme countries to encourage sound governance by administrations that are democratically representative and publicly account-able. But conditionality is an abnegation of those objectives. By its very nature, in seeking to impose policy direction from the outside, conditionality under-mines the domestic accountability it seeks to achieve. Ex ante, conditionality moves policy discussions 'off-shore' and ex post, it renders governments answerable to foreign and usually remote parties. Effectively, conditionality removes the responsibility of governments for development, while shoring up encumbent regimes whose political and economic power conditionality is often designed to limit. According to Joseph Stiglitz (cited in Uvin, 2004), ex-World Banker:

> *Rather than learning how to reason and developing analytical capacities, the process of imposing conditionality undermines both the incentives to acquire those capacities and confidence in the ability to use them. Rather than involving large segments of society in a process of discussing change, it reinforces traditional hierarchical relationships. Rather than empowering those who could serve as catalysts for change, it demonstrates their impotence. Rather than promoting the kind of open dialogue that is central to the democracy, it argues at best that such dialogue is unnecessary, at worst that it is counterproductive.*

POLITICAL CONDITIONALITY

Conditionalities have mostly been developed by economists and apply mainly to the sphere of economic management. But with the purging of the geopoliti-cal alliances of the Cold War from the early 1990s, and the rise of neo-liberal interpretations of the 'end of history', donors have attached growing impor-tance to broader governance concerns. Notwithstanding the ambiguities of the concept, democratic governance was lauded as an essential virtue for superior development performance. Donors have sought to tag aid with political condi-tionalities, applying criteria of democracy, human rights and, particularly since 1991, security.

Despite the ease with which the label is customarily applied, democracy is not easy to define, as we saw in the previous chapter. Better than static inter-pretations are the directions of change: are countries becoming more or less democratic? The most common surrogate for democratization is the holding of elections, and donors have attached increasing importance to the willing-ness of state leaders to submit themselves to a free ballot. Donors have been generous in extending technical support to balloting and there has been an impressive increase in the number of national elections. However, the freeness and fairness of balloting has come in for growing scrutiny. Elections are by no means a sufficient guarantee of good governance, nor even of legitimacy, as we have seen earlier.

Donors have also given aid to legislatures and the promotion of civil society organizations. In these technical senses, the instruments of democracy have been encouraged. But democracy itself cannot easily be 'purchased'. It has to come from within societies, engendering fundamental change and overturning tradition. As the author witnessed in the former Soviet Union, external partners can point the directions, but cannot order the speed. Based on an exhaustive study, Knack (2004) found 'no evidence that aid promotes democracy' and similar conclusions have been reached by others (for example, Bratton and van de Valle, 1997; Huntington, 1991–92).

Determining good and bad in the human rights records of countries is similarly elusive. For development purposes, rights can be divided into the two spheres encompassed by the UN Covenants drawn up in 1966: civil and political (CP) rights on one hand and economic, social and cultural (ESC) rights on the other. The former refer to individual freedoms and legal protections; the latter to the rights to development and cultural expression. Donors and recipients do not attach the same importance to each. For example, the US, which campaigned hard for the CP convention, has never ratified ESC. However, some developing countries (such as China, Cuba and Vietnam), which are accused of abusing CP rights, can legitimately claim better records on ESC. The reverse is also true: freer democracies such as India have been much less successful in guaranteeing development rights.

The most serious governance concerns stem from perceived threats to regional and global security. However, donors may have different perceptions of what those threats are. There has been much greater consensus about the dangers posed by Afghanistan during the era of the (democratically elected) Taliban government, Iran as a potential nuclear power or North Korea as an actual one, than there has been about Iraq. Some differences can be blamed on the quality of the intelligence, but in the case of Iraq, US perceptions were also more subjectively based on a dislike of the leadership.

Political conditionalities can take various forms. They may remain at the level of rhetoric, with individual donors choosing whether to engage or remain aloof from countries whose governance and human rights records they condemn. The impact of selective isolation is likely to be minimal, and widens policy differences among donors.

At the other end of the scale, donors may impose sanctions on developing countries subjecting them to economic or political isolation by the international community, or penalizing them through targeted restrictions on financial access, arms supplies or travel bans. Until 1990, only two countries (Rhodesia and South Africa) had ever been subjected to international sanctions. The 1990s, however, became the 'sanctions decade' and they were approved by the UN Security Council against governments (or opposing factions) in Afghanistan, Angola, Cambodia, Haiti, Iraq, Liberia, Libya, Sierra Leone, Sudan and Yugoslavia. Sanctions have been exhaustively analysed for their effectiveness and a full review is not entertained here (Cortright and Lopez 2000; 2002). Suffice it to say that sanctions – and just as often the threat of sanctions – have sometimes succeeded in persuading governments to accede to specific objectives demanded by the international community. The expulsion of Osama bin Laden from Sudan in 1996, the restoration of the elected government of Sierra Leone (through the Conakry agreement in 1997) and the ending of financial support to terrorism by Libya in 2003 were all precipitated by sanctions. However, sanctions have been much less effective in bringing about wholesale political change, for at least three reasons.

In the first place, in order to work effectively, sanctions require the universal approbation and commitment of the international community if they are to be effective. But rarely is there complete agreement in practice. Donor countries may diverge about the definition of a particular regime as egregious and the likely impact of sanctions. An example is Cuba. The US has imposed financial, trade and travel sanctions on the country for decades, at the urging of the vociferous lobby of Cuban exiles in some of the southern states. But few other donors have fallen into line. While they may object to the human rights record of the Castro regime, they can also recognize its achievements in the domain of human development. There is also a widely prevalent view that reform in Cuba is more likely to follow from engagement than isolation.

Donor solidarity is also undermined by subjective expediency of a commercial or other nature. The military junta in Burma (Myanmar) is widely reviled by the international community for its human rights record, but Japan and France (as well as other neighbouring countries) have declined to prevent their companies from working there and paying royalties to the regime.[5]

Second, even when agreement can be reached, the effect of sanctions is undermined because the targeted regimes almost invariably find ways of circumventing the restrictions or otherwise compensating for their losses. It required sanctions of increasing amplitude over more than 10 years on oil-rich Libya to exact a response on the Lockerbie bombing, although the overall economic impact was quite modest (despite the government claiming otherwise). Financial restrictions can increasingly be undermined through modern communications technologies, which allow unregistered cross-border transfers. An example is the informal *hawala* system that operates in South Asia and is largely out of reach of governments attempting to halt payments to and from terrorist organizations (Cortright and Lopez, 2002).

Third, sanctions are objectionable on ethical grounds because they tend to punish the most vulnerable in the population, in whose name the sanctions are designed. In Iraq, where sanctions imposed to persuade Saddam Hussein to disarm clearly did yield some positive results, the humanitarian costs to the general population were high and contributed to the unravelling of the programme.[6]

CAN CONDITIONALITY BE IMPROVED?

There is a mixed record on conditionality in its various forms. While democracy and rights have become a growing preoccupation for donors, they are areas in which an unequivocal determination of poor governance is difficult to make and where multilateral consensus is easily diluted by the individual commercial, political or other interests of donors. Sanctions, as an extreme form of punitive conditionality, have been successful in achieving some significant security-related objectives, usually under UN auspices. But in general, the influence of donors on the political nature and conduct of the administrations in developing countries has been limited. A review of African countries in the 1990s compared political with economic conditionalities and concluded that: 'donors have encountered considerable difficulty in ensuring that African governments adhere to economic reform agreements... There is no reason to expect recipient governments to comply any more fully with externally imposed political reform commitments' (Bratton and van de Walle, 1997).

In recognition of the limitations of conditionality, there has been a growing debate on how it might be improved. Three different examples can be cited to illustrate the avenues of change: fine-tuning, selectivity and ownership.

Fine-tuning

The IMF's 2001 report on its own conditionality, and other evidence, eventuated in new guidelines, approved at the end of 2002. They stress four changes: stronger national ownership, by involving the borrower more centrally in programme formulation; fewer conditions; more tailoring of programmes to the specific needs of borrowers; and more clarity on the exact terms of compliance.

Any roll-back from the increasingly invasive levels of conditionality reached at the end of the last decade is only to be welcomed. By reforming itself, the IMF also sends an important signal to other donors. However, even if some of the language is different, the new guidelines will not lead to a major departure from past practice unless they are interpreted more indulgently by the staff of the IMF. Some easing of conditionality is inevitable if rates of programme compliance are to be restored to higher levels. But if conditionality in all its forms has limitations, then fine-tuning will not address them.

Donor selectivity: The Millennium Challenge Account

After the Cold War, some bilateral donors began to narrow the number of their programme countries. The World Bank and others' findings that aid works best in the countries with the best policies has confirmed the trend. Donors are willing to lighten the touch of conditionality in countries already headed in the right policy directions.

A significant example of selectivity is provided by the Millennium Challenge Account (MCA), announced by the US President at the Financing for Development Conference in 2002. We discuss it at more length in Chapter 6. The MCA, to be managed by a new Challenge Corporation, separate from USAID and the State Department, may ultimately receive some US$5 billion per year and is to be disbursed in a limited number of the 'best-governed' countries. The first 16 recipients of MCA aid were identified in May 2004.[7]

Apart from its size and concentration – promising substantial increments of aid to the recipients – the MCA contains other important features. It enshrines a form of ex-ante conditionality. By prescribing in advance the criteria for MCA eligibility – governance, 'investment in people' and quality of economic policies – potential recipient countries are encouraged to burnish their policy profiles. Another key feature of the MCA, when it was announced, was a virtual absence of traditional kinds of conditionality: the chosen countries were expected to develop their own programmes for MCA funding.

It remains to be seen how the MCA will work out in practice. Beauty contests are never entirely objective. The absence of Uganda and Vietnam from the top choice may seem puzzling in terms of development performance, but for US tastes, their political scores were 'lower than others'. It is also already clear that the funds will not be free. A lot of hard bargaining is now expected to accompany the process of selecting projects and programmes in the 16 countries.

A much greater general concern with selectivity, however, is the principle itself. First, as with the MCA, selection by bilateral donors will always be overlaid by political considerations, which may not coincide with developmental criteria. Second, countries that are already doing well and earning commensurate support are further rewarded (making it all the harder to find new fundable projects within them).

There is now much backtracking from selectivity. Concentrating aid on the better performers – many of which are showing progress precisely because they have been able to lessen their dependence on aid – would mean ignoring the large number of developing countries variously described as 'fragile states' and 'difficult partnerships' in the language of OECD. These are the countries that lack the political commitment and the capacity to pursue pro-poor development because of egregious regimes or domestic conflict. While many of the familiar shortcomings of aid apply to this category of countries, many of them – and especially those in a phase of reconstruction – will have to depend on external assistance to regain viable statehood. The case for upturning selectivity and concentrating aid more exclusively on these fragile states is made in the next chapter.

Ownership and the PRSP

More 'ownership' of the development process is now strongly advocated as a counterweight to conditionality, the thinking being that if recipient countries can develop and commit themselves to their own national development strategies, they could persuade donors to respond to their needs, rather than the other way round. In 1999, the Bretton Woods institutions devised the Poverty Reduction Strategy Paper (PRSP) which, according to the World Bank, was to be 'country-driven and owned, based on broad-based participatory processes for formulation, implementation and outcome-based monitoring'. However, because the PRSP was also to be the sole basis for debt cancellation and new concessional lending from the Bretton Woods institutions, power in the partnership was strongly skewed in favour of the creditor.

From the start, even the notion of country ownership of the PRSPs was somewhat questionable. In the first place, the PRSP was a take-it-or-leave-it proposition. There was little time given for initial consultation with developing countries on the design of the instrument. All the heavily-indebted poor countries (HIPCs) were shepherded to a starting line, and given a tight timetable for completion. The Bank and the IMF made no secret of the fact that they wanted these papers done quickly.[8] It was another example of short-term banking rhythms superimposed on longer-term development processes. Second, because of the hastiness of the timetable, these country-owned instruments were never going to be adequately discussed and debated in 'broad-based participatory processes'. Just as in the rich countries, there is little tradition in developing countries of public participation in policy-making. Third, these 'country-owned' strategies had to be submitted to the World Bank and IMF for 'joint staff assessments', after which they were subject to approval by the boards of both organizations. Fourth, the World Bank proceeded to draw up an encyclopaedic compendium of PRSP guidelines, known as the Source Book, which recipient countries were encouraged to draw upon.

Nevertheless, by the time of the first comprehensive review of the PRSPs, in early 2002, the PRSP had become for many of the poorest countries what some have described as 'the only game in town'. The PRSP (complemented by the IMF's Poverty Reduction and Growth Facility) helped bring greater harmony to the Bank-Fund relationship and brought most of the bilateral donors on to the same platform. In fact, in terms of donor accord, the PRSP has been a significant achievement.[9] But the intimidating weight of donor interest, acting as an obligatory hinge on substantial new funding, has scarcely facilitated greater discretion and freedom of action by programme countries.

The 2002 review was mixed. The original deadlines for completion were missed by a long margin. But in countries where PRSPs were completed, they raised the prominence of poverty reduction as a policy goal, and helped to open up new spaces for discussion and dialogue on poverty issues. The finished products, however, reflect the central prescriptive processes that begat them, with some PRSPs bearing an unreassuring resemblance to each other. Like the pre-existing policy framework papers, they are often prefaced with the familiar Bretton Woods-style analysis of macro-economic frameworks.

Much more important, however, is whether PRSPs have actually been the best means – among other possible alternatives – to achieve the critical result of reducing poverty. This question was not adequately addressed by the review, although it was perhaps the most fundamental.[10]

CONCLUSION: THE NEED FOR DE-LINKING

The historical record has confirmed the findings of the World Bank and others about the limited influence of aid on policy change. The mechanism of conditionality is a poor lever for sustained policy reform, whether the policies are about economic management, governance or human rights. Money, in these circumstances, really does not talk. Where donors perceive the need for policy reform to be greatest and are willing to stake their resources on change, the results are limited. In the successful reforming countries, on the other hand, donors are pushing on an open door. It is tempting to conclude again from experience that where aid is needed, it isn't working and where development is working, aid isn't needed.

This chapter has examined the practical and ethical basis for conditionality. Analysis suggests that its failures are attributable to a variety of factors, among which is:

- the perception by recipient governments that their sovereignty is being undermined by the imposition of externally-conceived policy prescriptions; perceptions that are heightened by donor advocacy of unfamiliar and untried practices of popular consultation;
- the basic conservatism of all administrations, but more particularly the unwillingness of recipient governments to undertake policy change in the political, social, economic or other spheres because of the perceived risks to their own sustainability;
- the perception that all policy change is a desirable goal of external provenance that appeals mainly to donor ideologies, the full potential benefits of which have not been adequately explained nor quantified in comparison to the costs;
- the awareness that there are significant chinks in the neo-liberal boilerplate agenda, some aspects of which are vigorously contested by groups in international civil society;
- the imposition of artificial time-limits by donors on the achievement of results.

Aid conditionality is a poor lever for sustained policy reform, whether the policies are about economic management, governance or human rights. Change has to come from within, not without. Reform can be encouraged and catalyzed, but not enforced by external agents wielding a big financial stick.

The answer is to de-link aid from policy conditionality and to follow two tracks. On one track, there should be processes of policy and programme development, driven from within, and supported flexibly by trusted external partners. On a second track, external resources should be mobilized to meet the tangible needs outlined by each country's own strategy. The first track guides the second. The second funds the results of the first.

On track 1 the government undertakes a wide process of consultation within the country, leading to the formulation of an overall strategy of development, using goals that the country determines for itself. External partners act in this track as facilitators and sources of technical advice, where invited, but they do not impose their own agendas on it. The strategy is costed, assuming different funding scenarios.

On track 2 the government consults with the external partners of its choice – and those that are willing to assist – on the implementation of its strategy, soliciting support for different parts of it, to complement its own domestic resources. This way, all external aid is provided within the framework of the strategy, with minimal duplication.

In fact, there is nothing new in the two-track approach. An example was provided by Mali during the 1990s. Like many other developing countries, Mali had been developing its own poverty reduction strategy since mid-decade. Following more than two years of consultation and validation with a range of national actors within and outside the public sector, the government completed its national strategy in 1998 – track 1. The strategy was considered by the government to be a wholly home-grown document and submitted it to a donor round table in Geneva[11] as the basis for future assistance, which was duly pledged – track 2.

Unfortunately, this experience did not end happily. Not long after the approval of Mali's strategy and the donors' commitments to fund it, the PRSP was conceived and the World Bank and IMF asked Mali to start the whole process over again (focusing their attention – characteristically – around the finance ministry) and using the guidelines they brought with them from Washington. It was a repetitive and wasteful exercise.[12] The country's own strategy may not have been very sophisticated, and lacking in financial rigour, but it was developed from within and certainly could have been the basis for further strengthening by individual partners if necessary. Mali had demonstrated the art of the possible. But some of the donors had found problems to confound its solutions.

5

Aid to Fragile States

When countries give foreign economic aid, they have many motivations: humanitarian impulses, strategic concerns, interest group politics and simple bureaucratic inertia. We compared the amount of foreign aid countries receive per capita with the [Failed States] index ranking and found that the countries at greatest risk of collapse often get paltry amounts of aid. The exceptions appear to be countries that have been the recipients of large-scale international military intervention.

FOREIGN POLICY MAGAZINE, WASHINGTON DC, JUNE 2005

Although Australia has been a generous donor to East Timor, the Australian Government is reaping over $1 million per day from oil and gas in a disputed area of the Timor Sea that is twice as close to East Timor as it is to Australia. Australia has received nearly ten times as much revenue from Timor Sea oil and gas than it has provided in aid to East Timor since 1999...Australia has access to two-thirds of the known oil and gas deposits in the Timor Sea, even though a maritime boundary set according to international law could deliver most, if not all, these resources to East Timor.

OXFAM AUSTRALIA, 2004

Strong powers used to fear each other. Now their concerns emanate from states that are fragile and that threaten global stability. These states are still numerous – at least one-third of all developing countries. And they harbour up to one-and-a-half billion people, almost one-quarter of the world's population.

Fragile states are of universal concern because they are the source of many of the most challenging global problems. Many are chronically prone to conflict, with more than a dozen civil wars raging at any one time. Some are major exporters of narcotic drugs – Afghanistan, Burma, Colombia. Some are developing nuclear weapons and exporting the capability to develop them – North Korea and Pakistan. They are incubators of violence and terrorism, such as Afghanistan under the Taliban regime. In the zones of death, people are displaced, property is destroyed and natural resources are plundered. Weak states are also host to traffickers of people and to the still widespread practice of slave-labour. People quit failing states under the threat of persecution or economic deprivation and seek asylum or refugee status elsewhere.

Fragile states are also stalked by the silent crises of peacetime. People still starve to death in them – as in some of the West African countries in 2005 – and epidemic diseases can grow and spread alarmingly. The HIV/AIDS pandemic is the most obvious example, with 40 million carriers of the virus worldwide and 5 million additional infections every year. The much older disease of malaria – until recently the cause of even higher mortality rates in Africa than HIV/AIDS – has been almost completely eradicated in many tropical countries, but continues to afflict countries that have not applied the resources to sustain national campaigns. And polio, a disease spread by poor sanitation, but that can be controlled through universal immunization with a vaccine discovered 50 years ago, is still endemic in six countries (Afghanistan, Egypt, India, Niger, Nigeria and Pakistan). In 2005, it was carried across borders to several others, including Indonesia and Yemen.

Richer countries have more reasons than ever to address this new world disorder. But they are not doing a very effective job and, as donors, they have been inconstant partners. Many of the most fragile countries receive little assistance. Just as with all developing countries, donors have many criteria for allocating – or not allocating – aid. But even if need were the main incentive, trying to compensate for failure poses dilemmas. It is in the failing states where the intended beneficiaries of aid – the poor and marginalized – are worst off and who most urgently need to be reached. But under the prevailing orthodoxy, donors are inclined to withhold aid from governments with weak policy and governance records. Aiding fragile states carries high stakes. Aid driven by motives other than need can be destructive. But the right aid applied in the right manner can transform the prospects of millions of people.

This chapter examines state failure as an aid concern, and the failings of aid in the face of fragility. It first looks at poor development performance as a criterion for state failure. It then looks into the anatomy of failed states and enquires about some common causes, taking a closer look at three states in particular: Burma, Rwanda and Zambia. Finally, it asks how donor engagement could address the twin challenges of state failure: political will and incapacity.

FAILING DEVELOPMENT PERFORMANCE

The notion of development laggards is not new. In 1971, the UN identified a category of 25 least developed countries (LDCs) defined by three sets of criteria: low income levels (less than gross national income per head of US$775); a low human assets index (a composite of nutrition, health, education and adult literacy); and high economic vulnerability (volatility of agricultural production and trade, small economic size and proneness to natural disasters). Least developed status was consistent with the traditional orthodoxy of aid entitlement. It was equated with a priority for aid, as compensation for what was construed as inherent disadvantage. Within the overall target of 0.7 per cent of GNP for aid from the OECD countries, a target of 0.15–0.20 per cent was established for the LDCs, although it was never respected. (OECD aid for the LDCs actually fell by 20 per cent in real terms during the 1990s, which is much more than the overall aid decline.)

The sole graduate from this dismal club is the well-governed Botswana. Otherwise, the overall numbers of the LDCs have grown steadily and there are now 50, seeming to vitiate the criteria of natural disadvantage. Most LDCs would be unambiguously included among the poorest performers.

For many years, countries were compared using data of GNP growth and levels of income per head. From 1990, the UNDP broadened the income criterion and began analysing development performance by ranking countries according to a human development index.[1] The rankings immediately enlivened the development debate, especially because they were published at a time when many bilateral donors were reviewing their criteria for beneficiary selection.[2] A few years later, UNDP also published a ranking of countries in terms of poverty incidence.

Development results – and especially human development outcomes – provide an objective basis for determining individual country performance. There is now a wide range of indicators of overall performance available and in this section we look at a sample of empirical surveys. Depending on the definitions used, the number of poor performers ranges from around 30 to 60, which is a significant proportion of aid clients (see Table 5.1).

A study of poorly performing countries undertaken by the Overseas Development Institute (ODI) of the UK in 2004 examined performance in terms of two readily measurable development indicators (Macrae et al, 2004). It chose economic growth per capita and reductions in infant mortality over the separate decades of the 1980s and 1990s. Growth is a standard indicator of overall development performance, and the infant mortality rate (IMR) is a measure of social development that is highly correlated with income poverty. Both sets of indicators are available for most developing countries. Using these indicators, performance was determined for 126 low- and medium-income countries in absolute and relative terms. (Transition countries were excluded because full data for both periods were not available.)

The study examined performance in both absolute and comparative terms. It found that for each variable and each of the two decades, there were between 14 and 19 countries performing relatively poorly. However, the results reveal a lack of consistency in development performance. Over both decades, only four countries did poorly in growth terms (Democratic Republic of Congo, Niger, Saudi Arabia and Zambia) and only four did poorly in terms of IMR reduction (Afghanistan, North Korea, Rwanda and Zambia). The states that performed relatively poorly in growth, did better in IMR reduction, and vice versa. Only Zambia showed consistently poor performance on both measures in both decades.

Other contemporary research gives a different impression. Defining a failing state as 'a low-income country in which economic policies, institutions and governance are so poor that growth is highly unlikely', a more recent study suggests that almost all the countries in our table (for which data are available) show a consistently poor performance. Some are described as failing for more than 20 years (Chauvet and Collier, 2005).

The most comprehensive and widely acknowledged set of indicators for developing country performance tracking are the MDGs. The MDGs are based on the seven International Development Goals originally drawn up by the OECD in 1996, which were derived from a selection of targets defined by the global development conferences convened by the UN during the 1990s. There is nothing really new about these goals. A version of these OECD goals was incorporated into the Millennium Declaration that emerged from the Millennium Summit of world leaders called by the UN in September 2000.[3] Following the summit, an eighth goal, containing mainly the obligations of the developed countries was added.[4]

A comprehensive analysis of country performance in terms of MDG achievement was undertaken by the UNDP in 2003 (UNDP, 2003a). The report identified some 30 'top priority' countries, signifying failure to make progress towards achieving the goals from already very low starting levels, and a further similar number of 'high priority' countries, which either harbour acute poverty levels and are making moderate progress towards the goals, or have medium poverty levels but are regressing. Countries are designated as top or high priority according to different goals (see Table 5.2).

Of the countries in the poor-performers' table, 32 are included in the top priority category for MDG non-achievement in two or more areas. Unfortunately, even this figure is probably understated because of data shortfalls. Intuitively, Burma, North Korea and Somalia would probably belong here too. Some of the transition countries from the former Soviet bloc (such as Tajikistan) would also be included. On the basis of the data available, the worst all-round performers were Burundi, Central African Republic, Democratic Republic of Congo, Guinea, Madagascar, Sierra Leone, Tanzania and Togo, which all under-performed in three or more of the MDG criteria. The results confirm the predominance of Sub-Saharan Africa as the region of greatest concern.

Again, there are inconsistencies in MDG performance. Countries that perform worse on some indicators perform better on others. There are also variations over time. But while there is no definitive list of consistent under-performers, up to one-third of all developing countries are, by different measures, falling short of sustainable development progress.

Table 5.1 *Fragile states*

Country*	Least developed country status**	MDG Under-performer***	LIPPS†	Conflict-prone††	Corruption perception Index (out of 145 in 2004)
Afghanistan	✔	✔		✔	n.a.
Angola	✔	✔		✔	133
Bangladesh	✔		✔		145
Benin	✔	✔			77
Bhutan	✔				n.a.
Burkina Faso	✔	✔	✔		n.a.
Burma (Myanmar)	✔			✔	142
Burundi	✔	✔		✔	n.a.
Cambodia	✔			✔	n.a.
Cameroon		✔	✔		129
C. African Rep.	✔	✔	✔	✔	n.a.
Chad	✔	✔	✔		142
Congo DR	✔	✔		✔	133
Congo Rep		✔		✔	114
Equatorial Guinea	✔				n.a.
Eritrea	✔			✔	102
Ethiopia	✔	✔	✔	✔	114
Gabon					74
Gambia	✔	✔			90
Guinea	✔	✔	✔		n.a.
Guinea-Bissau	✔	✔			n.a.
Haiti	✔	✔	✔	✔	145
Indonesia				✔	133
Ivory Coast	✔			✔	133
Kenya	✔	✔			129
Korea, North		✔			n.a.
Laos	✔		✔		n.a.
Lesotho	✔	✔			n.a.
Liberia	✔	✔		✔	n.a.
Madagascar	✔	✔	✔		82
Malawi	✔				90
Mali	✔	✔	✔		77
Mauritania	✔	✔	✔		n.a.
Mongolia		✔			85
Mozambique	✔	✔		✔	90
Nepal	✔	✔	✔	✔	90
Niger	✔	✔	✔		122
Nigeria		✔	✔	✔	144
Pakistan			✔	✔	129
Papua New Guinea				✔	102
Rwanda	✔	✔	✔	✔	n.a.
Senegal	✔		✔		85
Sierra Leone	✔	✔		✔	114
Somalia	✔			✔	n.a.
Sudan	✔	✔		✔	122
Tanzania	✔	✔	✔		90
Timor-Leste	✔			✔	n.a.
Togo	✔	✔	✔		n.a.
Uganda	✔		✔	✔	102
Yemen	✔	✔	✔		112
Zambia	✔	✔	✔		102
Zimbabwe		✔	✔		114
TOTALS†††	**40**	**32**	**28**	**25**	

Notes: * Excluding the smallest states and the transition countries.

** Excluding: Cape Verde, Comoros, Djibouti, Kiribati, Maldives, Samoa, Sao Tome & Principe, Solomon Islands, Tuvalu, Vanuatu.

*** Countries listed as 'top priority' for attainment of two or more MDGs (Source: UNDP Human Development Report 2003).

† Low Income Poorly Performing States, defined by the Center for Global Development, Washington DC.

†† Open civil or international armed conflict since 1990 (see also Table 5.3 on countries with episodes of civil conflict).

††† Out of the 52 countries in the list above.

Table 5.2 *MDG poor performers**

	Top priority	High priority
Income poverty (*Goal 1*)	Angola, Burundi, Cameroon, Central African Republic (CAR), Chad, Congo, DR Congo, Gambia, Guinea-Bissau, Ivory Coast, Kenya, Madagascar, Niger, Nigeria, Rwanda, Sierra Leone, Tanzania, Togo, Zambia, Zimbabwe	Gabon, Mauritania, Senegal, Swaziland Pakistan Algeria
	Mongolia	Bolivia, Jamaica, Paraguay, Venezuela
	Ecuador, Haiti, Honduras	
Hunger (*Goal 1*)	Burundi, DR Congo, Kenya, Lesotho, Liberia, Madagascar, Rwanda, Sierra Leone, Tanzania, Zambia	Botswana, Burkina Faso, CAR, Congo, Gambia, Niger, Senegal, Swaziland, Zimbabwe
	Afghanistan, Bangladesh, Mongolia, North Korea	Cambodia, India, Nepal
	Iraq, Somalia, Yemen	Cuba, El Salvador, Guatemala, Panama, Trinidad, Venezuela
	Dominican Republic, Nicaragua	
Primary education (*Goal 2*)	Burkina Faso, Burundi, CAR, DR Congo, Mozambique, Niger, Tanzania	Botswana, Eritrea, Gambia, Ivory Coast, Mali, Namibia, Senegal
	Iran, Oman, Saudi Arabia	United Arab Emirates
		Chile, Honduras, Venezuela
Gender equality (*Goal 3*)	Burkina Faso, Burundi, Eritrea, Ethiopia, Guinea, Mali, Mozambique, Niger, Sierra Leone, Togo	Cameroon, Congo India, Laos
		Iraq
Child mortality (*Goal 4*)	Angola, Benin, Botswana, Burkina Faso, Burundi, Cameroon, CAR, Chad, Congo, DR Congo, Ethiopia, Ivory Coast, Kenya, Lesotho, Liberia, Mali, Mauritania, Nigeria, Rwanda, Senegal, Sierra Leone, Swaziland, Tanzania, Togo, Zambia, Zimbabwe	Eritrea, Equatorial Guinea, Gabon, Gambia, Guinea-Bissau, Madagascar, Malawi, Mozambique, Niger, South Africa, Uganda
	Afghanistan, Cambodia	Burma, North Korea, Papua New Guinea, Pakistan
	Iraq, Somalia, Sudan	Lebanon, Yemen
		Haiti
Access to water (*Goal 7*)	Ethiopia, Guinea, Madagascar, Mauritania, Togo	Cameroon, Malawi, Ivory Coast, Namibia, Niger, Nigeria, South Africa, Uganda
	Papua New Guinea	
	Libya, Oman	China, Philippines
	Haiti	Trinidad
Access to Sanitation (*Goal 7*)	Benin, CAR, Ethiopia, Guinea, Madagascar, Mali, Mauritania, Niger, Nigeria, Togo	Botswana, Burundi, Cameroon, Chad, Ivory Coast, Malawi, Namibia, South Africa, Zimbabwe
	Sudan, Yemen	
	Dominican Republic, Haiti	Bangladesh, China, India, Indonesia, Nepal, Papua New Guinea
		Brazil, Mexico

*Note:** Excluding the smallest states and countries in transition, and subject to availability of country data.
Source: UNDP (2003a).

FRAGILITY FACTORS: MATURITY, GOVERNMENT CAPACITY, LEADERSHIP, CONFLICT

What are the origins of fragility? And what are the conditions and circumstances that cause states to become and remain fragile? In this section we review several of the factors that help to explain why some developing countries are weaker and more poorly governed than others, starting with history.

Maturity

Some independent states have existed for many centuries – several millennia in the case of China. But most developing countries have led an independent existence for only a few decades, since the post-war end of colonialism. The so-called transition countries emerged (or re-emerged) when the Soviet Union splintered in 1991. Some states are even newer than that – such as Timor-Leste (2002) – and some are still emerging: Kosovo. Some states in the modern era have, in a sense, already come and gone: Somalia lasted for barely 30 years as a unified territory and is trying again to reconstitute itself.

Longevity confers confidence and identity, and while it does not guarantee capability, it is true to say that most of today's fragile states are among the newest. The experience of the post-war states has been highly variegated, however. Inevitably, the degree of colonial penetration was a major factor in these experiences, particularly in Asia and Africa, from where most of the post-war states emerged.[5] (In Latin America, decolonization had been much earlier). In Asia, colonial rule was broad and shallow. There were not the resources to maintain a large presence, and given the strength of culture and religion, local elites were empowered as much as they were co-opted. Mostly, states emerged strongly from the colonial presence, but statehood was under assault from Cold War rivalry in Indochina and the Korean peninsula, and by the contestation by minorities in several countries. The two states that were not formally colonized – Nepal and Thailand – were both under authoritative regimes, but adjusted very differently to the new era.

In Africa, states had in many cases been the original creation of colonial powers, with national boundaries clumsily etched across ethnic lines. Some were thus inherently artificial with fragmented national identities, within which the deeper colonial presence attempted to foster new (Western) traditions of education, religion and culture. Moreover, statehood was superimposed on the powers of local chiefdoms, whose authority had been determined in traditional ways, including heredity. Statehood was not underlined by 'nationhood' in the single-people sense and was an inherently unfamiliar concept. It tended to be identified with, and driven by, one strong man,[6] often a pioneer of the independence movement. Some of these states became what have been described as 'neo-patrimonial'. They depend on personalized exchanges, clientelism and politics by patronage. There is a strong executive – namely, the male head of state – a weak judiciary and parliament, and a corrupt and ineffective civil service (Bratton and van de Walle, 1997).

Government capacity

These executives were strong because much was expected of the state at independence. Worldwide, the growth of government had followed from the conduct of and recovery from two world wars. In the developing world, it was natural for the new governments to grasp the levers of political, social and commercial control. There was a patriotic attachment to big government and a prevailing sentiment of state nationalism.

In most of the newer states civil society was weak, or lacking altogether. There were no organized social groups or political parties that states were required to accommodate and adjust to. The authoritarian governments that most often emerged in the newer states were thus 'filling a vacuum that would have been filled in Europe by political parties, pressure groups, and a variety of autonomous bodies' (Pinkney, 2003).[7] In most developing countries, the emergence of civil society, which helped to dilute the monopolization of political power by the state, was to come much later.

The newly independent states also assumed wide-reaching economic powers made fashionable by the successful examples of state intervention in the West, epitomized by the Marshall Plan, the emerging welfare systems and Keynesian-style demand management. The Soviet Union also provided a central planning model for many countries. Newly independent states took responsibility for building infrastructure, developing infant industries, directing agricultural production and playing a large part in the allocation of resources, including through the administration of prices and subsidies and the control of labour, foreign exchange and financial markets (World Bank, 1997).

These extensive powers of the state were used to very different effect. In some countries (including the East Asian tigers: Korea, Taiwan, Hong Kong, Singapore), government built an efficient and well-coordinated planning system, while also investing in human resources through the social sectors. The private sector also thrived and was provided with incentives to develop. But in many other countries, state-led development turned out very differently. Public sectors became bloated and were run inefficiently, and the monopolistic powers of governments – often with political power overlapping with commercial and economic interest – left very little space for independent private enterprise and initiative to flourish. The 'dirigiste dogma' (Lal, 1983) was driven as much by form as by function. Big government seemed the natural accompaniment of development, and alternative means of public goods and service provision were never explored.

An acid test of state effectiveness was the use of resources. Some developing countries used the commodity price booms of the early 1950s as a basis to expand state activities, but never adjusted to the ensuing decline in revenues. The oil price shocks of the 1970s were a proving ground. Some oil exporters, such as Malaysia, built productively on their windfall, while others, such as

Nigeria and Angola, used it wastefully. For many oil importers, the shocks were disastrous. Many were driven into a level of indebtedness from which they have never recovered. But not all. In some, like South Korea, the government built economic strength through a deliberate policy of diversification.

Leadership

Leadership qualities have also played a critical part in determining development capacity, particularly in younger, institutionally immature states, where the character of the ruling elite – and particularly the head of government – can exert a major influence. Even in the absence of democratic institutions, enlightened and committed leadership can be instrumental in guiding countries on to paths of solid progress. But ill-motivated leadership will have the opposite result. Strong leaders can, for good or ill, create or influence policies and lay down norms of procedure and execution. Their personalities and examples are further guiding factors. In many developing states, strong leaders often emerged from within the most disciplined and cohesive institution – the armed forces – that then served to buttress the leader's position. The manner in which they have led, however, has then depended on their personalities and their patterns of co-opting support within the elite: in the best case, by soliciting individuals on the basis of merit; in the worst case, through family and crony relationships. The record of generals has mostly been egregious. From Argentina to Burma, from Liberia to Zaire, development has suffered the depredations of military men.

Compare the impact of military leadership in two Asian neighbours: Burma and Thailand. Each country is of similar geographical and demographic size, similar location and natural endowment. Both emerged from the Second World War with military-dominated governments and the challenges of communist insurgencies. Thailand developed the institutions of statehood, invested in human resources, maintained an open and relatively dynamic and unfettered economy, and succeeded in containing the insurgency. Burma, however, turned inwards under the unfortunate influence of parochial isolationism,[8] mismanaged its economy, failed to invest in people and decided on a hugely expensive military solution to separatism (communism was only contained by the late 1980s). The short flight from Bangkok to Yangon today reveals an extraordinary contrast in the relative fortunes of a prospering middle-income country and a failed state.

Damaging leadership has not been confined to military dictators; civilian leaders have also presided over self-interested kleptocracies. But there have also been some shining exceptions. Seretse Khama, the first President of Botswana, inherited an impoverished state from British tutelage in 1966. For the next 14 years, until his death in office in 1980, Botswana had one of the fastest growing economies in the world, turning revenues from beef, copper and diamonds into investments in infrastructure, education and health. President Khama used his authority to foster democracy and promote the rule of law, helping to set the country on a course of steady progress, which has been followed by his two successors (Quett Masire in 1980, and Festus Mogae in 1998).[9]

In pre-modern states, Weber (1946) emphasizes the significance of charisma and tradition in the vesting of authority. Charisma is the factor that precipitates the emergence of an individual leader, but tradition begets continuity and can reinforce dynastic tendencies, handing succession down the generations. It can also perpetuate authoritarian rule. The nature of leadership, and of its perpetuation, can take a very different hold over the fortunes of new states. Contrast the divergent fortunes of the two halves of the culturally homogeneous Korean society, led down different paths by strong but very differently motivated authoritarian regimes. The peninsular emerged from war in the early 1950s with per capita incomes among the lowest in the world and seemingly dismal prospects of early prosperity. The prognoses for North Korea were slightly more promising, since it had rich sources of key industrial minerals such as coal and iron ore. Yet today, it is South Korea that has joined the OECD club of rich democracies as a fully-fledged industrial power, while the North is a quintessential failed state. Its people continue to face repeated famines and impoverishment under a totalitarian regime that has diverted development resources into war matériel. It now constitutes one of the single greatest threats to global security.[10]

Some states that have benefited from strong and developmentally-effective leadership have never been democracies (Uganda, Vietnam). But most have become more democratic and clearly choice provides a better guarantee of good leadership. With very few exceptions, poorly led crisis states have remained undemocratic, and fragility and weakness are perpetuated where leaders are resistant to more democracy.

Conflict

There are over 70 states, North and South, that have suffered from some form of conflict-related state failure since the 1950s (see Table 5.3). Within the developing world, those states that have made the least progress and have remained mired in low-income and high-poverty levels have been the most prone to conflict, while those that have done relatively better have reduced the risks of conflict and insecurity. Here the statistical correlations are quite solid: there is a close empirical relationship between civil war and low income. Poverty increases the likelihood of civil war and war is a prime cause of poverty. Conflict vulnerability is also chronic: within five years, half of all countries securing peace slip back into conflict (Collier et al, 2003). In our table of fragile states, nearly half of the poor performers are listed as conflict-prone.

Over the last four decades – following completion of the main independence wave – there was a substantial increase in the number of civil wars. The 1990s saw a subsequent reduction. But while wars have been contained in Angola, Guatemala, Liberia, Mozambique, Peru and Sierra Leone, some long-standing conflicts have continued to fester (for example, in Burma, Burundi,

Table 5.3 *Countries with episodes of civil conflict, 1960–2000*

Country	Ethnic and religious wars	Revolutionary wars	Genocide/ politicide
Afghanistan	1992–X	1978–92	1978–92
		1992–X	
Albania		1997–97	
Algeria	1962–62	1962–62	1962–62
		1991–X	
Angola	1975–X	1975–X	1975–94
			1998–X
Argentina			1976–80
Azerbaijan	1988–97		
Bangladesh	1976–91		
Bosnia	1992–95		1992–95
Burundi	1972–72		1965–73
	1988–X		1988–88
			1993–93
Cambodia		1970–75	1975–79
		1979–91	
Chad	1965–94		
Chile			1973–76
China	1956–59	1966–69	1959–59
	1988–98	1989–89	1966–75
Columbia		1948–60	
		1984–X	
Croatia	1991–95		
Congo–Brazzaville		1997–99	
Cuba		1956–59	
Cyprus	1963–64		
	1974–74		
Dem.Rep.Congo	1960–65	1960–65	1964–65
	1977–78	1996–X	1977–79
	1992–X		
Dominican Republic		1965–65	
Egypt		1992–99	
El Salvador		1979–92	1980–89
Ethiopia	1961–91	1975–91	1976–79
	1963–64		
	1977–78		
	1999–2000		
Georgia	1991–93	1992–93	
Guatemala	1975–94	1966–96	1978–90
Guinea–Bissau		1998–99	
Hungary		1956–56	
India	1956–58		
	1967–71		
	1983–93		
	1990–X		
Indonesia	1967–71	1949–61	1965–66
	1975–91	1958–61	1975–92
	1981–84	1998–99	
	1997–99		
	1998–X		
Iran	1979–85	1977–79	1981–92
		1981–83	
Iraq	1961–70	1959–59	1963–75
	1974–75		1988–91
	1980–88		
	1991–98		

Country	Ethnic and religious wars	Revolutionary wars	Genocide/ politicide
Israel	1987–X		
Jordan		1970–71	
Kenya	1964–66		
	1991–93		
Laos	1961–79	1960–62	
		1963–79	
Lebanon	1975–91	1958–58	
Lesotho		1998–98	
Liberia		1985–85	
		1989–93	
Mali	1990–95		
Moldovia	1992–92		
Morocco	1975–89		
Mozambique		1976–92	
Myanmar	1961–X	1988–89	1978–78
Nepal		1996–X	
Nicaragua	1981–84	1978–79	
		1981–88	
Nigeria	1966–70	1980–85	
Oman		1970–76	
Pakistan	1971–71		1971–71
	1973–77		1973–77
	1983–98		
Papua New Guinea	1989–97		
Peru		1982–97	
Philippines	1972–X	1972–96	1972–76
Romania		1989–89	
Russia	1994–96		
	1999–X		
Rwanda	1963–66		1963–64
	1990–98		1994–94
Senegal	1992–99		
Sierra Leone		1991–X	
Somalia	1988–X	1988–94	1988–91
South Africa	1987–96	1984–90	
Sri Lanka	1983–X	1987–89	1989–90
Sudan	1956–72		1956–72
	1983–X		1983–X
Syria			1981–82
Tajikistan		1992–98	
Thailand		1965–83	
Turkey	1984–2000		
Uganda	1966–66	1983–85	1971–79
	1980–99		1980–86
United Kingdom	1971–82		
United States	1965–68		
Vietnam, South		1958–65	1965–75
Yemen, North		1962–70	
Yemen, South		1986–86	
Yemen		1994–94	
Yugoslavia	1991–92		
	1998–99		1998–99
Zambia		1964–64	
Zimbabwe	1981–87	1972–79	

Source: Based on data from the Center for International Development and Conflict Management, University of Maryland, US
Note: X = Continuing in 2000.

Colombia, Indonesia, Papua New Guinea, Somalia, Sri Lanka, Sudan and Uganda) and some new conflicts have started or been re-kindled (Afghanistan, Côte d'Ivoire, Haiti and Nepal).[11]

Civil war incurs huge costs and has been described as development in reverse. The human cost through loss of life is compounded by injury and permanent disability. There are also the psycho-social consequences associated with the destruction of livelihoods and the concern for survival. Economies are undermined, not just at the local level, but through the diversion of resources into expanded military budgets, at the expense of social development.

Unfortunately, the impact of civil conflicts is rarely confined within one country. Fragility is exacerbated by conflict in a contiguous state. Civil wars in recent years in Afghanistan, Angola, Burma, Colombia, Congo (Democratic Republic), Liberia, Rwanda and Somalia have all burst their borders, adding to refugee burdens and destabilizing their neighbours.

AIDING FRAGILITY

For the OECD's DAC, fragile states constitute 'difficult partnerships', a term coined to connote countries:

> *where development objectives play little role compared with prolongation of power, with the result that partner governments do not have credible commitment to effective policies and their implementation… corruption and political repression, among other characteristics, are commonly associated with such regimes.*
> (OECD/DAC, 2001a)

In 2002, the World Bank identified a category of 'low-income countries under stress' (LICUS), which pose liabilities for its lending portfolio. They include the delinquent debtors and the least bankable clients. Among bilaterals, the UK's Department for International Development (DfID) has defined a target group called 'poverty reduction in difficult environments' (PRIDE). DfID talks about 'difficult environments' where the state is 'unwilling or unable to harness domestic and international resources for poverty reduction'. The USAID refers to 'failing, failed and recovering states' and stresses concerns of conflict and security (USAID, 2005).

As these definitions imply, there are two dimensions of state fragility that donors seek to address: lack of political will and weak development capacity. State failure may reflect the unwillingness of a government to commit itself to policies of inclusion and human welfare, and to ensuring that available resources are utilized for productive purposes. Will may be bound up with political legitimacy. Where a regime is undemocratic and unrepresentative, its leadership is less likely to pursue a development agenda.

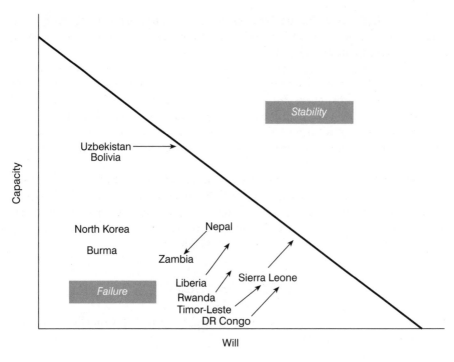

Note: Arrows indicate increasing/decreasing capacity and will, resulting in trends towards stability or failure. Countries without arrows are neither improving nor deteriorating.

Figure 5.1 *The two dimensions of fragility*

Capacity determines effectiveness in administration and service delivery, in the maintenance of order and security, and in economic and resource management. Both political will and capacity are important for effectiveness in the utilization of aid and for the quality of the relationship between recipients and donors.

Figure 5.1, above, attempts to plot the two dimensions of fragility for several states.[12] Bolivia and Uzbekistan are shown as relatively more capacitated states (with stronger institutions and human resources). Sierra Leone is shown as relatively less capacitated, but more willing in its post-conflict phase. Several states – such as Burma and North Korea – are shown as lacking both capacity and will. The arrows indicate the current trends towards or away from greater stability.

The role of donors is to help countries to move from the 'failure' to the 'stability' zone, by influencing political will and supporting development capacity. But there are no simple formulae linking aid and fragility, and the record of aid has been ambiguous. The examples of Burma, Rwanda and Zambia – three quintessentially fragile states embroiled in different kinds of development crises – are illustrative of this ambiguity.

THE CASES OF BURMA, RWANDA AND ZAMBIA

Burma: Donors at odds

Burma[13] emerged at independence in 1948 with seemingly bright prospects, based on rich endowments of minerals and natural resources, and highly fertile soil. It was widely regarded as having one of the most literate and educated workforces in the region. For most of its independent history, however, it has been ruled by military regimes, which have presided over impoverishment and internal conflict.

The first prime minister was U Nu, a statesman who helped found the non-aligned movement along with India's Nehru and Indonesia's Sukarno. He was replaced in 1962 in a coup by General Ne Win who came to dominate the government until the late 1980s. In 1988 a military junta formed the State Law and Order Restoration Council (SLORC) following widespread anti-government rioting that was brutally put down by the army. SLORC permitted elections in 1990 that were won in a landslide by the opposition National League for Democracy (NLD), led by Aung San Suu Kyi, daughter of the country's post-war liberation hero. The result was ignored by SLORC, which has continued its iron rule (since 1997 as the equally euphemistic State Peace and Development Council) under the chairmanship of Than Shwe, effectively the head of state.

Daw Suu, who won the Nobel Peace Prize in 1991, continues to retain iconic status within and outside the country and her treatment by the regime is considered by Western donors to be a bellwether of democratic progress.[14] She has been confined under house arrest for most of the period since 1988 and in May 2003 she was almost killed in a brutal massacre ('Black Friday') of NLD supporters orchestrated by the junta.

The country has been virtually isolated since the time of Ne Win who sought to take the country down the inward-looking 'Burmese way to social-ism'. The results in terms of human development indicators have been mostly disastrous and the country is probably much worse off now than at independence, belying the largely meaningless official statistics that purport to reveal significant progress.[15] According to UN figures, poverty rates may be over 70 per cent of the population, one-third of all children are chronically malnourished[16] and only 50 per cent of children complete primary education. There is a growing incidence of HIV/AIDS, tuberculosis and malaria.[17]

Burma is a collection of semi-autonomous states of many different peoples, including Shans, Karens, Rakhine, Mon, Chin and Kachin. Following independence, Burma took an initially tolerant attitude towards these minorities. But the military juntas have since sought to repress any moves towards autonomy or separatism. The armed forces, or Tatmadaw, number almost 400,000 and have used appalling brutality in their dual war on democracy and separatism. These internal wars have diverted considerable resources away from development and accelerated the impoverishment of the country, driving large numbers of people across the borders to Thailand and Bangladesh.

Burma is a comprehensively mismanaged military dictatorship. The junta runs much of the economy, including its key enterprises. There is little under-standing of a market economy and despite its apparent expressions of interest in foreign investment, it succeeds in deterring investors through the prepon-derance of regulations and licences, a multi-tiered exchange rate and the absence of a private banking system. The regime is also heavily involved in the gem trade and the exploitation of natural gas, as well as the fast-diminishing forest resources. The junta has locked up large numbers of those opposed to the regime. It indulges in rampant human rights violations and the Tatmadaw has been accused of the most inhumane acts of war. Burma is the largest producer and exporter of heroin, after Afghanistan, and although production has fallen in recent years with the help of a UN-sponsored crop-substitution programme, the junta has been accused of involvement in the drugs trade.

As Figure 5.2 indicates, Burma was a growing recipient of aid until the late 1980s when it reached over US$400 million per year. Since SLORC assumed power, aid has fallen sharply overall, but individual donors have taken rather different stances in their dealings with the country, reflecting their individual interests. The Western donors, for whom Burma holds little strategic signifi-cance, have shunned Burma because of its human rights record, its resistance to democracy and continuing incarceration of the main opposition leader. At one extreme is the US, which since 2002 has completely shut off all development assistance to the regime and tried to influence other donors to do the same. The Americans also seek to prevent the assistance of multilateral agencies such as the World Bank, IMF or UNDP going to any government recipients. The European donors have joined the US in imposing sanctions on Burma – mainly through a travel ban on the State Peace and Development Council (SPDC) leadership. But the investments by Unocal and Total in natural gas, which earn substantial annual royalties for the regime, are tolerated. Some European donors provide humanitarian assistance, mostly through non-governmental entities. The EU and the US provide assistance to refugees from the Burmese minorities along the border with Thailand. Japan has taken a more ambivalent stance. It curtailed its major aid programme after 1988. Since 2003, assistance has been limited still further. It has not applied sanctions, however, and contin-ues to provide aid to the regime. According to local sources, total official aid in 2005, including humanitarian, amounted to about US$25 million.

Burma's largest donors, however, are not from OECD/DAC, but from its neighbours, China and India. Thailand, Malaysia and Singapore are also signifi-cant partners. Chinese influence is most evident in parts of the Shan and Kachin states bordering China, where transactions are made in Yuan and even the school curricula are in Chinese. China (and particularly the Yunnan administra-tion) has invested in power plants and infrastructure, mainly in order to support its own investments in the northern and eastern parts of the country. Some of the aid is in military hardware provided through loans, repayable in kind in raw materials. China has been allowed to establish a military surveillance station off the coast of Burma, and probably hopes eventually to develop a corridor across the country to facilitate the access of Yunnan to the Bay of Bengal.

India's aid also carries influence. Politically, it has anxieties about China's growing role; economically, it is concerned to meet its growing energy needs. India has invested (with Korea) in a new off-shore gas field and it is providing infrastructure assistance, including the construction of a pipeline through which it intends to import natural gas. Thailand also benefits from Burmese gas and includes Burma in its programme of assistance to the three poorest members of the Association of Southeast Asian Nations (ASEAN) (including also Cambodia and Laos). Malaysia and Singapore also provide training and scholarships to Burmese as part of their own ASEAN assistance.

Western aid to this failing state is clearly not working. Humanitarian assistance is helping to support Burmese livelihoods, but it needs to be complemented by other forms of engagement, including active political dialogue. The regime has little capacity and little will, but it is more entrenched than ever. Short of another military invasion by the Western powers, therefore, the status quo will prevail. Certainly, the junta will not change its ways as a result of Western displeasure, as long as it enjoys the embrace of its neighbours (see also Chapter 7).[18] Just at a time when the US Congress is trying to isolate the regime further and tighten the screw on the multilateral organizations, observers in Burma are unanimous that exactly the opposite should happen. Western donors do not like to deal with egregious regimes but they should be concerned about turning failure – and its damaging consequences – around. If both capacity – in a country with chronically weak institutions of statehood – and political will are to be enhanced, there is no alternative to more, not less, engagement.[19]

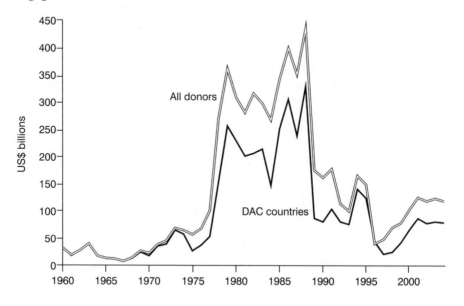

Source: OECD/DAC

Figure 5.2 *ODA to Burma, 1960–2004*

Rwanda: Complicity, oblivion and state collapse

Rwanda is a central African country of 8 million people. It is one of the world's most conflict-prone states, with which donors have maintained ambiguous and at times perilous relations. The story of rich country involvement was already a complex one before 1962 when it came to independence against a backdrop of seething ethnic conflict. Belgium, the colonial power, had decided to prepare the ground by abolishing the monarchy and switching patronage from the minority Tutsi elite to the Hutu majority 'in the name of a suddenly discovered attachment to democracy' (Uvin, 1998). On assuming sovereignty, the regime of President Kayibanda chased down and eliminated most of the Tutsi elite. In 1973, he was removed by his cousin General Habyarimana in a coup that ushered in a military dictatorship for the next 20 years.

A modicum of stability was maintained, but it was a lid firmly battened on the ethnic Hutu–Tutsi rivalries beneath, a situation characterized as 'structural violence' (Galtung, 1969). Open conflict broke out in late 1990 with incursions from Uganda by a force of Tutsis who were exiled there. Civil war continued with sporadic outbreaks of fighting until April 1994 when Habyarimana was killed and the world's worst genocide in the post-war period began, resulting in the slaughter of some 800,000 people – nearly all of them Tutsis – in the space of 100 days.[20] Nine-tenths of the Rwandan population was dispersed by the fighting, within the country and over the border, and it was several years before resettlement was completed.[21]

Against this turbulent background, Rwanda nevertheless had made reasonable development progress in its first two decades. Per capita income, food production and the manufacturing sector all showed positive growth. The HDI improved quite significantly between 1975 and 1985. Rwanda seemed to be on a solid path. But from the mid-1980s, progress started to unravel. There was drought in 1984 and from the following year, the export prices of coffee and tea began to slide. These factors caused the primary sector to shrink and set off a period of profound crisis that continued up to and beyond the genocide. Rwanda had recourse to the international financial institutions to shore up a yawning external deficit. From modest levels in the early part of the decade, the country's debt grew to more than 60 per cent of GNP by 1993, a long way beyond sustainability levels, since this was equivalent to more than 8 times the value of its exports.

From the mid-1960s, development assistance from the donor community flowed freely and showed a steady upward trend (see Figure 5.3) as the donors considered Rwanda something of a model among African developing countries. Up until the 1980s crisis, the country had been thought to be doing many things right. Although democracy was not practised and human rights were beneath the vision of the despotic first and second republics, the government was credited with a developmental orientation. Reports from the pre-genocide period talk of stability and discipline. As the economy deteriorated, some development assistance yielded to humanitarian aid, but the amount continued to grow.

The general sense of goodwill towards Rwanda was one of the factors favouring high aid levels. Habyarimana was rewarded for maintaining stability. His popularity was not in question, and donors overlooked the autocratic nature of the regime whose mandate was regularly renewed with near-unanimity. The existence of a growing NGO sector was noted positively. For some donors, Rwanda was also linguistically strategic. Being at one of the borders between francophone and anglophone Africa, it was favoured by France, Belgium and Switzerland.

But as history has subsequently told us, the donor community suffered a massive deception in Rwanda. In the early 1990s, a few concerns had begun to surface about the nature of the Habyarimana regime. But the international community neither spoke out against nor acted on the perpetration of structural violence that led directly to the massacre of 1994 (Uvin, 1998). Rwanda was constructed on a foundation of institutionalized racism that marginalized the Tutsi minority. The regime also sanctioned an ill-intentioned militaristic elite (the *Akazu*) that manipulated the social and political processes to its own ends. Observers have been astounded by the rapidity of the call to arms by the Hutu and the incredible vehemence of the 100-day slaughter. But it can be at least partially explained by the existence of the genocidal edifice that Rwandan society had become.

The donors missed the signals or chose to ignore them. The awful probability of either complicity or oblivion only compounds the sin of vacillation by the UN in 1994 that denied Rwanda a peacekeeping force, which many feel would have been able to forestall the genocide.[22]

The aftermath of the genocide brought substantial humanitarian aid, which also ran immediately into controversy. Very large numbers of Hutu people fled with the militias who had committed the genocide into eastern Zaire, where they would undoubtedly have perished through hunger and disease. The first wave of humanitarian assistance was therefore concentrated on these perpetrators of the genocide, rather than the victims who remained in Rwanda. This bias was only gradually corrected, partly as a result of the enforced repatriation of the Hutus in 1995.

In the development phase that followed, a somewhat different set of donors – more anglophone in profile – has emerged to champion Rwanda, which again continues to benefit from high levels of assistance. As the author witnessed in the late 1990s, there are some frightening echoes of the earlier ethnic myopia in some aid programmes. However, donors are more aware of the underlying social tensions and there is support for the rebuilding of a justice system and for fostering reconciliation.

But Rwanda exposed many fallabilities of the 'development enterprise'. The country has also proved to be a jousting field for donor influence. Some donors were historically and sentimentally loyal to the Hutu cause and acted accordingly. After the genocide, they played a limited role. Other donors emerged as supporters of the Tutsi government, whose leadership emerged from Rwanda's anglophone neighbours. But then these new donors also became politically indulgent patrons. They maintained their high levels of

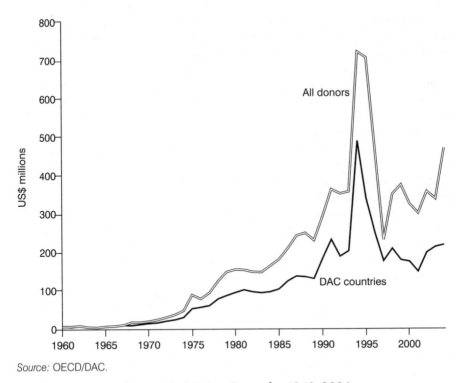

Source: OECD/DAC.

Figure 5.3 *ODA to Rwanda, 1960–2004*

assistance even after it became known that the new regime was actively perpetrating rebellion across the border in the Congo on a scale that went beyond mere self-defence.

Donor divisions linger as a result of differing perceptions of this aid client. They have made their own assessments of the intentions of the government and there is no collective view of where Rwanda is placed on the 'will' scale (Uvin, 2001). Aid follows influence and is at least partially related to the degree to which individual donors believe Rwanda is amenable to their own agendas.

Zambia: An unsuitable case for Bretton Woods treatment

Zambia is a land-locked country of 10 million people in southern Africa. It came to independence in 1964 under the presidency of Kenneth Kaunda who ruled Zambia as a one-party state continuously for 27 years. His vision was of a dominant government with widespread ownership of productive assets. Soon after assuming power he nationalized many key enterprises, as well as all private land. Following the adoption of a multi-party constitution, Frederick Chiluba was elected president in 1991. But accusations of corruption and mismanagement dogged his decade-long tenure.

Zambia has been a consistent poor performer almost throughout its independent existence. Economic growth has been paltry, well below rates of population increase. During the 1990s, growth fell almost to zero (0.3 per cent per year). Consequently, per capita income has fallen from over US$750 at independence in 1964 to about half that level now. Poverty rates are close to 70 per cent of the population and rose during the last decade. The HDI, measuring income, education and health, has fallen from 0.47 in 1975 to 0.39 today, ranking Zambia 164th out of 175 countries. Zambia is further than ever from achieving the Millennium Development Goals, which span the 25-year period 1990–2015.

Several factors have played a part in Zambia's poor performance. Kaunda's attempts to run the economy as a bureaucracy was a dampener on enterprise and efficiency. The economy was also heavily dependent on mineral production and exports (mainly copper, but including zinc and cobalt) and was seriously undermined by long-term falls in international prices, which have brought the purchasing power of copper down to barely one-quarter of the level of the 1960s. Zambia did not succeed in diversifying its economy away from the mining sector, but continued to incur loans in the expectation that copper prices would revive. The country is also disaster-prone. Droughts have been a persistent affliction and more recently HIV/AIDS – which the government was very slow to recognize and act upon – has ravaged the population. One in five adults are infected, life expectancy has fallen below 40 years, and more than half a million children have been orphaned.

When it comes to aid, the country is an extreme example of why poor countries with falling export revenues, geographic disadvantage and a proneness to crises make highly unsuitable banking clients. Its international indebtedness began soon after the collapse of copper prices in the mid-1970s. The price never revived, no other significant sources of foreign exchange were ever developed, and the country has been saddled with the huge additional burdens of debt repayment and servicing ever since. By the late 1990s, international debt owed to donors and the Bretton Woods institutions was larger than the country's entire GNP. The cost of servicing this debt has mounted in spite of 'emergency interim' debt relief but by 2004, the amount owed was close to US$400 million – more than the combined health and education budget of the government. Debt has dominated all other development efforts. It has been claimed that in 2004 an additional 9000 available trained teachers – urgently needed for the expanding education programme – could not be hired because of spending restrictions imposed by the IMF-led macro-economic programme.[23] Aid has been generous, but fickle. At its peak in 1995, it reached the equivalent of 30 per cent of GNP, but fell back to one-third of the level soon afterwards (see Figure 5.4).

In fact, Zambia did not intend to remain a one-commodity economy. After independence, it established a domestic textile and garment industry, which by 1970 comprised more than 80 companies employing 10,000 workers (World Development Movement, 2004). Like its agriculture, the manufacturing sector was walled off from foreign competition by high import tariffs – a strategy of incubation successfully followed by the dynamic economies of Southeast Asia. Much of the economy was in state hands and it was managed inefficiently. However, it was a broader-based economy in the making.

When copper prices collapsed in the early 1970s, accompanied by huge hikes in the costs of imported oil, Zambia was forced to borrow. But the lending programmes of the Bretton Woods institutions came with the familiar prescriptions of privatization and trade openness. During the 1990s, the state was urged to sell factories and lower import tariffs. The textile sector could not compete. During the decade, the number of textile manufacturers fell from 140 to 8 and the number of employees from 34,000 to 4000. Zambia became a large importer of tariff-free second-hand clothes from the US. The manufacturing sector as a whole did not fare much better. More than 300,000 jobs were lost out of 800,000.

That Zambia has been economically mismanaged is not in doubt. Yet trying to direct Zambia's economic affairs from Washington with the support of some of the major bilateral donors has not succeeded in building capacity within the country. Numerous donors have brought their many forms of project assistance to bear. But the large bilaterals have tended increasingly to line up with the Washington agenda, cheerleading when the agenda advanced and withdrawing support when it foundered. In 1983, Zambia agreed to a structural adjustment programme and bilateral aid flowed generously (see Figure 5.4). After the abandonment of that agreement in 1987, some of the major donors reduced their assistance and the US, UK and Germany temporarily suspended disbursements entirely. Aid again grew in the early 1990s as a positive response to the holding of democratic elections, and there was a spike in 1995 with the release of substantial IMF assistance (under the Structural Adjustment Facility and the Extended Structural Adjustment Facility). Aid levels again dropped off, however, during the 1990s as the country was perceived to be slipping off the good governance track (Carlsson, 2000).

Zambia was one of 14 developing countries (8 of them fragile) recently included in an OECD/DAC survey of donor 'harmonization and alignment' – a report card on the Rome process (OECD/DAC, 2005). The survey maintains that Zambia has begun to take control of its development agenda. But it is an agenda based on a PRSP and underpinned by a 'medium-term expenditure framework' (MTEF) and a 'public expenditure management and accountability review' (PEMFAR) – all instruments (and acronyms) invented by, and developed in very close consultation with the donor community.

Today, Zambia is trying again to steer itself back to the donor agenda. But the 40-year aid balance sheet has scarcely been propitious. The country has received aid at some of the highest levels in Africa and it has borrowed well beyond the limits of debt sustainability. Yet its people are considerably poorer than at independence. In the matrix of fragility, capacity has remained stubbornly low, while the government has moved up and down the x-axis of willingness. There is no doubt that government attempts to run the state like a

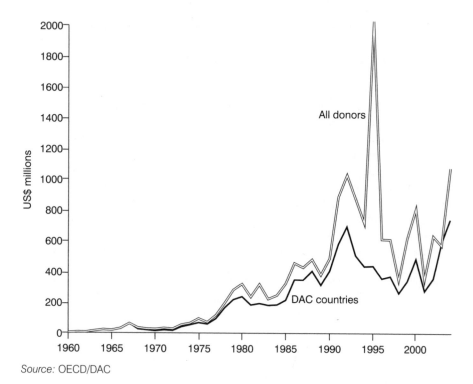

Source: OECD/DAC

Figure 5.4 *ODA to Zambia, 1960–2004*

huge public sector utility sapped the economy of some of its dynamic potential. However, trying to force on the state a series of uncompromising reform agendas has been politically unpalatable and has resulted in a growing, not a diminishing, dependence on external assistance.

In summary, each of these three states has suffered from some of the major causes of fragility, including the four adumbrated above, but to differing degrees. All of them can be described as new and relatively immature states, their boundaries determined by colonial powers, vesting them at independence with a degree of artificiality. All three have also attempted to go down development paths characterized by excessive statism, from which Rwanda and Zambia are beginning to retreat. Burma is an extreme example of a monolithic state, having not developed either political or economic institutions of any significance outside the auspices of the current regime.

Each of the three has also suffered from different kinds of leadership crisis, usually with a single strongman at the helm. In Burma, a more enlightened leadership in its early days soon gave way to a series of security-obsessed and self-interested regimes. In Rwanda, the leadership showed a distinct ethnic bias, which led to serious distortions and created a 'structurally violent' society. Zambia had more benevolent but developmentally incompetent leadership. In both Rwanda and Zambia, however, the advent of more democratic openness will provide a counterweight to the risk of autocracy. Rwanda is the most conflict-prone of the three, but in Burma regional ethnic aspirations have been harshly suppressed at enormous cost.

In each of these states, donor engagement has been a very mixed blessing. It has not been very successful in altering political will, nor in building capacity. In fact, there are all too few examples of fragile states transported from failure to stability by aid. We need to know why if we are to propose how aid could become more effective.

As the examples of three countries help to illustrate, the circumstances of every fragile state is unique. However, the two-dimensional challenge of overcoming fragility and backwardness applies to all: how much are they *willing* to change and how much are they *able* to improve? The most egregious regimes are the unwilling, those whose leaderships have impoverished their countries and are resisting change, whatever the reasons: dogma, greed, military paranoia, but invariably a determination to hold on to power whatever the development cost. In other fragile states, the leadership may be more amenable, but capacity is limited. Such would be the case in Liberia, Rwanda, Sierra Leone and other countries emerging from conflict, or Mali, Nicaragua, Niger, Zambia and others seeking to compensate for poor management and the adversities of HIV/AIDS, natural disaster or global economic conditions. We shall look respectively at these challenges for donors.

AID AND POLITICAL WILL: ENGAGEMENT AND CONSISTENCY

In Chapter 4, we examined the limited effectiveness of donor conditionality. Some of these arguments apply *a fortiori* to fragile states that are not in open conflict, but where the leadership is more entrenched and plays an unchallengeable role in steering the direction of the country. Conditional aid has limited impact in countries where the leadership is developmentally inclined and is even less likely to lead to beneficial change in the circumstances of fragile states. However, *political engagement* by donors can stimulate change if certain conditions are met.

First, engagement can help to connect cynical regimes with global values. While it may be premature to talk of universal convergence, those values are becoming increasingly centred on more open democracy and market principles. This growing consensus can play a helpful framing role in advocating for political and economic change.

Advocacy is being driven by demonstration, in a world in which globalization has sharpened the sense of inter-state competition and when development performances are compared more overtly than before. For example, reform in India has been goaded in part by a desire to catch up with the growth and income levels of China. South Korea has set its sights on Japan. Brazil,

Malaysia, Nigeria, South Africa, Thailand and others aspire to middle-income status. All these countries have been finding their own way to the democratic free-market road.

Demonstration effects have become extremely powerful for at least two reasons. One is the spread of global information and media via new information technologies, which allow people in one country to learn about and compare life in almost every other. The second is the rise of the global civil society movement, which has helped to connect people within and between countries and act as an alternative voice to governments.[24] In the West we now take technologically-facilitated networking for granted, but connected civil society has become a redoubtable force for change. In the late 1980s and early 1990s, it helped turn Eastern Europe from autocracy and accelerated the demise of the Soviet Union by piercing the barriers to information exchange. It has raised the aspirations of people in the developing world by making millions more aware of how much better their lives could be.

Connectedness is specifically denied in the more abject examples of state failure such as Burma and North Korea, where governments have permitted very limited internet access and placed drastic restrictions on the media. As in the states of the Soviet Union before the break-up, isolation is taking a heavy toll. If these barriers cannot be broken down, then the role of donors should be to encourage more engagement and dialogue, and not reinforce a country's isolation. The process needs to start with this same cynical leadership.

Engagement – through dialogue and demonstration – should then be the conduit of value change. Minds cannot be altered from behind unbroken walls, but they can see through the cracks. In the northern parts of both Burma and North Korea it is – almost ironically – China that is encouraging a furtive encroachment of capitalism via the development of free enterprise enclaves. These small bridgeheads could become significant forces for change, and could precede a wider opening of these societies.

In the second place, solidarity and consistency are important. The impact of US and European sanctions on Burma are already diluted by the breaches in their own foreign investment ban. But more importantly, the country's immediate neighbours are willing to engage. To be effective, Burma's partners should – at least with respect to influencing political will – speak with a single voice. Similar arguments apply to Zimbabwe. The political (if not the economic) impact of US and European sanctions is undermined by close and generally uncritical relations that the country enjoys with South Africa and China. On Cuba, the world is similarly divided – the US and Canada cannot agree on relations with the regime (even to the extent of the US threatening to impose sanctions on Canadian and European companies that continue to do business with Havana). The chinks must be mended, not only between the rich states, but among all the partners of fragile states.

An OECD consensus around fragile states has often proved elusive. But aid from the rich West is losing its influence anyway. Trade and economic relations within developing regions are growing in importance, and non-DAC donors, such as India, China and Brazil have entered the stage (see Chapter 7). India looms large on the strategic horizons of its neighbours, including the fragile states of Burma and Nepal. China has long been a significant donor to recipient countries in Asia and in Africa (where it has built a sports stadium in virtually every country[25]). Through aid, it actively supports weak states such as North Korea, Burma, Laos and Zimbabwe. Like India, China's aid is strongly influenced by commercial interest, currently driven by the need to secure supplies of energy and raw materials to fuel its voracious expansion. The desire for influence leads to aid, and vice versa. In 2005, China succeeded in preventing Sudan from a harsher censure by the UN Security Council over Darfur, and it is an important counterweight to Western donor interest as a member of the 'Group of 77' developing countries.

In some circumstances, regional organizations could play a role in influencing states. For Burma, ASEAN, to which it belongs (along with Thailand, Malaysia, Singapore and others), could help the international community to forge a common position on a desirable political roadmap for the country. An opportunity has already been provided by the agreement by Burma not to take up chairmanship of ASEAN in 2006, in order to save the grouping from an embarrassing boycott by Western countries. A similar position with respect to Zimbabwe could be taken by an African sub-regional grouping (such as the South Africa Development Community (SADC) to which South Africa and Zimbabwe both belong) or by the African Union, which plays a more political role in the continent.

Third, donors need to stay engaged with the people of fragile states. Their humanitarian needs should be met even though they are exacerbated by the actions of misguided leadership. Humanitarian engagement is important for several reasons. One is obviously altruistic. Others are more political. Aid connects people in need with the international community and is a foundation for building longer-term goodwill beyond periods of crisis. Humanitarian aid has its own beneficial demonstration effect from the sacks of USAID wheat and UNHCR tenting to the selfless toil of the camp doctors. Humanitarian aid and the development aid that follows it can, if carefully applied, hold bad government up to scrutiny.

In sum, first, engagement is better than isolation, particularly where fragile states are already seeking to isolate themselves; second, engagement should be consistently applied and based on collective action, preferably backed by the authority of a regional grouping and by globally acknowledged norms of international comportment; and third, donor engagement should take full cognisance of, and attempt to compensate for, the humanitarian plight of the populations in fragile states who are the victims of wrong-headed policies that are driving them to impoverishment.

AID AND CAPACITY

The record of aid in building sustainable capacity has been a very mixed one, even where leadership is committed. The record is unfortunately no better in the building or reconstruction of fragile states, where failure comes at much higher costs, but where the dividends of success can be enormous.

In this section, we review the impact of aid on capacity in three different scenarios: during what may be described as 'pre-conflict' periods; during conflict; and during periods of reconstruction and state-building (which are quite often post-conflict).

Pre-conflict

Somalia in the mid-1980s was a country at peace, and Mogadishu was one of the safest capitals in Africa. But all was not well. A despotic president ruled with total intolerance of dissent as well as indifference to the process of development. The country was one of the most generously aided in the world but the donors were having a negligible impact on both the policies of the regime and the capacities of the country. Supply-driven aid carried the donors' trademarks and the landscape was littered with some of the starkest relics of aid failure: broken tractors, silted pumps, fuel-less turbines, vacant schools, darkened hospitals and crumbling new roads to nowhere. Typical of 'capacity building' was a large bilateral programme at the National University of Somalia, costing much more than the total national education budget. The main beneficiaries were the expatriate professors from the donor country who enjoyed lucrative six-monthly tours of duty in the capital.

Somalia began to implode in the late 1980s as the president sought with mounting desperation to hold onto power, favouring his own and discriminating against unfriendly clans. A country in which so much hope had once been vested as an example of unique ethnic, cultural, linguistic and religious uniformity, splintered into domains of warlordism and remains divided today.[26] In 1960, the international community had successfully reunited Somalia under a UN mandate but subsequent donor interests were dominated by Cold War competition. First the Russians sought to bring the country into their sphere and then, quite abruptly, the Western camp gained ground as allegiances switched in 1977. When the country began to fall apart, the Western donors departed, except for the hardiest humanitarian agencies. Unluckily for Somalia, the Cold War was ending and most of the remaining strategic interest in the country evaporated. Italy – the former colonial power – decided to back one of the warlords attempting to form a new government, but he was virulently opposed by other factions and civil war raged openly from 1991. The international community returned to Somalia in 1993 but in different guise.

Through complicity in or oblivion to state collapse, Rwanda has also taught us that aid can do harm in the wrong circumstances, with deadly results. The nexus between aid and conflict is extremely delicate and deserves much closer and more subtle consideration than it has received in the past (Andersen, 1999). To the sounds of stable doors closing, there has been considerable donor introspection on Rwanda, Somalia, Bosnia, Angola and the many other war-torn states. It has led to the development of increasingly sophisticated methodologies for analysing conflict-proneness,[27] as well as whole new 'crisis' departments. This new-found conflict sensitivity among donors is only to be welcomed. As with much that is good about donor intention, however, it is important that it is followed in practice.

During conflict

Attempts by the international community to stop civil wars have had mixed success. An analysis by the Rand Corporation (2005) found that of seven UN-led peace-keeping operations since 1989, all had been partially or wholly successful (see Table 5.4) (Dobbins et al, 2005).[28] Where the US led the missions, or was heavily involved, there were successes in Bosnia and Kosovo, but failures in Somalia and Haiti (Dobbins et al, 2003).

Somalia was a watershed because troops were sent in for the first time under a Chapter VII UN Charter mandate to try to quell a civil conflict through force, without a government invitation. The intervention was, as we know, spectacularly unsuccessful. Soldiers under UN command were killed, prompting the US to send troops to join them. But when the US lost 18 of its own men,[29] they began to withdraw. By 1995, there were no UN troops in Somalia, but civil conflict – albeit at a more subdued level – still simmered.

Rwanda was another failure when, in April 1994, the UN did not deploy peace-enforcing troops which by all accounts could have stopped the slaughter of 800,000 civilians. Unquestionably, failure in Somalia was a factor in dissuading intervention in Rwanda, although the two situations and the antic-ipated results would have been very different. Again in 2004, a UN mandate could not be forged in time to quell genocide in Darfur, Sudan.

Whatever the outcomes of these peace-enforcing initiatives, an important threshold was crossed in the 1990s. For the first time since the beginning of the post-war independence movement, sovereignty is being subordinated to the notion of wider responsibility. As the UN High-level Panel on Threats, Challenges and Change puts it: 'successive humanitarian disasters....have concentrated attention not on the immunities of sovereign governments but their responsibilities, both to their own people and to the wider international community' (UN Panel, 2005). The Panel – comprising eminent persons from both North (7) and South (9) – goes on to provide the rationale for engage-ment: 'while sovereign Governments have the primary responsibility to protect their own citizens from such catastrophes, when they are unable or unwilling to do so that responsibility should be taken up by the wider international community'. In effect, the right to intervene under Chapter VII is reinterpreted as responsibility to protect:

Table 5.4 *The UN history of state-building since 1989*

Country or Territory	Years	Peak Troops	Lead Actors	Assessment	Lessons Learned
Namibia	1989–1990	4493	UN-led	Successful. UN helped ensure peace, democratic development, and economic growth	Compliant neighbours, a competent government, and a clear end state can contribute to successful outcome
El Salvador	1991–1996	4948	UN-led	Successful. UN negotiated lasting peace settlement and transition to democracy after 12-year civil war	UN participation in settlement negotiations can facilitate smooth transition
Cambodia	1991–1993	15,991	UN-led	Partially successful. UN organized elections, verified withdrawal of foreign troops, and ended large-scale civil war. But democracy did not take hold	Democratization requires long-term engagement
Mozambique	1992–1994	6576	UN-led	Mostly successful. Transition to independence was peaceful and democratic. But negative economic growth	Cooperation of neighbouring states is critical to success. Incorporation of insurgent groups into political process is key to democratic transition
Eastern Slavonia	1995–1998	8248	UN-led	Successful. Well-resourced operation and clear end state contributed to peaceful and democratic transition	UN can successfully conduct small peace enforcement missions with support from major powers
Sierra Leone	1998–present	15,255	UN-led, parallel UK force in support	Initially unsuccessful, then much improved. Parallel British engagement helped stabilize mission	Lack of support from major power can undermine UN operations. But even a badly compromised mission can be turned around
Timor-Leste	1999–present	8084	Australian-led entry followed by UN-led peacekeeping mission	Successful. UN oversaw transition to democracy, peace and economic growth	Support of neighbouring states is important for security. Local actors should be involved as early as possible in governance

Source: Rand Corporation (2005)

> *We endorse the emerging norm that there is a collective interna-*
> *tional responsibility to protect, exercisable by the Security*
> *Council authorizing military intervention as a last resort, in the*
> *event of genocide and other large scale killing, ethnic cleansing or*
> *serious violations of international humanitarian law which sover-*
> *eign Governments have proved powerless or unwilling to prevent.*
> (UN Panel, 2005)

In spite of mixed outcomes, international engagement is morally correct where regimes have lost control. There is also an important economic rationale. While enforcing and keeping the peace can be expensive, the prospect of reducing the catastrophic costs from civil conflict can easily be justified. By way of illustration, an economic study has attempted a cost–benefit analysis of peace-keeping initiatives (Collier and Hoeffler, 2004). It yields an impressively positive ratio. Based on the record of recent civil wars, it finds that US$4.8 billion spent on peace-keeping could yield almost US$400 billion in benefits.

Reconstruction and state-building

After conflict, and in all other circumstances where states are attempting a fresh start, the role of development assistance can and should be of primordial importance in building sustainable new capacity. As conflicts are resolved, as wills turn, and as persistent non-performance finds fewer excuses, there is a keener edge to the realization that rich countries hold some of the keys to the prosperity of the recipients. The constant refrain of this book, however, is that more-of-the-same aid will perpetuate failure because it has for so long pursued the wrong objectives.

We visited the do's and don'ts of capacity building in a previous chapter. A recent verdict on the role of gap-filling is less than sanguine: 'the international community is not simply limited in the amount of capacity it can build; it is actually complicit in the destruction of institutional capacity in many developing countries' (Fukuyama, 2004). And speaking of the public sector in fragile states, the same author goes on to say that the 'deterioration in capacity has happened precisely during a period of accelerating external aid flows'. The correlation may not be robust, but the fact is that donors' efforts in capacity development have failed to arrest failure.

The author's own conclusions from a study (Browne, 2002) of aid and capacity development in six major aid recipients, two of them on our 'fragile' list (Bangladesh and Uganda), are also sceptical about the sustainability of the results of past aid:

> *The outputs of aid projects have abounded and these are manifes-*
> *tations of development. But they are also in part a substitute for*
> *it... many countries have not been able to use technical assistance*
> *as a tool to build sustainable capacities and manage their devel-*
> *opment independently. The word sustainable is important.*

> *Inappropriate TA, far from building sustainability, may under-mine it.*

But if it is not to be more of the same, then more of what? The analysis of this book suggests that there are several ways in which aid could be better applied to the reconstruction of fragile states.

1. Treat every case as unique and know thy subject

No two fragile states are similar. They are not similar in current profile, and there are always unique sets of causes of fragility. We should therefore beware of standard typologies, as well as the kind of standardized solutions that have undermined aid effectiveness in the past. Donors have an uncomfortable tendency to consider some fragile states as ailing patients amenable to standard types of treatment, whether humanitarian, reconstructive or developmental. There are some common general manifestations of fragility, however, and these can be used to determine appropriate types of donor engagement. As mentioned earlier, they include: institutional maturity; nature of leadership; size and role of state; and proneness to conflict.

The proclivity for standardization is related to a poverty of learning that must also be addressed. Donor and development agencies are notorious re-inventers of wheels. There are many thousands of development practitioners who have worked in or on any one of the recipient countries, fragile states included. There is a vast and rich experience to draw on, but it is rarely captured, codified and shared even within individual agencies, let alone between them. (The UN system itself is one of the worst offenders.) Because this knowledge is not tapped, standardized clean-slate solutions are often applied to states in crisis by donor staff who actually have very limited experience of the countries in question and who make limited attempts to discover and build on the experience of others.

2. Understand what state capacity means

The challenge in fragile states is the reconstitution of basic state functions of three general kinds: political and institutional; economic and social; and security. All are important and they are interconnected. Table 5.5 outlines some of the main challenges that need to be addressed in these three spheres, implying that any aid effort should be both broad based and finely tuned.

An understanding of the different dimensions of state capacity is also vital, but there has been a tendency in the past for donors to concentrate on state size as of primordial importance. It is true that oversized public sectors, in concentrating too many resources and powers to themselves and using them inefficiently, have been a detriment to development progress. But the alternative is not simply the dogmatic pursuit of small government and the wholesale reduction of state capacity. There are activities of governments that may be better in private hands, but there are important functions of government that

Table 5.5 *Major characteristics of fragile and war-torn states*

	Fragile states	Plus conflict proneness
Politics	Lack of regime legitimacy	Exclusionary policies; discrimination against ethnic/other marginal groups
	Concentration of government power	
	High centralization	Poor/non-existent communications with regions
	No opposition parties	Armed insurgency
	Lack of transparency; no access to information	
	High levels of corruption	
	No access to justice	
	Weak/no civil society	
	No fair elections	
	Incapacity to provide services	
Economic & social	Poor human development indicators	Civilian casualties; refugees; internally displaced people; child soldiers
	Low income; low growth	
	Dependence on single export commodity	
	Severe income/asset inequalities	Competing claims to assets/resources
	High HIV/AIDS incidence	HIV spread by armed forces
	Excessive state control of productive sectors	
	Chronic budget deficit	Excessive military spending
	Chronic external indebtedness	
	Poor/deteriorating infrastructure	Extensive damage through conflict
	Absence of economic opportunities; high unemployment	Economic disruption; livelihoods based on war conditions
Security	Weakened social capital	Destruction of communities; culture of violence and mistrust
	Armed forces control over internal security	
	No accountability of armed forces	
	Culture of impunity	

Sources: Author and Debiel and Klein (2002)

also need strengthening. The planning and formulation of national policies; the promulgation and enforcement of laws; the guaranteeing of basic social services – these are just a few of the indisputably essential state functions. Fukuyama (2004) makes the useful distinction between the *scope* of state activity – some of which could be reduced – and the *strength* of state power – which often needs strengthening.

As part of the Washington paradigms, many Western donors have been overzealous in their advocacy of privatization in developing countries (reduction in state scope). But there has been inadequate attention to the development of adequate checks and safeguards under public auspices (state strength) to ensure that privatization results in better and more affordable services and that public good (for example, universal service) is not sacrificed to private gain (von Weizsacker et al, 2005).

3. Build up not down

One of the more serious illusions in donor approaches to capacity development is the notion of gap-filling, a subject we broached in Chapter 3. The build-down fallacy is based on the assumption that there are 'levels' of capacity that can be prescribed in advance, that the gaps between these levels and present levels can be determined, and aid provided as the filler. All too often gap-filling approaches lead to the artificial grafting of 'capacity solutions' on to unwilling institutional hosts. Where these solutions amount to a significant diversion for these institutions, long-term capacity may actually be undermined.

In reconstructing fragile states especially, building up, rather than down is all the more imperative. Where governments are weak, or where they barely exist as in the first stages of rebuilding after conflict, humanitarian assistance through multilateral organizations and through international NGOs provides for populations directly. But as stability is restored, appropriate local partners – within or outside the state sector – should be brought in and their capacity to administer services gradually be built up.[30]

4. Cancel debts and forgo new lending

Zambia is not the only unsuitable case for lending. Low-income countries as a whole owe more than US$600 billion, even after recent relief deals. From developing Africa, there is a reverse transfer of capital (new borrowing minus debt service on past loans), which amounted to US$11 billion during the last decade (Boyce and Ndikumana, 2002).

To pay off the World Bank and IMF, funds have to be raised elsewhere. Whether Somalia in the 1980s or Haiti in the 1990s, countries scramble to find donor grants. This 'rob-Peter-to-pay-Paul' merry-go-round has continued for over two decades. And the momentum is maintained because even where multilateral debt is cancelled through new gifts of aid, the lending process repeats itself. The July 2005 G8 meeting in Scotland, like almost every other before it, began with the familiar hand-wringing on indebtedness and ended with another declaration on debt cancellation. But among the big bucks, the small penny hasn't dropped: many countries, and most of the fragile ones have never been suitable clients for the Washington Consensus. The results are eloquent enough evidence.

There are also reasons of principle to drop the debt for fragile states. Under the law in many countries, companies are not liable for contracts that their former managers entered into on their personal authority. It is ethical banking practice to acknowledge that debts should not be repaid by current governments where the proceeds were dissipated for non-developmental purposes by previous regimes. The Rwandan government used development loans to buy weapons prior to the 1994 genocide; the former presidents of Nigeria, Democratic Republic of Congo (Zaire), Nicaragua and other highly indebted countries diverted loans into their personal bank accounts.

In fact, the World Bank has begun to provide more grant assistance – an average of around 20 per cent – out of its International Development Association (IDA) programmes for the poorer countries. Donors, outside and within the multilateral system, should provide only grants to fragile states and they should also retreat from imposing their agendas. Rather, as part of ground-up capacity development, they should allow consensus to build around national strategies. Encouragingly, this idea comes out quite strongly in numbers 4, 8 and 9 of the latest OECD/DAC principles of engagement with fragile states (see Box 5.1).

5. Choose an intermediary

Donors do harm by bringing their own agendas to their support for weak states, and one of the hardest principles to try to enforce is one of donor disinterest. Over Rwanda, donors have manifested their strong individual interests, and there is baggage of different shape and bulk associated with many other fragile states. Many of these interests relate to the old colonial ties of European countries (mainly UK, France, Portugal, Belgium, Italy and the Netherlands) and Russia.

In circumstances of chronic administrative weakness and high insecurity, donor engagement with fragile states needs to be mediated, preferably through multilateral means, until the governments concerned can gain the strength and confidence to play the mediation role themselves. The UN, OECD or a suitable regional grouping can play such a role – even a bilateral – but not an organization with a significant financial stake or other special interest in a country. Smart mediation is not just about managing the aid but managing the transition process cohesively across the whole range of state capacity: political and institutional; economic and social; and security.[31]

The UN can claim some success in concerting the management of recovery processes following serious conflict. The UN Transitional Authority for Cambodia (UNTAC) was set up following the signing of the Paris Agreements in October 1991. With the support of different donors, it organized elections, maintained security, helped re-establish the civil administration, rebuilt some infrastructure and repatriated and resettled refugees and displaced people. In Timor Leste, the UN established another transitional authority following 1999 elections to lead the country to independence in May 2002. The UN Transitional Administration in East Timor (UNTAET) administered the territory, exercised legislative and executive authority and helped build capacity towards self-government. It was succeeded after independence by the UN Mission of Support in East Timor (UNMISET), which continued to provide assistance to core administrative structures of the new country.[32] After conflict, the UN also assisted in the establishment of an interim administration in Afghanistan in 2001 – led by Afghans – to guide the country to elections and rebuild capacity. The organization of these arrangements could be further improved.[33] For post-conflict states, the UN Secretary General has accepted the proposal of the High Level Panel for the establishment of an inter-governmental Peace Building Commission. It would seek to improve UN planning and coordination in the immediate recovery phase, help to ensure predictable financing, encourage donors to share information about their programmes, monitor progress and – importantly – 'extend the period of political attention to post-conflict recovery' (UN, 2005).

These arrangements are possible and necessary where governments are chronically weak or virtually non-existent, and where even country representation is unclear. In other circumstances, local administrations should be supported. They should be assisted at an early stage of rehabilitation to develop comprehensive strategies that lay down a clear itinerary, setting out tasks and timing, and identifying resources and responsibilities. A monitoring mechanism is also needed, and there have been proposals for 'transitional results matrixes' to track progress.

6. Coordinate aid

This principle is all of a piece with the preceding one. If assisted rehabilitation is to succeed, then donors need to subsume their individual programmes for a country within a coordinated framework. This could mean the adoption by individual donors of specific parts of an agreed recovery programme, or the contribution of unearmarked resources into a central pool.

Donors have been agonizing for many years about coordination and harmonization and some progress is being made.[34] There are agreements by a growing number of bilateral agencies to untie their assistance and mingle it more flexibly with that of others. But to be effective aid needs to move a radical step beyond the adaptation of individual practices by donors to each other. There should be in each instance complete alignment with the frameworks and management capacities of recipients. However, the principle of country alignment needs to be reaffirmed, especially in the context of recovery and rehabilitation.

7. Sustain the support

Being to a significant degree supply-driven, aid is subject to the vagaries of donor circumstances and preferences. Individual recipients are often subject to ebbs and flows.[35] For recovering fragile states, capacity development cannot be realized without an assurance of resources over the long term, and donors need to sign up to multi-year engagements. It is beginning to happen in countries, such as Mozambique, where donors judge that political will has become positive and sustained. But there are too many exceptions.

To encourage sustained support, aid planning needs to become more open ended. Even while broad objectives need to be defined to permit the monitoring of progress, planning should not be narrowly tied down, project-style, to fixed costs within strict time boundaries. Indeed, traditional project approaches should be avoided entirely. Facilitating the renewal of capacity is fundamentally an unpredictable, even idiosyncratic, trial-and-error process, especially in the more hazardous contexts of fragile states.

8. Be coherent

Donors give with one hand and take with the other. Surprisingly, the necessity to view donor engagement in terms of the totality of economic and other interactions with recipients has virtually eluded the analysis of aid effectiveness until very recently. Yet, the impact of bilateral trade terms, investment patterns, migratory flows and other factors can have consequences that outweigh, and often directly detract from, the potential benefits of aid. One of the central tenets of this book is to press the case for more even-handed partnerships as an alternative to aid.

An interesting attempt to gauge the comparative impacts on developing countries of a range of donor policies has been undertaken by the Center for Global Development since 2003. A 'commitment to development index' is calculated for the 21 richest donor countries, ranked according to their policies on aid (relative amount, destination, aid tying, project density), trade (import tariffs and domestic agricultural subsidies), investment (incentives to invest in the South), technology (share of research and development in GDP), security (contributions to peacekeeping), environment (levels of pollution emissions, commitment to multilateral agreements) and migration (net immigration flows from the South).[36]

Fragility is exacerbated by these uneven terms. Any comprehensive solution to the challenges facing fragile states must take into account not only the non-aid inflows of resources, but also the outflows and the financial and other impediments for which the same donor countries are responsible. This must be done, not globally, but on an individual country basis. Balance sheets should be drawn up, calculating with respect to each major donor the total financial value of the bilateral relationship. The trade/aid nexus alone is important. The rich countries collect in tariffs on the imports of some of the poorest much larger sums than they provide in aid to the same countries. The subsidies provided to rich country farmers distort global markets against the interests of lower cost producers in the poorer countries.[37]

Manifestly, donor engagement with fragile states cannot just be about aid. It has to encompass the totality of bilateral economic and other relationships. Our analysis concurs with most of the OECD principles for 'good international engagement' (see Box 5.2), although there is insufficient stress on these non-aid policies.[38]

Box 5.1 How do the donors rank on 'commitment to development'?

In 2005, the Center for Global Development calculated its third annual 'commitment to development index' for 21 of the richest countries (the OECD/DAC members minus Luxembourg). In addition to aid, the index takes into account six other factors: openness to developing country exports, investment facilitation, migration policies, environmental policies, security policies and creation and dissemination of new technologies. The index is thus a composite calibration of government policies towards development. The top scorer was Denmark and the bottom was Japan, with the US in the middle (see Table 5.6).

The *aid* index takes into account 'quality' factors such as destination (Mozambique scores much higher than Israel), frequency of aid missions (the lower the density the better), and amount of private giving facilitated by tax incentives.

Trade takes into account the extent to which donors encourage (through aid for trade) or inhibit (through tariffs, quotas and domestic subsidies) access to their markets. Here the top scorer is Denmark and the lowest are Japan and Norway, which both maintain heavily protected agricultural markets. The UK's policies on foreign direct and portfolio *investments* get the highest mark in this category, which is based on destination of investments, tax provisions and risk protection. The *migration* index rewards rich countries that are open to immigrant labour – unskilled more than skilled because of the deleterious effects of the brain drain – and that facilitate asylum. Austria and Switzerland do best here because they permitted the largest numbers of immigrants relative to their size. The US is only modestly placed because no account is taken of non-legal immigration.

The Europeans do best, Japan and US worst, on the *environment* index that measures contributions to greenhouse gases and levels of interest in international environmental agreements. *Security* is intended to measure the contribution of the rich countries to the security of the developing world. Multilateral peacekeeping commitments, the securing of international sea-lanes and arms trading (positive if to responsible states) are the three main factors considered. Australia and Norway score best; the US and UK are penalized by their Iraq involvement (which was not internationally authorized). Finally, rich countries are judged according to the amounts they spend on *technology* research and their policies on intellectual protection.

Table 5.6 *Donor commitment to development (2005)*

Rank	Country	Aid	Trade	Investment	Migration	Environment	Security	Technology	Average
1	Denmark	12.3	5.9	5.5	5.3	6.5	7.2	4.4	6.7
2	The Netherlands	8.7	5.9	6.8	5.7	6.6	6.8	5.8	6.6
3	Sweden	9.8	5.8	5.5	6.4	6.4	5.2	5.3	6.4
4	Australia	2.5	7.3	6.5	6.5	5.4	8.5	5.0	6.0
5	Norway	10.8	1.0	5.8	4.9	4.2	8.5	5.2	5.8
5	New Zealand	2.1	8.8	3.4	7.1	5.9	7.8	5.1	5.8
7	Finland	4.9	5.8	5.9	2.5	6.1	6.6	6.3	5.4
7	Austria	3.0	5.8	3.0	10.5	6.5	4.7	4.6	5.4
7	Germany	3.4	5.7	6.7	6.8	6.7	3.8	4.7	5.4
10	United Kingdom	5.6	5.9	8.1	2.8	7.9	2.1	4.6	5.3
10	Canada	2.9	7.3	7.6	4.9	4.3	3.5	6.3	5.3
12	United States	1.9	7.2	6.7	4.7	4.0	6.2	4.7	5.0
13	Switzerland	6.0	3.3	4.6	10.5	4.7	1.6	3.8	4.9
13	Portugal	2.8	5.9	5.5	1.4	6.7	6.4	5.3	4.9
15	France	4.1	5.8	6.0	2.7	6.2	2.8	6.2	4.8
15	Belgium	5.4	5.8	5.0	2.9	6.3	3.6	4.5	4.8
17	Spain	2.6	5.8	5.2	5.1	5.1	3.6	5.4	4.7
18	Italy	1.6	6.1	6.8	2.5	5.4	4.1	5.3	4.5
18	Ireland	5.6	5.6	2.5	3.2	5.9	6.1	2.8	4.5
20	Greece	2.8	5.8	3.6	1.8	6.3	5.8	3.2	4.2
21	Japan	1.4	-0.2	5.1	1.8	3.7	2.8	5.0	2.8

Source: Center for Global Development

CONCLUSION

How donors meet the challenges of fragile and failing states provides the acid test for aid. While most aid has been a vehicle for donors to build relationships with individual developing countries, the predicament of the fragile states presents two outstanding justifications for activism. One is obviously humanitarian, since development failure has continued to impoverish the lives of many hundreds of millions of people. The other is self-interest, given the dangers posed by the fragile states to global security and health.

The donor record is patchy to say the least. And the closer you come, the worse it looks. Donors bear some responsibility for not being there, but that is not the worst accusation. Donors also appeared at the wrong times with the wrong attitudes. Working within their own scripted agendas, they succeeded in sometimes unpicking and undermining development progress.

Now, being there in the right frame is the urgent order of the day. Failure demands constructive engagement, in some cases to save people from their leaders, and in all cases to save some of those failing states from circumstances they cannot control. These adversities are in some cases natural, such as isola-

Box 5.2 OECD/DAC principles for good
international engagement in fragile states*

1. *Take context as the starting point.* All fragile states require sustained international engagement, but analysis and action must be calibrated to particular country circumstances. It is particularly important to recognize different constraints of capacity and political will.
2. *Move from reaction to prevention.* Action today can reduce the risk of future outbreaks of conflict and other types of crises, and contribute to long-term global development and security.
3. *Focus on state-building as the central objective.* States are fragile when governments and state structures lack capacity – or in some cases, political will – to deliver public safety and security, good governance and poverty reduction to their citizens.
4. *Align with local priorities and/or systems.* Where governments demonstrate political will to foster their countries' development but lack capacity, international actors should fully align assistance behind government strategies.
5. *Recognize the political-security-development nexus.* The political, security, economic and social spheres are interdependent: failure in one risks failure in all others.
6. *Promote coherence between donor government agencies.* Close links on the ground between the political, security, economic and social spheres also require policy coherence within the administration of each international actor.
7. *Agree on practical coordination mechanisms between international actors.* In these fragile contexts, it is important to work together on upstream analysis; joint assessments; shared strategies; coordination of political engagement; multi-donor trust funds; and practical initiatives such as the establishment of joint donor offices and common reporting and financial requirements.
8. *Do no harm.* International actors should especially seek to avoid activities that undermine national institution-building, such as bypassing national budget processes or setting high salaries for local staff that undermine recruitment and retention in national institutions.
9. *Mix and sequence aid instruments to fit the context.* Fragile states require a mix of aid. A vibrant civil society is important for healthy government and may also play a critical transitional role in providing services, particularly when the government lacks will and/or capacity.
10. *Act fast...* Assistance to fragile states needs to be capable of flexibility at short notice to take advantage of windows of opportunity and respond to changing conditions on the ground.
11. *...but stay engaged long enough to give success a chance.* Investments in development, diplomatic and security engagement may need to be of longer duration than in other low-income countries.
12. *Avoid pockets of exclusion.* International engagement in fragile states needs to address the problems of 'aid orphans' – states where there are no significant political barriers to engagement but few donors are now engaged and aid volumes are low.

Note: *Based on 2005 draft.

tion and drought. But mostly they are man-made, whether triggered by internal demagogy, HIV/AIDS and strife, or resulting from conditions that the rich countries themselves can ameliorate. Aiding the fragile states means more and better forms of engagement. It also means lifting some of the impediments to progress.

6

Aid and Imperialism

The word 'empire' has come out of the closet. Respected analysts on both the left and right are beginning to refer to 'American empire' approvingly as the dominant narrative of the twenty-first century. JOSEPH NYE, *FOREIGN AFFAIRS*, 2003

I am not interested in using the word imperial as an epithet. I would prefer to use it as a description and to explore how American imperial power is actually exercised.
MICHAEL IGNATIEFF, 2003

For globalism to work, America can't be afraid to act like the almighty superpower that it is...The hidden hand of the market will never work without a hidden fist – McDonald's cannot flourish without McDonnell Douglas, the designer of the F-15. And the hidden fist that keeps the world safe for Silicon Valley's technologies is called the United States Army, Air Force, Navy and Marine Corps.
THOMAS FRIEDMAN, *NEW YORK TIMES*, 28 MARCH 1999

We may say that we shall not abuse this astonishing and hitherto unheard of power. But every other nation will think we shall abuse it. EDMUND BURKE ON THE BRITISH EMPIRE, 1770

It is dangerous to be America's enemy, but fatal to be America's friend. PAT BUCHANAN, US REPUBLICAN PRESIDENTIAL CANDIDATE

Large nations do what they wish, while small nations accept what they must. THUCYDIDES, GREEK HISTORIAN, 5TH CENTURY BC

While there have been dominant powers throughout history, at no time has there been a single superpower with the size and global reach of the US. Its economy is larger than the combined value of the four other permanent members of the UN Security Council. In 2003, the *increase* in the US defence budget was equivalent to total UK defence spending. In 2006, US defence spending is equal to that of the rest of the entire world. There are 350,000 US troops deployed in over 90 military bases outside the US. Some 250,000 of them are combat troops, two-thirds (150,000 in late 2005) in Iraq, but with major deployments in Korea (37,000 troops in 28 camps and bases) and Afghanistan (11,000). Twelve aircraft carrier fleets ply the world's oceans.[1]

The sheer economic might of the US is also reflected in its appetite for imports. Every month, it buys over US$50 billion more from the world than it sells.[2] American corporations like Exxon, ChevronTexaco, General Motors, Ford, General Electric and Coca Cola are among the world's largest, and their products can be found on every continent.

Even without aid, the US is globally preponderant. But it has also again become the world's largest donor – by a large margin. Using the OECD definitions of official aid, the total value of its assistance in 2004 was almost one-quarter of global ODA and more than twice that of Japan, the next largest donor (see Table 6.1 and Figure 6.3). Some leading aid proponents are, nevertheless, highly critical of the US government for devoting one of the smallest shares of GNI to aid among rich countries (0.16 per cent – see Figure 6.4). But if the 'stingy' US decided today to suddenly respect the UN target of 0.7 per cent of its GNI for its aid,[3] as it is being exhorted to do, then US assistance, at more than US$90 billion per year – while still only 20 per cent of military spending – would be significantly larger than the total of all other OECD donors combined. As the head of USAID said in June 2005: 'if we ever reached 0.7 per cent we would be the dominant force in all aid and be accused of imperial development'.[4]

Indeed. Influence is the quintessence of US aid, which is more closely wedded to home interests than that of the other major donors. More US aid would mean added reach and influence, driven by motives that are at least as much commercial, geopolitical and security-related, as they are developmental. The record of US aid – particularly in recent years – supports one of the main theses of this book: seeking aid effectiveness in purely developmental terms is looking down the wrong alley.

But – and this is part of the paradox of American power (Nye, 2002) – it is by no means certain that more aid actually translates into more influence. The reasons why are the subject of this chapter.

FROM TRUMAN I TO BUSH II

Aid as influence has a solid pedigree in the US. The Marshall Plan, which ran from 1948 to 1951, was not only a very generous aid programme, it was a spectacular example of enlightened self-interest. As we saw in Chapter 2, it

Table 6.1 *OECD countries: ODA, 2001–2004*

	Country	ODA in US$ (millions)				ODA as GNI Percentage			
		2001	2002	2003	2004	2001	2002	2003	2004
1.	Australia	852	962	1237	1465	0.25	0.25	0.25	0.25
2.	Austria	457	475	503	691	0.25	0.23	0.20	0.24
3.	Belgium	866	1061	1887	1452	0.37	0.42	0.61	0.41
4.	Canada	1572	2013	2209	2537	0.23	0.28	0.26	0.26
5.	Denmark	1599	1632	1747	2025	1.01	0.96	0.84	0.84
6.	Finland	389	466	556	655	0.33	0.35	0.34	0.35
7.	France	4293	5182	7337	8475	0.34	0.36	0.41	0.42
8.	Germany	4879	5359	6694	7497	0.27	0.27	0.28	0.28
9.	Greece	194	295	356	464	0.19	0.22	0.21	0.23
10.	Ireland	285	397	510	586	0.33	0.41	0.41	0.39
11.	Italy	1493	2313	2393	2484	0.14	0.20	0.16	0.15
12.	Japan	9678	9220	8911	8859	0.23	0.23	0.20	0.19
13.	Luxembourg	142	143	189	241	0.80	0.78	0.80	0.85
14.	The Netherlands	3155	3377	4059	4235	0.82	0.82	0.81	0.74
15.	New Zealand	111	124	169	210	0.25	0.23	0.23	0.23
16.	Norway	1346	1746	2043	2200	0.83	0.91	0.92	0.87
17.	Portugal	267	282	298	1028	0.25	0.24	0.21	0.63
18.	Spain	1748	1608	2030	2547	0.30	0.25	0.25	0.26
19.	Sweden	1576	1754	2100	2704	0.76	0.74	0.70	0.77
20.	Switzerland	908	933	1297	1379	0.34	0.32	0.38	0.37
21.	United Kingdom	4659	4749	6166	7836	0.32	0.30	0.34	0.36
22.	United States	10,884	12,900	15,791	18,999	0.11	0.12	0.14	0.16

Source: OECD

brought substantial benefits to the Western European recipients, setting them on a solid course of economic revival that the ideologically differentiated East was denied. Healthy economies meant healthy markets and George Kennan – an influential director in Marshall's State Department and the architect of containment – justified the plan by arguing that the money for the Europeans was needed 'so that they can buy from us' (Layne, 2003).

But Marshall was not the only model for bilateral aid, which began under the auspices of President Truman's 'doctrine', enunciated in March 1947, to support 'free peoples who are resisting attempted subjugation by armed minorities or by outside pressures'. The doctrine was a political response to perceived Soviet aggression in Europe and was the basis for assistance (a then huge US$400 million) to Greece and Turkey, considered in danger of falling into the communist sphere. In 1950, the Congress passed an Act for International Development. While this act was certainly inspired by the altruistic sentiments of Truman's Point Four statement (from his 1949 inaugural speech), it was followed one year later, as the Marshall Plan was terminating and the Cold War was beginning, by the Mutual Security Act, which regrouped economic and technical assistance with military aid under a new Mutual

Security Agency. Aid could be provided if it 'strengthened the security of the United States'. It was Truman I rather than Truman II that was to prevail.

Another feature of the decade was the start of commodity assistance, which came with its own gift-wrapping. In 1954, Public Law 480 authorized food aid, justified according to President Eisenhower because it would 'lay the basis for a permanent expansion of our exports of agricultural products with lasting benefits to ourselves and peoples of other lands'. US food aid was also distinguished from that of other donors by the fact that almost all of it was produced in America and bagged and shipped by US companies. The source was clearly branded.

In 1958, William Lederer published *The Ugly American*, a poignant attack on US policy in Southeast Asia. The renewed debate on foreign assistance that followed brought an attempt at a fresh start and the Kennedy administration created the US Agency for International Development, to be governed by a new Foreign Assistance Act (FAA) passed in 1961. The 1960s were the heyday of US assistance. Several programmes were regrouped under the single agency, USAID, and it was given a relatively free hand, within some broad-brush foreign policy interests. In Latin America, the Alliance for Progress was designed to roll back the appeal of revolutionary politics in Cuba and elsewhere. In parallel with aid there was police and military assistance to help governments fight communist insurgency. But the preoccupation was mainly with Asia, the principal theatre of the Cold War. Through the 1960s, the countries of that continent were by far the largest recipients.

From the early 1970s onwards, US aid again came in for much introspection. The US was about to exit Indochina and a much wider debate was being joined on the effectiveness of aid, partly in terms of development, but mainly according to the strategic goals of the US. In 1971, Congress made a fist by knocking back a foreign assistance bill for the first time.[5]

Aid was now firmly a tool of US foreign policy and security interests. But as aid was batted back and forth among different interest groups in Washington, a confusing set of prescriptions emerged on how and by whom it should be administered. In the late 1970s, an International Development Cooperation Agency (IDCA) was set up with an anticipated oversight role over USAID. At around the same time, a Development Coordination Committee was revived with the mandate to harmonize the activities of the different departments with aid responsibilities, including USAID, the Department of State and the Treasury. But it never functioned properly. A legacy of poor coordination has carried over into the present.

There have been repeated attempts to review the FAA, but none has succeeded, partly due to Congressional inertia. However the processes of introspection and enquiry have continued and these have reaffirmed the self-serving nature of aid. In 1988, in one of these reviews, the House Foreign Affairs Committee determined that 'the public has very little concept of the aid program as an instrument of foreign policy, *used to advance US interests*' (author's italics).

Notwithstanding erratic aid policies and politics – a feature of most major donors – US assistance continued to climb steadily during the 1980s. On the surface, a rise of more than 100 per cent over 10 years seems surprising given the known scepticism of President Reagan about foreign aid. However, geopolitics continued to give aid its own momentum. In the 1990s, this rationale disappeared with the end of the Cold War and, in common with other major donors, aid volume fell markedly between 1992 and 1997.

Then there was a turning point in 2000. US aid growth accelerated to 12 per cent in real terms in 2001, 15 per cent in 2002, 20 per cent in 2003 and 14 per cent in 2004.[6] This series of increases is completely without precedent and bigger, lumpier aid has become a hallmark of the Bush era.

WHO GETS IT?

The geographic pattern of US patronage reflects the evolution of strategic and commercial interests. For much of the post-war era, aid being a Cold War instrument, the US favoured a number of large Asian countries encircling the Soviet Union and China, including India, Indonesia, Korea, Pakistan and Vietnam (see Table 6.2). During the 1960s, Taiwan was also an important beneficiary. Assistance to Vietnam was generous until 1975, ending abruptly with the fall of Saigon. Aid to South Korea was also substantial in the 1960s. It began to diminish steadily after 1972 and ended in the 1980s, but a large military presence has been maintained.

The Middle East has also retained an intensive US interest. The assumption is often made that aid in that region has always been driven by oil interests, but the original American motivation was the same, namely rivalry with the Soviets. America was determined to ensure that declining European influence would not allow the Soviet Union to extend its reach there, as had happened in Asia. The US certainly understood the significance of the region's oil resources.[7] But at the time, the US produced half the world's output and imported very little. A pro-Arab policy was belied by support for Israel, which has consistently been a beneficiary of US aid from the time of its recognition in 1948, even though US foreign policy has often been quite ambivalent about Israel, which initially found deeper political support in Europe. It was the powerful pro-Zionist lobby in America that helped to sustain generous flows of aid.

Support to Egypt was first motivated by Nasser's aggressive version of a 'non-aligned' policy, which sought aid from both ideologies, but gave special favour to the Russians. The US was concerned about Egypt's role as a Russian stooge and American aid also began to flow into Jordan – for a long time a regional UK military base – when it was feared that it might fall under Egyptian influence. Nasser, the Arab socialist, died in 1970. Three years later, his successor Anwar Sadat expelled his Russian advisers and shortly afterwards launched an attack on Israel, in an attempt to regain some of the territory occupied in the six-day war of 1967. Sadat's independent boldness earned him

Table 6.2 *Top 10 recipients of US aid*

	1960	1970	1980	1990	1995	2000	2001	2002	2003
1.	India	India	Egypt	Egypt	Egypt	Russia	Pakistan	Russia	Iraq
2.	Korea	Vietnam	Israel	Israel	Haiti	Israel	Russia	Egypt	DR Congo
3.	Pakistan	Pakistan	Turkey	Poland	Israel	Egypt	Egypt	Israel	Jordan
4.	Vietnam	Indonesia	Bangla-desh	Philipp-ines	Russia	Ukraine	Colombia	Serbia	Colom-bia
5.	Egypt	Korea	Indonesia	El Salvador	Iraq	Jordan	Ukraine	Afghan-istan	Russia
6.	Taiwan	Brazil	N. Marianas	Honduras	Palau	Indonesia	Serbia	Colombia	Ethiopia
7.	Turkey	Colombia	India	Bangla-desh	El Salvador	Ethiopia	Honduras	Jordan	Afghan-istan
8.	Jordan	Turkey	Nicaragua	Pakistan	Philipp-ines	Bulgaria	Israel	Ukraine	Israel
9.	Morocco	Laos	Somalia	Sudan	S. Africa	Mozam-bique	Peru	Indonesia	Egypt
10.	Tunisia	Northern Marianas	Sudan	Jamaica	Jordan	Honduras	Jordan	Pakistan	Bolivia

the respect of the Americans and aid to Egypt rose steeply from 1974 onwards. Since that year, Israel and Egypt have almost continuously been two of the top three recipients of US assistance.

From the 1970s, aid was brought closer to home with support to Latin and Central American countries. Brazil became a major recipient during the 1960s, the early phase of military dictatorship; Colombia until 1977, then again after 1995. Nicaragua and Honduras were mirror images. When the hostile President Ortega came to office in 1984, aid switched from Nicaragua to Honduras, which also hosted a large US military presence. When Ortega was voted out in 1990, Nicaraguan aid was resumed while in Honduras it dropped by half. Increased aid to El Salvador coincided with the accession of a military government and continued during the civil war that lasted 12 years until 1992.

The largest per capita recipients were in the Pacific: Northern Marianas and Palau. The former has been receiving over US$2000 in aid per head per year after opting to continue as a US dependency in the 1970s. Palau, which hosts a US military base, has also been generously aided since its independence in 1994.

In Africa, Somalia was suddenly a new beneficiary after it expelled its own Russians in 1977. Sudan was a major recipient during the 1980s, and then again during the last few years. Mozambique has seen a steady build up from the 1990s after its own civil war and the Congo (Democratic Republic) received a huge one-off injection of debt relief (over US$1 billion) in 2003. But the most developmentally deserving continent received very limited US assistance until quite recent years. For most of Africa, aid flows have been modest and fickle. From the 1970s to the 1990s, more than 40 countries in Sub-Saharan Africa received less aid than Israel and Egypt together.

From 1990, attention turned from containment to the conversion of new 'transition' countries to markets and democracy. There were many new recipients among the former Soviet satellites: Russia itself and Ukraine – where the US also helped fund the very expensive disarmament process – Poland, Bulgaria, Serbia and Montenegro, among others. The 1990s were also politically opportunistic. The US sponsored the return of former President Aristide to Haiti in 1994 and provided substantial aid for just two years. Aid was also briefly resumed to Iraq in mid-decade. Bangladesh was an important beneficiary at the beginning and end of the decade. By 1998, total ODA was rising again, in part to complement growing US military operations in Colombia, Haiti, Bosnia and Kosovo.

AID AND THE 'WAR ON (ISLAMIC) TERROR'

After 2001, a suddenly stronger new security focus was restored to US aid with the 'war on terror'. After 1990, the difficulties of justifying aid on grounds of national interest and security had brought a long period of expansion to an end, with aid volumes levelling off and falling during the decade. Now the Afghanistan intervention turned around a new US administration and provided a basis for substantial aid expansion. As Richard N. Haass, Director of Policy Planning Staff, put it:

> In the conduct of the global campaign against terrorism, the military has often been the most visible aspect to the outside world. However, over the long haul the military tool will almost certainly not be the most important contributor to our success.... Our tool kit must also include effective foreign assistance. (Haass, 2002)

President Bush had arrived in 2001 on a platform of non-intervention and disengagement. In his first months, he withdrew from the Middle East and North Korea peace processes. He reduced anti-terrorist funding. He also distanced the US from several multilateral treaties: the new Kyoto Protocol designed to limit global warming; the 1997 Mine Ban Treaty; and verification measures for the 1972 Biological and Toxic Weapons Convention. He spoke the Cold War language about his concerns for Russia and China.[8]

September 11th did not change anything of the 'new unilaterism'[9] in US foreign policy, but it radically altered the earlier reticence about intervention. President Bush was ready to 'fight for freedom and against terror', making no distinction between 'those who planned those acts and those who harbour them'.

Intervention in Afghanistan, and the huge challenge of rebuilding a country, all with a solid team of allies, built considerable confidence into US foreign policy. There was a new belief in the ability of military might and economic resources to remake the world order. After regime change in Afghanistan there was now a focus on an 'axis of evil' (January 2002) comprising Iran, Iraq and North Korea. Old allies also experienced verbal censure, including top aid recipient Egypt and oil-friendly Saudi Arabia – the original home of Osama Bin Laden and 15 of the 9/11 terrorists. These were the sentiments that have stimulated the debate on imperialism.

The invasion of Iraq was part of the logic instilled by 9/11 and the Afghanistan response.[10] Although a former ally, assisted by the US in the war with Iran during the 1980s and a significant source of oil imports (from 1988 to 1990 and again from 1998), Iraq had become defiantly anti-American and construed by the US as a danger to world security. The real contest over the invasion turned on perceptions of the legitimacy of superpower prerogative, for which the yardstick was UN endorsement. But for the US, Iraq seemed to signify the triumph of hard power over soft. As Joseph Nye describes it, Americans were told 'that their unipolar moment will last and that they can do as they will because others have no choice but to follow' (Nye, 2003). Imperialism?

Aid was destined to follow in the wake of war as the needs for reconstruction became evident. Afghanistan and Iraq began to tie up unprecedented levels of resources for 'nation-building'. In 2003, US$2 billion of new ODA was appropriated for these two countries and this figure jumped to US$3.8 billion in 2004. As the USAID head of programmes in Kabul put it in 2002: 'We're not here because of the drought and the famine and the condition of women. We're here because of 9/11' (quoted in Ignatieff, 2003). Prosecuting the war on terror also benefited other countries. Aid to Pakistan rose almost ten-fold in 2001 to US$780 million; Jordan received close to US$1 billion in 2003.

But aid was also becoming again a new currency of influence in other spheres. Soon after September 2001, a campaign began among some donors to make significant commitments of aid at the UN's international conference on 'financing for development' in March the following year in Monterrey, Mexico. President Bush, whose Texan ranch was a short distance over the border, agreed to attend, but was under mounting pressure from other Western donors and international non-governmental organizations to make his own offer. He did not disappoint the aid proponents, for in invoking a new 'fight against poverty', he announced plans to increase American aid by US$5 billion to US$15 billion per year.

NEW DEVELOPMENT AID

It was the birth of an interesting innovation: the grandly-titled Millennium Challenge Account. The MCA was designed to be a separately funded and managed programme, applying different criteria to aid eligibility and disbursement. Most importantly, the MCA is the closest the US has come to a purely developmental fund but with a distinct good governance slant. It is designed specifically to reward well-performing countries.

To qualify for funds, countries must, in President Bush's words, be considered to be 'ruling justly, investing in their people and establishing economic freedom'. These conditions have been refined into 16 criteria using indicators developed by the World Bank, Freedom House and other sources (see Table 6.3).

Table 6.3 *16 criteria for Millennium Challenge Account eligibility*

	Indicator	Source
Ruling justly	Control of corruption	World Bank Institute
	Rule of Law	World Bank Institute
	Voice and accountability	World Bank Institute
	Government effectiveness	World Bank Institute
	Civil liberties	Freedom House
	Political rights	Freedom House
Investing in people	Immunization rate (DPT and measles)	World Health Organization
	Primary education completion rate	World Bank
	Public primary educ. spending (percentage of GDP)	World Bank
	Public expenditure on health (percentage of GDP)	World Bank
Economic freedom	Country credit rating	Institutional Investor
	Inflation rate	IMF
	Regulatory quality	World Bank Institute
	3-year budget deficit	World Bank
	Trade policy	Heritage Foundation
	Days to start a business	World Bank

Source: Brainard and Driscoll (2003)

The MCA has been very slow starting. It took nearly two years for the enabling legislation to pass Congress and for a new agency, the Millennium Challenge Corporation to be set up. It is now (2006) headed by a business friend of President Bush with no aid or development experience. The appropriations were also delayed. It had been envisaged that there would be a three-year build-up to the additional US$5 billion of assistance. The actual appropriations for the fiscal years 2004–06 have been US$1 billion, US$1.5 billion and US$1.75 billion respectively.

The first MCA programmes were finalized in 2005 for just five recipients:

- Madagascar at US$110 million over four years;
- Honduras at US$215 million over five years;
- Cape Verde at US$110 million over five years (largest with Portugal);
- Nicaragua at US$175 million over five years;
- Georgia at US$295 million over five years (largest with Germany).

These 5 countries were selected from an initial list of 16 (augmented to 17), which were judged to have met the criteria. The other 12 are: Armenia, Benin, Bolivia, Ghana, Lesotho, Mali, Mongolia, Morocco, Mozambique, Senegal, Sri Lanka and Vanuatu.[11] There is also a list of 13 so-called 'threshold' countries,[12] which are judged to have made significant progress towards meeting the indicators, but are still falling short. These countries will be eligible to share 10 per cent of the total MCA allocations. The first allocation was made in July 2005 to Burkina Faso for a girls' education programme (US$13 million).

The amounts of the MCA grants are potentially quite substantial, even though spread over four to five years. An objective of the MCA is to make the US one of the preponderant donors in the recipient countries and this will be achieved in Cape Verde, where the US will rival only Portugal, and in Georgia, where Germany is the other major donor.

The MCA has its critics. It threatens to duplicate the aid programmes of USAID to the same countries, while being managed independently. It entails a rather elaborate oversight structure in the beneficiary countries. It uses relatively narrow criteria for eligibility, reflecting a conservative American ideology, and the indicators themselves are open to quite wide interpretation, making it difficult to determine unambiguously when a country is 'justly ruled' for example. Being selective, it ignores many of the poorest and neediest countries. And actual disbursement has been very slow. Out of the first two years' allocation of US$2.5 billion, only US$50 million (2 per cent) had been expended by the end of 2005.

But the MCA has also received praise from some quarters. The programmes so far agreed have been developed collaboratively with governments as well as potential beneficiaries in the selected countries. In fact, the lengthy consultation process is one of the reasons for the delays in finalizing the first grants. The orientation of the aid is also pro-poor: for example, rural roads, land rights and business development in the poorer provinces of Nicaragua; rural development and transport in Honduras; land rights, banking and rural business development in Madagascar. Another significant advantage is that the aid is also untied to sources in the US and procurement is the responsibility of the recipient country.

Above all, while the MCA is highly selective, the aid is provided to countries that are among the most likely to use it well. Even the prospect of generous assistance among the potentially eligible countries has provided an incentive to governments to reform. In sum, the MCA is one of the better examples of bilateral aid as influence. There is country ownership, a continuing commitment to reform and a reasonably high chance of success.

AIDS AND INFLUENCE

The same cannot be said, however, for a rather different and even larger new aid initiative: the President's Emergency Plan for AIDS Relief (PEPFAR) launched and rapidly enacted by President Bush in 2003. The new programme projects total spending of a huge US$15 billion over five years (with more than half appropriated for 2004–06). With the MCA, it has been seen as another part of the response to the scepticism of some European donors about American commitment to development.

Unfortunately, PEPFAR is bedevilled by dogma and self-interest and has been heavily criticized by development specialists. It has three fundamental flaws. In the first place, the US has again taken a unilateral route, despite the existence of the multilateral Global Fund to fight AIDS, Tuberculosis and Malaria (GFATM), established at the beginning of 2002. At a pledging conference in late 2005, the Global Fund attracted an additional US$3.7 billion in funding, of which the US contribution was US$300 million, a modest part of the PEPFAR. The programme has been established under the auspices of the State Department, but separate from USAID, which is an implementing partner. Second, PEPFAR, initially headed by the former chief executive officer of a major US pharmaceuticals company,[13] is seen as doing the bidding of the US pharmaceuticals companies, led by their lobby group PhRMA, which opposes the use of cheaper generic anti-retroviral drugs for AIDS treatment. Third, the programme is strongly influenced by conservative faith-based groups. It promotes an approach to HIV/AIDS prevention with the epithet 'ABC' inspired by the example of Uganda: Abstinence, Being faithful, Condoms. But it is all about keeping the problem in the family. Controversially, it also forbids grants to organizations with programmes that involve prostitutes and sex workers,[14] also requiring grantees to have an explicit policy opposing prostitution and sex trafficking. Since sex workers are in the forefront of the battle against AIDS, it is obvious that one of the most effective means of control is to encourage the use of condoms in commercial sex. Moralistic dogma will unfortunately do nothing to rid the world of its oldest profession, but it will undermine a key front in the global AIDS campaign. This is aid at its least influential in any positive sense.[15]

There have been several other initiatives. Also under the State Department – and again separate from USAID – is the Middle East Partnership Initiative (MEPI), established in 2002. The MEPI has four pillars – economic, political, educational and women's empowerment – and its funding of US$70–100 million per year supplements other US aid programmes in the region.[16] In 2003, two new discretionary funding initiatives, under the auspices of the White House Office of Management and Budget, were announced: a US$200 million Famine Fund, 'to provide emergency food, grants or support to meet dire needs on a case-by-case basis'. The fund would be a supplement to the more than US$1 billion per year of food aid that is regularly appropriated. There is also to be a US$100 million presidential Emerging Crises Fund 'to respond swiftly and effectively to prevent or resolve unforeseen complex foreign crises', but more of a geopolitical than humanitarian or developmental nature.[17]

SIX AID DRIVERS

In late 2003, a coalition of 160 private aid groups and NGOs working in the US called InterAction, published a policy paper critical of many aspects of US aid. It spoke of 'increased fragmentation of resources and responsibilities,

Table 6.4 *Major US aid programmes with 2005 appropriations*

Bilateral Economic Assistance	US$million
USAID	
Total development assistance	4234
of which, Child Survival and Health	(1538)
USAID/Department of State	
Economic Support Fund	2481
Assistance for Eastern Europe and the Baltic States	382
Assistance for the Independent States of the Former Soviet Union	482
Department of State	
International Narcotics Control and Law Enforcement	326
Andean Counter-Drug Initiative	734
Migration and Refugee Assistance	764
US Emergency Refugee and Migration Assistance Fund	30
Nonproliferation, anti-terrorism, demining and related programmes	399
Global HIV/AIDS	1970
Middle East Partnership Initiative	100
White House (Office of Management and Budget)	
Famine Fund	200
Independent agencies	
Peace Corps	317
Inter-American Foundation	18
African Development Foundation	19
Millennium Challenge Account	1488
Department of the Treasury	
Treasury technical assistance	19
Debt restructuring	99
Agriculture	
Food aid (PL480)	1173
Multilateral Economic Assistance	*US$million*
International Financial Institutions	1219
United Nations and other international organizations	1492
International peace-keeping	483
Military Assistance	5012

Sources: USAID, Office of Management and Budget (2005); Federation of American Scientists, http://www.fas.org/asmp/profiles/aid/fy2006/F150budget.pdf

confusion externally about who is in charge, and a loss of coherence in the field as multiple federal agencies pursue similar goals with little coordination' (InterAction, 2003). A seasoned analyst of US aid told lawmakers it had become a 'hodge-podge of uncoordinated initiatives... too many actors, with little clarity on overall objectives' (Radelet, 2004). The further proliferation of new programmes addressing different aspects of global concern has presented additional challenges. This fragmentation has occurred as a result of many new commitments by the present US administration to expand its engagement with developing countries and it contrasts with the earlier meek pronouncements that seemed to presage isolation. The problem is with the nature of these engagements. Aid does not have one overall objective, it has many – in fact more than ever – and they each pursue different aspects of American interest.

The 9/11 attacks marked the definitive end of any incipient inclination towards isolation and girded US foreign policy into a 'war on terror'. The reprisals in Afghanistan were seemingly inevitable but there was no stopping a growing belief, within the conservative establishment, in the impact of shock-and-awe and in the power of the US to manipulate world affairs – if necessary without many of its traditional allies. As long as Osama bin Laden is still at large and the threat of terror growing, it will be difficult to convince this administration of the inefficacy of hard power.[18] Curiously, it was the same Bush who had expressed fears in 1999 about his 'arrogant nation'. But even if he has since changed his mind, events may have proved him right about humility.[19]

It was the determined spirit after 9/11 that begat big aid, with the lumpy targeted increases we have described. It was aid with influence written all over it, but there were multiple interests and objectives, of which six stand out and can be used to rationalize most US assistance. With one exception, these are not developmental. It is not even clear that they meet their non-developmental purposes.

Military power

Security has been a governing principle of American aid since the beginning and, more than any other major donor, aid from the US is strongly correlated with military assistance (see Figure 6.1). Development aid accompanies and helps to sugar military assistance. It helps countries in the American front-line to absorb the economic shocks of conflict and rewards their loyalty. Infrastructure is also built specifically to help with US military logistics: roads, housing and communications in the immediate vicinity of American bases is always built and maintained to a high standard.

Afghanistan and Iraq have been the principal focus of aid and military spending since 2001. Substantial assistance has been directed towards reconstruction, including as a first priority the rebuilding of infrastructure destroyed by American bombs. (Massive procurement of goods and services from favoured US suppliers in the rehabilitation has also given a commercial edge to this assistance.) There has been more assistance for the countries surrounding Afghanistan. Pakistan enjoyed a ten-fold increase in 2001, and aid was doubled in Tajikistan and Turkmenistan. Similar increases were enjoyed by Kyrgyzstan and Uzbekistan between 2000 and 2002. Aiding contiguous countries can bring complications, however. Pakistan has been generously rewarded for its role in facilitating regime change in Afghanistan, but support

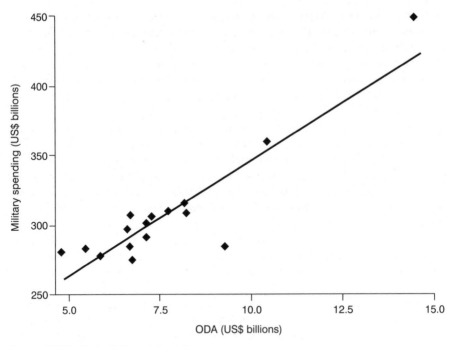

Source: US Center for Defense Information

Figure 6.1 *US aid and military expenditure, 1988–2003*

from its territory for the ousted Taliban is having a serious destabilizing impact on the country, increasingly decried by Afghan President Karzai. Pakistan could do more to hunt down American global enemy number one, Osama bin Laden, who is thought to be more popular there now than in the aftermath of 9/11. But it is alleged that they have as much incentive not to.[20]

In other regions, many countries have been rewarded by the US in military and economic aid for taking up arms against terrorists, including Colombia, Indonesia, Philippines, Yemen and Mauritania. But such support can have its limitations. In Mauritania, where aid has risen seven-fold after 2000, President Taya was a willing adherent to a regional coalition against Islamist rebels in the Sahara. But his popularity waned rapidly as a result of his over-zealous suppression of militant rebels. In August 2005, he was ousted in a coup after 21 years in office. His link with the US – the 'fatal friend' – has been cited as one of the major reasons for his downfall.[21]

There are other cross-overs from military interests to aid. Since the International Criminal Court – set up by the UN as a permanent body to try crimes against humanity – became operational in 2002, the US has actively sought to persuade as many countries as possible to sign immunity agreements intended to protect US soldiers serving abroad from prosecution. Over 100 of these agreements have been signed, but 20 countries – half of them in Latin America – have declined to do so, and in many cases they have been punished

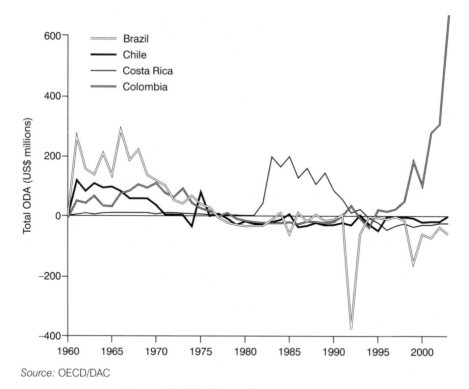

Source: OECD/DAC

Figure 6.2 *US's Latin American recipients*

with cuts in military and development assistance. One example is Ecuador, which houses US military bases and has been used as a staging ground for surveillance of the drugs trade. It has suffered significant aid reduction in 2004 and 2005.[22]

Commercial interest

The commercial pay-back from foreign assistance has also been another consistent feature. In 2004, according to the OECD, some 70 per cent of US assistance was tied to procurement from US sources, the second highest proportion among donors, behind only Japan.

Tying is also a feature of humanitarian assistance. As noted earlier, the US is the only donor to provide food aid solely in kind, rather than cash, because PL480 is used as a means of disposing of domestic agricultural surpluses. There are three domestic interest groups that derive substantial benefits: four major grain traders (including Cargill and Archer Daniels Midland), five shipping companies and a group of non-governmental aid organizations (including CARE and Catholic Relief Services). The aid groups – rather than the recipient governments – distribute the food.[23] But they can also sell it on local markets in order to generate revenues. Tied food aid is slow to reach its destinations and excessively costly because of all the interested middlemen. In a 2005 report, the OECD criticized the US for 'substantial cost inefficiencies associated with tied food aid' (Clay et al, 2005).

If development value were the governing criterion, PL480 would never have begun. But it is the strong home interests that prevail. Like PEPFAR, discussed above, which is used as a vehicle for procurement from US pharmaceutical companies (that themselves use their influence by making major contributions to the main political parties[24]).

Not all ODA is free. The US has also provided significant proportions of its development aid (and military assistance) in the form of loans and export credits, along with many other donors, making aid a significant commercial proposition from the financial viewpoint too.[25] Currently, the US is the largest net recipient of ODA loan repayments among the OECD countries, the flow turning negative – against the developing countries – in every year after 1989. In some years, the return flow to the US has exceeded US$1 billion. According to the OECD, the return in 2003 (latest data) was $1.7 billion. Figure 6.2 shows the Latin American origins of some of these repayments. Brazil and Chile became 'negative recipients' (namely, net donors) of the US in terms of total aid flows in the 1970s and Costa Rica joined them in the mid-1990s. Colombia was a net donor to the US for all of the 1980s, but has benefited from growing net inflows over the last ten years.

Oil security

The US is by far the largest consumer of oil in the world. Its 21 million barrels per day are equivalent to the consumption of the five next largest consumers combined: China, Japan, Germany, Russia and India (2004 figures).[26] The US is also an oil producer, but depends on imports for 60 per cent of its needs: over 11 million barrels a day – the single largest import item. Not surprisingly, therefore, assured oil supplies are a major preoccupation in America's international relations. Oil imports have grown by 20 per cent over the last 5 years. Without an energy policy that seeks conservation or a switch to alternatives, this preoccupation will only grow.

The main foreign suppliers of US oil are Canada, Saudi Arabia, Mexico and Venezuela, together accounting for over half of all imports.[27] But the US is seeking to diversify its sources even further and West Africa is likely to grow in importance as a regional supplier. Angola, Gabon and Nigeria already account for 15 per cent of US imports and in each case they have benefited from a three-fold increase in aid since 2000. Other beneficiaries in the region include Congo (Democratic Republic) that saw aid increase by more than 100 times between 2000 and 2003, and Cameroon (5 times).

This book is not going to enter the speculation of others on the oil-related motives of the Iraq invasion. However, there has been a notable softness of approach in America's relations with other major oil producers – like Sudan and Venezuela – that might have been expected to incur more political hostility.

Freedom and democracy

'We see development, democracy and security as inextricably linked... the United States cannot win the war on terrorism unless we confront the social and political roots of poverty', said Colin Powell after stepping down as secretary of state (Powell, 2005). He also stressed the importance of 'representative government' and 'bringing justice to people'. These were sound words, but under his watch US assistance had a patchy record of promoting democracy. The 'war on terror' – as during the Cold War – entailed support for, and moral encouragement to some distinctly undemocratic regimes. The drive against autocracy among the Arab states through the Middle East Partnership Initiative, which Powell himself launched in 2002, has taken an approach akin to the Soros Foundation in Eastern Europe, by patronizing non-governmental groups. But it too appears like an orphan in the foreign policy establishment, being criticized for its scatter-shot approach and absence of cohesive strategy (Wittes and Yerkes, 2004).

The Millennium Challenge Account remains the best contemporary example of US attempts to foster good governance and liberal democracy. The choice of beneficiary countries is bound to remain somewhat subjective, and the criteria of eligibility reflect standardized conservative notions of the well-governed state. But the MCA can have a positive influence, and deserves to receive the amount of funding that had been originally promised to it.

Political influence

Through its aid programmes the US has maintained a heavy presence in the Middle East over more than three decades. Since the mid-1970s, Egypt and Israel have been two of the top beneficiaries of US assistance – with ODA alone (net of military assistance) exceeding a cumulative US$25 billion in each case. Here the intentions were primarily of political influence, maintaining bridges with influential regional powers.

In practice, the political 'influence' has been rather ineffective. Notwithstanding the enormity of the two aid programmes, one state remains an oppressive and undemocratic society,[28] the other a democracy blemished by its occupation of Palestinian territory, and sometimes quite impervious to US pressures.[29] In fact in both these relationships, it is not clear that patronage and influence always flow in the same direction.

Unilateralism

Going it alone is nothing new to the US. In the world's only universal forum, the US has often wielded the sole veto in the Security Council and been in a tiny minority against resolutions of the General Assembly. Since 2000, unilateralism has tightened. The US has backed out of several global agreements, some of which were designed – ironically – to enhance security, and it is using bilateral free-trade agreements with developing countries to get around the

BOX 6.1 TRADE AND INFLUENCE IN THAILAND

The US has negotiated several bilateral free-trade agreements (FTAs) with developing countries (among them, Cambodia, Jordan, South Korea and Vietnam) and is negotiating others, including with Thailand, where there has been considerable opposition within civil society. On the positive side, the FTA will result in lower tariffs for a range of Thai imports into the US. But Thailand will also have to agree to a number of measures that abrogate existing multilateral agreements. These include Thailand's enforcement of environmental laws in the US interest, but which violate the Kyoto Protocol (on global warming), the Convention on Biological Diversity and the Basel Convention (on hazardous waste), all of which Thailand has ratified, but which the US has not.[30] They also include Thailand's agreement to impose stricter controls on patent medicines that will restrict Thai firms' ability – permitted under the WTO – to produce much cheaper generic drugs for its HIV/AIDS patients, and allow the US to import into Thailand patented genetically-modified (GM) products, which could greatly increase the exclusive dependence of Thai farmers on US companies. Negotiations have been going on for 18 months, but during a recent round in northern Thailand (January 2006), they were brought to an abrupt halt by 10,000 protesters.

restrictions that multilateral conventions impose on the freedom of action of American corporations (see Box 6.1).

In September 2005, the US succeeded in weakening the global consensus around the Outcome Declaration of the largest-ever gatherings of world leaders at the UN. One of those compromises concerned intervention in cases of genocide, which one year previously the US had nevertheless been quick to highlight in Darfur, Sudan. Since the summit, President Bush's own representative to the UN, John Bolton (who once stated that 'there is no United Nations') has argued that 'either we need to fix the institution, or we'll turn to some other mechanism to solve international problems'. The former house speaker has also summed up the relationship with the UN in the following manner: 'the fact that the UN has no democratic preconditions for membership limits America's *ability to render the UN's infrastructure and its decisions compatible with American values and interests*'.[31]

There are, however, circumstances in which the US sees the merits of a multilateral approach to humanitarian assistance, and it is an active supporter of UN peace-keeping operations (17 of which around the world cost less in a year than the US presence in Iraq for 1 month). Multilateral channels have also been used as a bilateral bypass. One example is aid to the Palestinians. The Palestinian Authority – officially stated to be tainted by ties to terrorism – receives no direct assistance, but, nevertheless, benefits from about US$150 million per year from the US through the United Nations.[32]

But 9/11 reinforced the Manichaean sentiments of 'for us or against us', which went beyond verbal bravado and sparked the language of those 'willing coalitions'. While there are circumstances in which strong global leadership can be beneficial, even without a large like-minded coalition, the US conveys a strong sense that policy is currently driven less by a sense of collective global good, and more by the desire to press home the advantages of its unique comparative strengths.

CONCLUSION: BUT DOES US AID WORK?

From the outset, US aid has been interlaced with security concerns, and with keeping as much of the world as possible friendly to the American economic system. As the quotations in this chapter illustrate, the US has always been rather frank about these intentions – and more sincere than if it had claimed that aid was solely motivated by development. Of the six aid drivers – security, commerce, oil, democracy, politics and the unilateral agenda – only one is developmental. Whatever other analysis shows, the commitment to develop-ment is therefore weak, and it would be inappropriate to apply normal criteria of development effectiveness to US bilateral aid.

The question is whether the US is meeting its own objectives through its multi-dimensional programmes of patronage, and whether the world is safer and stronger as a result. The disturbing conclusion of this chapter is that on both these counts, the answer appears to be as much negative as positive and that bigger aid still yields small results. The explanations are both specific and general:

- Security-related assistance has had mixed results in co-opting individual countries into a 'war on terror', has been politically destabilizing in some instances and has associated the US with some notably untoward bedfel-lows.
- Commercial patronage and aid-tying are seen as doing the bidding of already-powerful US companies and are not perceived as charitable.
- Oil-based aid is also transparently self-serving and brings its own relational distortions.
- The drive for 'freedom and democracy' has been clumsy and uneven, and America's potential star programme is insufficiently funded.
- Political bridge-building is selectively targeted and relatively ineffectual.
- Unilateralism heightens divisions and makes it harder to build coalitions.

But perhaps the major factors undermining impact are those founded on more general perceptions. When you are large and forceful and perceived even by the most reasoned and moderate of US commentators as imperialistic, then – to paraphrase Burke (1793) – every other country will assume that power is being abused. There are unfortunately too many signals to reinforce that perception.

One is manifested by the dogmatic application of a particular set of moral values, which are by no means universal even in the rich countries. This percep-tion has its mirror in attitudes to other religions. To state, for example, that the US is not specifically waging a war against Islam may be accurate, but being unable or unwilling to understand the growing prevalence of this perception in large parts of the developing world is potentially disastrous.

Consistency also counts for a lot and some countries have felt let down by their sudden abandonment by the US when they lost their strategic value. During the 1980s and 1990s, the US switched into and out of some Central American countries according to the ideological flavours of successive regimes. America turned away from Pakistan and Afghanistan in the 1990s following the Soviet Union's retreat – and then returned after the vacuum had been filled by new enemies of the West. The patterns of support following the Asian financial crisis of 1997–98 are also symptomatic of subjective interest. Two staunch US allies against Indochinese communism in the 1970s – Thailand and Indonesia – received little more than moral support for their collapsing economies, but for South Korea, with its 37,000 American troops, the US worked with the IMF to secure a US$57 billion rescue plan (Mahbubani, 2005).

The world does need a value-centric superpower, but one that is willing to propagate norms and standards that have universal recognition (such as those enshrined in many UN conventions, or the Millennium Declaration of 2000 signed by all the world leaders). Many people feel a certain nostalgia for the post-war period, when the US helped to found the UN and played such a critical role in establishing the mechanisms of global governance. Since then, the country has seen its economic and military strength increase further, but its influence has not grown commensurately. Joseph Nye (2002) uses the term 'soft power' to describe the espousal of values that are universal and that the US should reclaim. Rather than going it alone, Nye says, the US should be building and leading coalitions by listening as much as telling. It should also mean taking a more inclusive approach to developing countries: not labelling them by 'axis' or 'rogue' status but being willing to engage with even the least fragrant regimes. For every Burma and Zimbabwe (isolation), there is a Libya (successful engagement).

Unlike the empire builders of the 18th and 19th centuries, the world's superpower is not after the wholesale subjugation of other peoples and the clumsy maintenance of overseas administrations. However, the perception of America's motives as the pursuit of a world serving its commercial and strategic interests prompts many inside and outside the country to tout the imperialist epithet. Influence cannot be bought by might and money, even where – perhaps especially where – military and development assistance are seen to be linked so closely. Less hardware traded for more inclusion, engagement for rebuke, consistency for tied assistance, these could be the alternative ingredients for influence.

But time is not on the side of the US. However the power and influence relation develops, the US position of single superstate will gradually come in for challenge. If their economies continue to expand rapidly, China and India will become major powers in their own right over the coming decades. Already, their developmental influence is being felt within Asia and it is spreading to

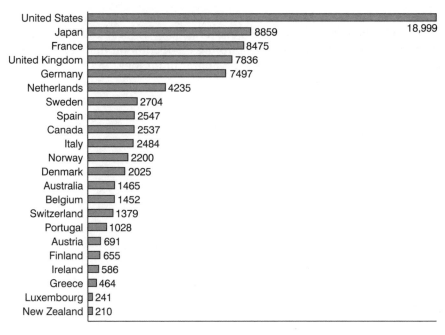

Source: OECD/DAC (2005)

Figure 6.3 *OECD countries: Net ODA in 2004*

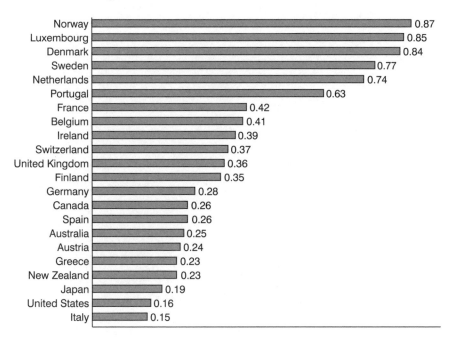

Source: OECD/DAC (2005)

Figure 6.4 *OECD Countries: Net aid as percentage of GNI in 2004*

other regions as well. They represent large markets and growing sources of investment. They have also been donors for as long as most OECD countries. Their existence is one reason for doubting the likelihood that single-power 'liberal imperialism' (Ferguson, 2004) will prevail for long.

7

Donors from the South

China knows that Indonesia needs highways, bridges, and ports. We are ready. We have tremendous capacity in construction, enormous number of engineers and technicians, to help. What does China need? [We need] oil, natural gas, palm oil and other natural resources, which Indonesia has in abundance. The deal is easily made.   CHINESE GOVERNMENT SOURCE, 2005

We normally think of donors as the rich countries of today, which industrialized first. These are the countries that set up the multilateral aid architecture after the Second World War and established their own bilateral aid agencies. Several of those in Europe were recipients of Marshall Plan aid from the US in the late 1940s and early 1950s. As recipients, they formed their own association, which subsequently became the OECD. The OECD hosts the rich donors' club, the Development Assistance Committee, now with 21 members (plus the European Commission).

The DAC countries together provide the major part of total ODA, but not all of it. By the OECD's own estimate about one-tenth – perhaps between US$5 billion and US$10 billion per year – is accounted for by donors from the South. Like the European donors, they all have been – and mostly still are – aid recipients themselves. These countries are sometimes called the 'emerging donors', but the term is misleading, for it excludes some of the largest, like China and India, that have been donors for as long as the DAC countries – and that were the world's two largest economies in the 19th century.

Surprisingly little analysis has been done on the Southern donors, in spite of their importance for several individual developing country aid recipients. These donors have no club like the OECD/DAC and no statistics are systematically collected. One of the only non-OECD countries to produce its own analysis of its aid programme – in 2005 – has been Thailand (UN, 2005).

Data are in any case hard to come by. There is both reticence and ambiguity. Most of the Southern donors have been quite furtive about their patronage, and most do not have transparent parliamentary systems that request accountability. The reticence is related to the often intimate degree of political patronage that is bound into much Southern aid. Governments keep these cards close to their chests. The ambiguity is in the definitions of aid. Since there is no OECD/DAC to carefully sort what is ODA from the rest, the numbers that do exist cannot easily be compared. Southern aid often combines humanitarian with developmental, and the developmental component may not all be soft (namely, loans with minimum grant equivalent). Also, gifts and transfers in kind may be mixed in, or they may be excluded. There are other problems.

In this chapter we look at Southern donors mainly from three developing regions: Asia, Middle East and Eastern Europe. The choice is dictated in part by available information, but ensures that most of the largest donors are included. Notwithstanding the difficulties of measurement, there are several reasons for taking a closer look – albeit a selective one – at Southern aid. One is to see how similar or different have been the aid motivations, compared with the rich countries, and the extent to which aid from this provenance is also subject to influence-seeking. Another is to trace the growing significance of aid from the South, and assess the ways in which aid recipients are exposed to different and sometimes countervailing pressures from this direction.

WHAT ARE THE ORIGINS OF SOUTHERN AID?

There have been several motives behind Southern aid, some political, some economic and some commercial. China, as one of the oldest of all donors, began its assistance at the founding of the People's Republic in 1949 (Zhang, 2005) and the motivation was partly Southern solidarity. India was also an early starter and linked its aid to its prominent role in the non-aligned movement (NAM) that emerged from the Bandung South–South summit of newly independent states in 1955. The principles of NAM emphasized sovereignty, but also Southern cooperation.

Political aid

Ideology was soon helping to sharpen and differentiate Southern aid. China being firmly in the socialist bloc, its assistance was directed at friendly countries like North Korea and North Vietnam at a time when their southern halves were major recipients from the Western donors. (Today, North Korea's other major donor is South Korea, for very pragmatic security reasons.) Military hardware was then – and remains now – a significant component of Chinese aid. In Europe too, the Cold War drove the Soviet Union and its satellites (especially Czechoslovakia, Hungary, Poland and Yugoslavia) to provide assistance to their socialist cousins worldwide, including Angola, Mongolia, South Yemen and Vietnam. Cuba was also a beneficiary, but has since become a significant donor of technical assistance in its own right.

On the other side of the political divide, Saudi Arabia became a key sponsor in the 1960s and 1970s of strategic Western friends like Afghanistan, North Yemen, Oman, Somalia and Zaire that were, at different times, repulsing Soviet interests. Saudi Arabia was also very strongly aligned politically to the Arab world as a whole for political and cultural reasons.

In 1964, the then Chinese Premier Zhou Enlai, who was on a long tour of many developing countries in Asia and Africa, enunciated the eight principles of China's aid (see Box 7.1). These were intended to give a friendly flavour to the patronage, and emphasize the recipient countries' 'ownership'. The aid was condition-free but it was all tied to Chinese origins and was often in the form of loans rather than grants.

From early years, although there were some favoured destinations within Asia, Chinese aid was remarkably widely spread geographically. After 1971, this diversity increased for other political reasons. China took over Taiwan's seat in the UN Security Council and the rivalry sparked one of the most overt examples of aid as political influence. China (People's Republic) declared its one-China policy and through 'cheque-book diplomacy' each country tried to win the allegiance of other developing states. Taiwan, with its small size but greater economic success, was suddenly a significant donor for more than 30 countries that were willing to acknowledge Taipei and spurn diplomatic recognition of China. The aid bidding involved significant sums and has continued up to the present. In recent years, for example, Grenada in the Caribbean and Senegal each received substantial assistance from Taiwan, immediately before switching their diplomatic allegiances and becoming Chinese aid clients.[1] In these circumstances, while aid-as-influence is clearly not driven by developmental considerations, the client countries would at least have got what they wanted.

The four Visegrad countries[2] of Europe all quite significant donors before – began to develop modest aid programmes in the 1990s. Mostly the motivation has been the desire to impart some of their experience of transition to other states in the Eastern European region with which they have some affinity. Poland's aid, for example, is directed at countries 'with which it maintains a significant level of political, cultural and economic relations; that are under transformation in eastern and south-eastern Europe; and with large populations of Polish origin' (Hanspach, 2004).

Economic aid

Economic motivations have also been important among Southern donors. The most obvious example of resource-driven aid is the emergence of the Organization of Petroleum Exporting Countries (OPEC) as donors in the 1970s, following the huge oil price rises during that decade (Neumayer, 2004; Cotterrell and Harmer, 2005b). Saudi Arabia, Kuwait and United Arab Emirates (UAE) were the most prominent countries and they established their own aid funds. The Kuwait Fund for Arab Economic Development had already been established in 1961. The Saudi Fund for Development was established in 1974, and the UAE's Abu Dhabi Fund for Arab Economic Development followed in 1975. Several multilateral institutions were also launched during the 1970s: the Arab Fund for Economic and Social Development (AFESD), the

---

Box 7.1 Eight principles for China's
aid to foreign countries

1. The Chinese Government always bases itself on the principle of equality and mutual benefit in providing aid to other countries. It never regards such aid as unilateral alms but as something mutual.
2. In providing aid to other countries, the Chinese Government strictly respects the sovereignty of the recipient countries, and never attaches any conditions or asks for any privileges.
3. China provides economic aid in the form of interest-free or low-interest loans and extends the time limit for repayment when necessary so as to lighten the burden of the recipient countries as far as possible.
4. In providing aid to other countries, the purpose of the Chinese Government is not to make the recipient countries dependent on China but to help them embark step by step on the road of self-reliance and independent economic development.
5. The Chinese Government tries its best to help the recipient countries build projects that require less investment while yielding quicker results, so that the recipient governments may increase their income and accumulate capital.
6. The Chinese Government provides the best-quality equipment and material of its own manufacture at international market prices. If the equipment and material provided by the Chinese Government are not up to the agreed specifications and quality, the Chinese Government undertakes to replace them.
7. In providing any technical assistance, the Chinese Government will see to it that the personnel of the recipient country fully master such techniques.
8. The experts dispatched by China to help in construction in the recipient countries will have the same standard of living as the experts of the recipient country. The Chinese experts are not allowed to make any special demands or enjoy any special amenities.

Source: Principles formulated by Premier Zhou Enlai of China in 1964

Arab Bank for Economic Development in Africa (BADEA), the Islamic Development Bank (IDB) and the OPEC Fund for International Development. Two UN-related multilateral funds were also created with large injections of Arab money: the International Fund for Agricultural Development (IFAD) in 1977 and the Arab Gulf Programme for United Nations Development Organizations (AGFUND) in 1981. All these organizations provided either grants or loans on a concessionary basis (see Table 7.1).

Saudi Arabia and Kuwait were already contributing some US$1 billion to aid in 1970. In the next five years, however, aid from the OPEC grouping rose by nine times in real terms. For the decade as a whole, OPEC aid was equal to about one-quarter of DAC assistance and at its peak accounted for 3 per cent of the GNI of these new donors (against a DAC percentage of 0.35). In 1973, Saudi aid actually reached the equivalent of 15 per cent of the country's economic value (Browne, 1990).

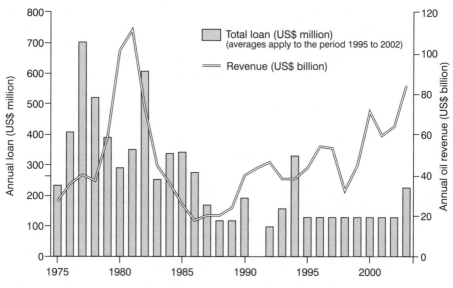

Source: Cotterrell and Harmer (2005b)

Figure 7.1 *Saudi Fund for Development: Loans and oil revenue, 1975–2004*

But what goes up, comes down, especially if it is substantially supply-driven and tied to the fortunes of the provider. OPEC aid has been exceptionally volatile. Taking the Arab countries and their funds as a whole (and excluding, for example, Iran) for which some data are available, aid fell markedly during the second half of the 1980s and during the 1990s. By the late 1990s, some Arab donors were recording a negative balance, meaning that net repayment of loans from beneficiaries exceeded new capital. The rise and fall is well illustrated by data for the Saudi Fund for Development, showing revenue and lending between 1975 and 2003 (Figure 7.1). In 2005–2006, however, rising oil prices have again led to an upturn in Arab patronage.

Aid from South Korea has also been closely linked to its growing economic strength, as a mark of which it became a member of the OECD in 1996 (but not the DAC). The hosting of the Olympic Games by Korea in 1988 provided a stimulus for the country to enlarge its global presence. Its aid programme has grown steadily, but still appears as relatively modest, partly because a substantial amount of resources – in grant and in kind – are channelled to its ailing northern neighbour, where it is one of the top two providers (with China).

Commercial aid

The pursuit of commercial interest – also part of Korea's agenda – has been another stimulant of South–South patronage. Not surprisingly, this interest has usually been concentrated on countries near to, or contiguous with, donors as they seek to expand trade and investment within their own sub-regions. While Korea looks to Southeast Asia, India looks to South Asia. It is a major donor for Nepal and Bhutan, where it has invested heavily in hydroelectricity, but it provides assistance to all its neighbours (and Afghanistan), with the exception of Pakistan, with which it has maintained a territorial rivalry since the partition of the sub-continent in 1947. India makes few bones about its own aid intentions. A recent official document seen by the author intones about 'projecting India's growing economic strength... a positive image of India will pay off by attracting investments in key sectors and at the same time assist Indian industry in projecting itself as a viable and technologically sound partner in other countries'.

The new phase of China's assistance, which can be roughly dated from the mid-1990s, adopts a rubric of 'mutual economic cooperation' and 'co-development' in which the state mingles its resources with those of Chinese companies (Zhang, 2005). China's investment and trade concerns are increasingly focused on essential raw materials to help drive its voracious economy. The emerging patterns of its aid reflect these concerns and have led to new cooperative arrangements with Burma, Iran, Sudan, Zimbabwe and the Central Asian republics.

Thailand is another Southern donor that links its aid closely to commercial ends. Its aid programme began as long ago as 1960, but has only recently attained significance (over US$250 million per year, equivalent to 0.13 per cent of GNI). Almost three-quarters of the aid is destined for three of its neighbours: Cambodia, Laos and Burma (Myanmar), from where Thailand obtains a substantial part of its energy and raw materials, including agricultural products for its food-processing industries. Thailand is the largest investing country in Laos and one of the largest in the other two countries (UN, 2005).

ADMINISTERING SOUTHERN AID

For all donors, their ministries of foreign affairs (MFA) play a key role in determining the nature and destinations of assistance programmes. This is to be expected and the same is true of the Northern donors. Within the MFAs there is usually a department responsible for aid, but they have not taken on the size and sophistication of the fully-fledged aid agencies of the OECD/DAC countries. Korea set up the Korea International Cooperation Agency (KOICA) in 1991. Among the Arab States, Kuwait, Saudi Arabia and UAE have agencies, but only the longer-established Kuwait Fund (1961) has a modicum of independence. Saudi Arabia provides a significant proportion of its aid outside the Saudi Fund for Development, relying also on discretionary payments by the ruling families (Neumayer, 2004).

Given the commercial bent of much of the Asian assistance, trade ministries play a role, along with finance ministries, in the major donors (see Figure 7.2). Besides KOICA in Korea, the Ministry of Finance and Economy is the major player. China's Ministry of Commerce has a very central position,

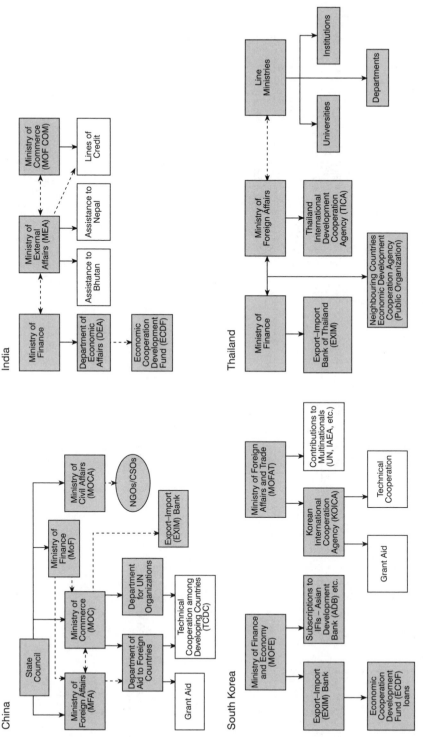

Figure 7.2 *Aid management structures: China, India, South Korea and Thailand*

Table 7.1 *Overview of Arab funds*

Donor	Date established	Net disbursements in US$millions (1975–1995)	Gross cumulative disbursements since establishment (US$ millions)	Geographical pattern	% to Arab states	Sectoral pattern (top two sectors) (%)
Kuwait Fund	1961	188.9	9300 (by 1997)	Varied	53.8 (to 2000)	Transport and telecommunications (35), Energy (21)
Saudi Fund	1974	149.6	6500 (by 1997)	Varied	45.0 (to 1996)	Transport and telecommunications (33), Agriculture and Livestock (20)
Abu Dhabi Fund (ADF)	1971	76.9	1700 (by 1997)	Varied	81.6 (to 1996)	Transport and telecommunications (92), Agriculture and livestock (4)
Arab Fund for Economic and Social Development (AFESD)	1974	108.2	8600 (by 2002)	Arab states	100 (to 2002)	Energy (29) Agriculture and Livestock (22)
Arab Bank for Economic Devt. In Africa (BADEA)	1975	29.6	1300 (by 2002)	Non-Arab African countries	0 (to 2002)	Transport and telecommunications (51), Agriculture and livestock (29)
Islamic Development Bank (IDB)	1975	108.4	18,000 (by 2002)	Islamic countries	54.5 (to 1996)	Energy (23) Industry and mining (20)
OPEC Fund for International Devt (OFID)	1976	111.6	4300 (by 2002)	Non-OPEC developing countries	n.a.	Transport and telecommunications (24) Energy (21)
Arab Gulf Programme for UN Development Organizations (AGFUND)	1980	n.a.	200 (by 2002)	UN Agencies, Int. Orgs, Arab NGOs	n.a.	Health Education
Arab Monetary Fund (AMF)	1976	n.a.	n.a.	Arab states	100	Balance of Payments Trade

Source: Compiled by author from various sources

Table 7.2 Asian and Eastern European donor aid in summary (US$ millions)

Country (start of aid)	1990	1995	2000	2001	2002	2003	2004	Main recipients (priority sectors)
China (1949)							3000†	Over 100 countries, 50 in Africa, most of the rest in Asia (infrastructure, sports stadiums, loans)
India (1950)							1000(?)	Bhutan (hydropower, roads, hospitals) Nepal (hydropower, various)
Korea (1976)	(63)(14)	116(59)	212(135)	265(195)	279(222)	366(245)	397	Over 100 countries, with emphasis on poorer Asian countries, China (various)
Thailand (1960)						167		Cambodia (hotels) Laos (hydropower) Myanmar (roads) Maldives (housing)
Taiwan (1958)							500††	30 countries in Africa (6), Asia-Pacific (9), Caribbean and Central America (11), Middle East (2), Latin America (2) (Small manufacturing, rural sector, micro-finance, health, human resources)
Poland*	3		29 (15)	36 (33)	14 (9)	35 (19)	(23)	Eastern and Southeastern Europe (institutional reform, NGO support) Afghanistan, Angola, Cameroon, Congo, Iraq, Kenya, Rwanda, Senegal (various)
Czech Republic* (1995)			16 (10)	26 (21)	20(32)	26 (80)	(56)	Eastern and Southeastern Europe (environment, agriculture, industry, health, education) Afghanistan, Angola, Iraq, Mongolia, Vietnam, Yemen, Zambia (various)
Slovakia* (1999)			8 (2)	(5)	(5)	(8)	(9)	Eastern and Southeastern Europe (institutional reform) Afghanistan, Kenya, Mongolia, Mozambique, Sudan (various)
Hungary						(14)		Eastern and Southeastern Europe (institutional reform) Afghanistan, Cambodia, Ethiopia, Iraq, Laos, Mongolia, Palestine, Vietnam, Yemen (various)
Slovenia* (1991)			3	2	n.a.	25		Southeastern Europe
Turkey	(2)	(93)	(29)	(27)	(33)	(26)		

Notes: Numbers in parentheses = OECD statistics. *excluding multilateral contributions to the EU, date refers to re-establishment of aid programme
† Based on an announcement that China intended to provide $10 billion over 3 years in concessional loans and export credits to developing countries.
†† Based on an announcement by an official Taiwanese source that aid is equivalent to 0.14% of total GNI – at the low end of the percentages for rich countries
Source: compiled by author from various sources

defining policy, signing bilateral aid agreements and managing most of the funds (Zhang, 2005). In India the Ministry of External Affairs gives guidance to the Department of Economic Affairs in the Ministry of Finance and works with the Ministry of Commerce on trade loans (Cotterrell and Harmer, 2005a). In Thailand, there is also a distinctive commercial bias, but it is the Neighbouring Countries' Economic Development Agency, under the joint auspices of the Ministries of Foreign Affairs and Finance, rather than the Commerce Ministry, that plays the more central role, with responsibility for the three major recipient countries (Burma, Cambodia and Laos).

The Asian donors also give a key role to their export–import banks, mostly operating under the auspices of the ministries of finance. As funders of exports and outgoing investments, the export–import banks underscore the commercial interests of the donors, with public finance following private. Aid through these channels is 100 per cent tied, in DAC parlance.

In the Arab region, as we have seen, the three major donors – Kuwait, Saudi Arabia and the UAE – have set up bilateral and multilateral aid agencies ('funds') to manage surplus oil revenues. These funds administer a mix of instruments including loans, grants and technical assistance, and the aid is substantially untied to domestic sources. However, although their total disbursements have been quite significant, they receive only a minority of the total resources disbursed by these three donors as aid, the balance being channelled through finance and other ministries and under other discretionary arrangements (Neumayer, 2004). To a high degree, therefore, the three donors[3] are subject to subjective criteria of allocation determined by the rulers of the states. In 1975, the AFESD set up a Coordination Secretariat regrouping the eight largest Arab Funds (Abu Dhabi, Kuwaiti and Saudi Funds, AFESD, BADEA, IDB, AMF [Arab Monetary Fund] and OFID [OPEC Fund for International Development]). The secretariat facilitates co-financing among these agencies, but does not otherwise coordinate assistance systematically, nor does it publish statistics.

The aid programmes of eight of the Eastern European donors have developed alongside their assimilation into the European Union, to which they are expected to become growing contributors of multilateral assistance. For this group, responsibility for aid typically resides with a number of different ministries, but with foreign affairs tending to assume growing roles in determining national development assistance frameworks (Hanspach, 2004). The Czech Republic (with the longest aid pedigree[4]) and Poland are the largest donors in this group[5] and they have laid the foundations of an aid administration. The Czechs have established a Development Centre and the Polish a Department for Development Cooperation in its Ministry of foreign affairs, to help guide aid policy. These new EU donors are expected to gradually develop aid infrastructure like their western neighbours. In this process they have received some external advice and assistance from the UNDP (phasing out its presence in all the new EU members) and Canadian bilateral aid.

THE SIGNIFICANCE OF SOUTHERN AID

Applying the OECD/DAC's definition of ODA, which includes gifts and concessional loans (with a minimum of 25 per cent 'grant equivalent'), it is probable that aid from the non-DAC donors lies somewhere in the range US$5 billion to US$10 billion per year. Estimates are inevitably quite rough, for a number of reasons. An uncertain proportion of aid is undeclared – even described as 'secret' in the case of some of the Arab donors (Neumayer, 2004). Many of the Southern donors hold back information, especially where the aid is predominantly political in character and closely interwoven with bilateral foreign policy. Also, the distinction between humanitarian and development assistance, both of which are provided increasingly by Southern donors, may be ambiguous. The line between commercial and non-commercial assistance is also difficult to draw where, for example, aid from a public source is used to subsidize commercial-type loans from an export–import bank.

Where unambiguous data can be found, however, they reveal that in the case of some of the Southern donors – among them the Czech Republic and Thailand – their aid programmes are already equivalent in value to 0.1 per cent or more of their GNIs, signifying that the comparative resource effort entailed by their ODA is approaching that of the traditional donors like the US and Italy. For the new EU member countries, the collective aid target has been set at 0.11 per cent by 2006, rising to 0.17 per cent in 2010 and 0.33 per cent in 2015. As we saw earlier, some Arab donors achieved much higher ratios in the 1970s.

For the arguments of this book, the exact amounts of Southern aid are less important than the scope and nature of the influence that the aid purchases. In this respect, the three geographical groups of donors we have chosen to examine are rather different.

Eastern European donors

Let us start with the Eastern Europeans, where there is a strong element of benign political influence. The eight new adherents to the European Union – the three Baltic states, the four Visegrad countries and Slovenia – have begun to align themselves with the aid structures and policies of the older members. Their geographical priorities are to some degree already influenced by the priorities given by the EU to the 79 African, Caribbean and Pacific (ACP) countries that were originally colonial dependencies of EU members. But there are at least two other features of their aid which are original. In the first place, some have resumed cooperation with countries to which they were linked during the socialist era, such as Angola (Czech Republic, Poland), Mongolia (Czech Republic, Hungary, Slovakia), Vietnam (Czech Republic, Hungary), as well as the Central Asian states that emerged from the former Soviet Union. These links will help to broaden the scope of interest in these countries by the EU and its principal aid agencies.

The other concentration of interest is much closer to home, and results from a deliberate policy by the EU to loosen the edges of the union and extend assistance to countries in the queue for later membership. All eight countries have successfully made the (mostly painful) transition from central planning to market democracy, generating lessons that can be emulated by the countries of South Eastern Europe. In 1999, the EU established the Stability Pact for South Eastern Europe principally in order to help maintain peace and encourage democracy and development in the eight countries of the sub-region.[6] The pact has been a focus of attention for several of the new European donors.

Arab donors

Although the amounts have fallen off from the levels of the 1970s and 1980s, the Arab donors provide much more substantial amounts of development assistance. The main beneficiaries by far are other Arab or Muslim states, first in the Middle East, next in Africa and then in Asia. During the 1990s, some 60 per cent of Arab bilateral and multilateral aid stayed in the Arab region, with about 20 per cent going to Africa, and most of the rest to Asia. Barely 5 per cent went to Latin America and Eastern Europe (Neumayer, 2004). At least for bilateral aid, the developmental patterns of this assistance are hard to discern. While the Arab donors have largely eschewed the fashionable development agendas of the West, they do not seem either to have followed criteria of income, poverty or other objective need in their patterns of patronage. Even the multilateral funds have tended to shift their assistance away from the poorest countries.

Politics and a sense of cultural solidarity would seem to have been the prevailing motivations. Much aid has concentrated on the countries surrounding Israel: Egypt, Jordan, Lebanon and Syria. But in addition, the sympathetic stance of countries in other regions towards the Middle East crisis can bring aid rewards. Given the potentially volatile nature of the relations among Arab states, it has also been suggested that aid by the main donors has been used to placate envious and threatening neighbours that do not enjoy the same benefits of bounteous oil resources (Hunter, 1984). This is a more cynical version of solidarity. Islam, through the principle of zakah,[7] one of its five pillars, encourages charitable donations for the benefit of the poor and aid has been partly inspired by a sense of religious duty. The major donors – and Saudi Arabia in particular – have contributed to the building of mosques and religious schools (madrasas) in many developing countries with large Muslim populations.

Asian donors

For the major Asian donors, there has been a mixture of aid motives. First and foremost these have been political. What is perhaps insufficiently appreciated is the extent to which long-standing tensions along the Himalayan belt among India, China and Pakistan – flaring periodically into open conflict – have affected patterns of patronage. For much of the period since 1950 (when China annexed Tibet), the rivalry has been territorial. India has extended considerable patronage as well as military assistance to its landlocked neighbours, Nepal and Bhutan, which also have borders with China. Strategically, China has sided with Pakistan – backed with assistance – in that country's unresolved dispute with India.

Since the early 1990s, a new political and commercial 'front' has opened in Burma (Myanmar), with which both China and India have been building increasingly cosy relations. Both have interests in that country's energy and other rich natural resources and China is using Burmese territory to establish military surveillance capacity. The military and commercial aid channelled to Yangon benefits the regime there more than the population at large.

Among the Asian non-DAC donors, China has also promulgated a policy of global influence over a long period. Partly, its influence was a show of socialist-leaning solidarity with the developing world. From the 1970s, it also became a means of cementing its one-China policy with most of the globe. Much more recently, with the huge growth of China's economy, the country's relations with individual countries in all regions are also influenced by trading patterns – sources of energy and raw materials, as well as markets. There is a curious irony in this metamorphosis from revolutionary advocate to capitalist partner. But whatever the motivations, the governance considerations that are of concern to Western donors are overlooked. China's increasingly urgent search for oil sources drives its friendship with Iran, from where it purchases one-third of its oil, and from Angola, Gabon, Nigeria, Sudan and other states in Africa, from where it gets another third of its supplies.

India and the other Asian donors we have chosen to examine – Korea and Thailand – have strong commercially related aid interests that are mainly confined to the region, with the bulk of their aid directed at neighbours: for India, it is the other South Asian countries, for Korea its northern neighbour, and for Thailand it is Burma, Laos and Cambodia. All the Asian donors have supported and in some cases (like Thailand) actively sponsored regional cooperation arrangements. China has pledged US$20 million to start a fund to promote cooperation in the region under the auspices of the Asian Development Bank.

In sum, while there are clear regional characteristics within each of the three groups of Southern donors whose assistance is concentrated in their own backyards, these groups are quite different from each other in their approaches to aid. The new European donors are helping to widen and deepen the assistance regime of the EU. Apart from official (ODA-style) aid that is steadily growing, this group also encourages assistance through non-governmental organizations, partly in recognition of the fact that a vibrant civil society is important for recipient countries still coming through the transition from central planning. The Arab donors – formerly substantial contributors of aid on a much wider scale – now exert a rather confused pattern of patronage, much influenced by its informal and discretionary nature. With the recent oil price rises, however, Islamic developing countries are beginning to receive increases in Arab aid. While it has an obvious cultural and religious orientation, the commercial content of the aid is weak, in strong contrast to Asian sources where economic interest drives other forms of influence.

Because of the nature and scale of their engagement, the Asian donors are the most influential and among them, China is of course predominant. Its economy is already huge – and it could again become the world's largest in only 20 years. It has widespread trading and investment interests. Its foreign exchange reserves could top US$1 trillion in only a few years. It also has considerable political clout as a fifth of the permanent membership of the UN Security Council, with veto power over resolutions that might be critical to one or other of its clients or partners. In this sense, China can act as a counter-weight to the influence of the traditional rich donors.

With the other Asian donors, it is also bound to the fates of several of the region's fragile states. Sanctions or other forms of pressure and influence from the richer states will not prevail in North Korea without China and South Korea; in Burma, without China, India, Korea and Thailand; in Nepal without India; in Laos and Cambodia without China and Thailand, and so on. The Asian donors, in particular, will ensure that influence through aid – at least in their own region – becomes increasingly multipolar.

8

New Beginnings: A Market for Aid

By many measures, it's been a great year for Africa, with debt relief, awareness-raising concerts and G-8 leaders pledging more aid. As an African, I'm gratified that the world has turned so much attention to my continent. But at the same time, a voice inside me wants to shout: 'Wait. This is not the way real development happens!'...It's what Africans do themselves that will determine how far and how fast we move forward.

GEBRESELASSIE Y. TESFAMICHAEL,
FORMER FINANCE MINISTER OF ERITREA, JULY 2005

We in the developing countries must own the development agenda, and our partners have to align their support to our agenda, our priorities and the sequencing we have set for ourselves. Development cannot be imposed, it can only be facilitated. PRESIDENT BENJAMIN MKAPA OF TANZANIA, 2004

At the beginning of this book, we described the two factors that have conditioned aid. First, it has always been pre-financed – paid by donors – either as grant or loan. Second, it mostly consists of transfers from public sectors in the North to the public sectors of the South.

Before the aid era countries never modernized this way, yet we have come to take these conditions of public patronage for granted. Aid has been administered along the lines of former central planning systems: developing countries are perceived as the passive recipients of state bounty, rather than active consumers with independent tastes and choices. Such systems have been discredited, it would seem, everywhere but in the aid business. This book has tried to show why delivering aid in this manner has compromised its own effectiveness, all the while purporting to provide the resources that developing countries are supposed to require.

Allocative efficiency can only be achieved through markets. They offer choices to the consumer. They encourage lower prices and better quality through competition. They are better at matching demand and supply. In this concluding chapter, we review the specific failings of the centrally administered approach to aid and propose how market principles can and should be applied.

Six features of 'centrally-planned' aid

1. Most aid is administered by many large public bureaucracies each with procedures of their own

There are at least 80 public aid agencies employing more than a quarter of a million bureaucrats, and a substantial number of consultants and employees of non-governmental organizations who are aid-financed. Each agency – even those within the UN 'common' system – has its own reporting and account-ability procedures prescribed by each of their governing bodies, to which the agencies are mainly accountable (upwards – to the paymasters – rather than downwards to the ultimate beneficiaries of aid).

2. Supply is excessive and duplicative

Supply-driven means more rather than less. Many of the aid organizations offer similar services, which are delivered in parallel, rather than being selected on the basis of competitive choice. The existence of many well-resourced aid agencies leads to considerable duplication of services as each agency seeks to market its own technical development 'solutions'. The problem is illustrated by examples from three African countries. Kenya has received from donors 18 different types of pump for its domestic water programme, each one requiring its own service manual and spare parts. Donor missions are excessive in number. Over 200 to Ethiopia were reported to the OECD/DAC in 2003, but this represents only one-quarter of the donors (ActionAid International, 2005). Some developing countries in Africa receive as many as 20 donor missions per week on average throughout the year. Each mission works with its own proce-dures and styles and develops its own outputs. Tanzania is said to turn out 2400 reports annually for the donors (Easterly, 2002), most of which have no direct impact on development processes.

3. Recipient countries are chosen according to the instincts of Northern politicians and donor self-interests

The destinations of aid are determined according to eligibility criteria, which the political governors of the agencies determine according to country interest as much as recipient need. Even in the multilateral system, the donor countries can influence the choice of aid recipient by conditioning and targeting their contributions. These criteria include commercial, historical, geopolitical and security considerations. Consequently, developing countries with the most impoverished populations – some of which are fragile or failing states – are often not those that attract the most assistance.

4. The content and terms of aid are strongly influenced by the needs and interests of the suppliers rather than the recipients

Agencies have their own preferential agendas, which reflect the latest development paradigms of their academics and researchers. These developmental paradigms have provided the frames within which donors have inserted their own technical solutions.

These foreign solutions are not fully absorbed. More often they are grafted on to local institutions without strengthening them from within. Or they remain as enclaves. The proliferation of donor-funded 'project implementation units' (PIU) is a widespread symptom of this grafting process. PIUs are there to ensure that the donors' projects are carried out to donor specifications. They employ foreign and local staff who are remunerated at levels well above local scales. When the project has run its course, the PIUs disband leaving little behind in terms of sustainable capacity. Enclaves are similar. They include, for example, some of the withering fruits of capital assistance: empty schools and hospitals, unmaintained highways and silted dams.

5. The rules of engagement are stacked in favour of the providers, whether in global governance, creditor–debtor relations or trade practices

Bretton Woods

The operations of the two most powerful multilateral organizations – the World Bank and the IMF – are strongly influenced by their richest Western members through systems of weighted voting. For most of their existence, the membership has also not been global, since it excluded all the states in the Soviet sphere until recent years. Largely in consequence, their own development approaches have been strongly influenced by Western neo-liberal thinking. Bretton Woods debts cannot be forgiven,[1] so the developing countries, which provide all the borrowers, have virtually no room to manoeuvre within the rigidly conservative prescriptions emanating from Washington. It is the most draconian and disciplined system of administering assistance that could have been devised, and it has been applied to a clientele with widely varying competence, to support development processes that are themselves highly variegated and unpredictable. This book has referred to the shortcomings of this arrangement and the resulting indebtedness several times.

Debt

Elementary economic projections of worst-case commodity export scenarios – long foreshadowed by trade realists decades earlier (as shown in Chapter 2) – could have confidently predicted the chronic unsustainability of external debt. But fundamental institutional weaknesses have compounded the non-viability of many poor countries as banking clients.

Substantial amounts of development assistance have been provided as loans – albeit at concessional rates – particularly by Japan, the US, France and Italy. For these and many of the DAC donors, loan repayments from developing countries have been building steadily over the years, beginning to outweigh new financial aid. In 2004, Japan was repaid US$900 million for ODA loans by both Thailand and Indonesia, and US$800 million by India. In each case, these amounts were more than the value of incoming assistance to those countries. In the same year, Brazil, Costa Rica, Morocco, Tunisia and Turkey were also net creditors of the US, thanks to loan repayments.

Chronic indebtedness has grown steadily for the developing countries. External debt was less than US$60 billion in 1970 but by the mid-1990s, it was over US$2 trillion (US$2000 billion) – close to half their total GDP. Since 1985 (and the so-called Brady Plan), the rich countries have been devising measures to reduce commercial debts, and donors have become more indulgent about forgiving ODA loans. Debt relief has become a major component of additional ODA. (But it does not represent new financing, only reducing future repayments.[2])

A major concern highlighted by this book, however, is multilateral lending to the poor countries that has become the predominant external obligation. When their obligations fall due and cannot be paid, the World Bank and IMF pay themselves back and extend new loans – a process known as defensive lending.[3]

Under G7 auspices, the rich countries have devised a series of schemes in order to maintain the bankability of the poorest countries vis-à-vis the Bretton Woods through debt rescheduling. In 1996, they came up with the Heavily-Indebted Poor Countries Initiative (HIPCI) for the benefit of 41 developing countries (most in Africa). Eligibility was linked to client performance in the reform programmes devised by the World Bank and IMF. HIPCI went through a further iteration before Washington came up with the Poverty Reduction Strategy Paper in 1999, the most comprehensive debt reduction and compliance instrument to date, open to all countries willing to seek concessional loans.

But the donors keep breaking their own rules as the merry-go-round of new and exceptional debt reduction measures goes on. Indebted countries remain as stubbornly in hock as before, and are bailed out with cancelled debts amid self-laudatory G7 declarations of new-found generosity. By this time, the monarch is without clothes. For decades, the development finance institutions have proceeded on the assumption – which provided a core rationale – that the poorest countries suffered from problems of liquidity. Yet in many cases their clients have become and remained fundamentally insolvent, for which heavily conditional loans have proved inappropriate. As a US academic (Lerrick, 2005a) put it recently:

> *for decades, the multilateral agencies have played a shell game with what they privately acknowledged were worthless developing-nation loans by recirculating funding on fantasy*

balance-sheets. The money is long gone, the debt is uncollectable, and rich lenders and international financial institutions must move on from denial to a new life as donors.

The most unfortunate aspect of unproductive lending is that it places the burden of failure on the recipient. If a policy-based programme goes awry – often because it never had the full approbation of the borrower at the outset – its benefits are not realized, yet the costs of repaying the loan still redound fully on the borrower.

Trade
The World Trade Organization – the almost-global trade forum – at least works through consensus of all its 149 members, giving potentially more bargaining bite to developing countries. Successive rounds are slowly grinding down tariff rates and opening markets, while promising to reduce (eventually) the farm subsidies on which rich countries spend US\$300 billion per year (OECD, 2004) and which hinder fair competition in the global market for agricultural goods. But barely 2 per cent of the imports of the six largest industrial economies come from the low-income countries and the proportion has scarcely progressed at all overall. Markets are only opening very slowly.

Agricultural imports into US, EU and Japan still attract average tariffs of over 20 per cent, and for individual items the rates are much higher. The EU rate on imported cereals that the Europeans produce goes up to 180 per cent. Japan virtually bans all imports of rice that could compete with its own domestic production. Developing countries have progressively moved from commodities into processed goods, but tariff rates then go higher – a practice known as escalation. Industrial goods have fared no better. The donors collect in tariffs from low-income countries several times more than they provide in aid.

6. The current aid system encourages leakages and corruption

Aid's most vocal critics contend that government-to-government transfers result in diversion and waste by corrupt recipients with weak institutions. Unfortunately, they are not wrong. For all the talk of accountability, aid has been poured in substantial quantities through the coffers of unreliable regimes, and the donors – whether bilateral or multilateral – have usually succeeded in justifying it by claiming mitigating factors. Bilateral donors have overridden these preoccupations by appealing to concerns about the strategic significance of the recipients, or the commercial opportunities they offer. Multilateral reasoning is obfuscated by attention to the technical details of the assistance and the perpetual belief that governance is about to improve. These excuses demonstrate the limits of upward accountability.

The OECD/DAC (2003) has cited a number of factors that incite corruption in aid programmes:

policy failure (particularly structural adjustment policies); failure to understand or to react to the environment in which they were operating, for example patronage and elite systems which support corruption; over-funding and then pressure to disburse; focus on infrastructure; poor supervision; reluctance to intervene in domestic affairs; reluctance to admit problems or failure as well as lack of transparency; and pressure to recover loans.

APPLYING THE MARKET

Our central thesis in this book has been that aid has no adequate market signals and that supply and demand are heavily distorted by donor domination. The suppliers pay and the consumers often do not get what they want because they did not ask for it.

Development experts have for too long been focusing on the bad policies of the South and have barely begun to notice the policy motes in their own eyes. The OECD now correctly blusters about donor policy coherence, for it is the 'incoherent' policies of the North that are aid-market distorting. Only by reducing the impacts of donor cartelization and restoring the tenets of a fairer market environment can aid be made more relevant and responsive. It means bringing market rules to bear on trade, finance and technical assistance.

A better trade market

In Chapter 2, we saw that trade was destined to become an Achilles heel for many of the developing countries. At independence, they lost some of their privileged access to donor markets. More importantly, falling commodity prices were identified early on as a critical impediment to increasing the purchasing power of the exporting countries. These disadvantages have been compounded by policies of rich countries that specifically target the agricultural and labour-intensive goods that are primarily exported by the South, through the imposition of tariffs, quotas and other restrictions.

In truth, the rich countries, which are so ready to exalt the virtues of market principles in domestic economies, are impeding fairer markets internationally. Slowly, these impediments are being unwound as the stark 'incoherence' of trade and aid policies gets more attention. Take the case of textiles and garments, which are very important exports for many developing countries. In the 1970s, the developed countries devised the Multi-Fibres Arrangement that imposed import quotas on textiles and garments. It was finally phased out at the end of 2004, but the rich countries are re-imposing quotas on a case-by-case basis. And if quotas have been eased, garments are still heavily taxed in order to protect developed country producers. For example, the US rates vary from 5–30 per cent depending on the item.

There is also a rash of special trade deals that offer new opportunities to developing countries, but they come with their own constraints and conditions. In 2000, the US granted duty-free access to 35 African countries, which induced more exports to America. But only 'non-sensitive' goods were permitted and all garments from these countries had to use US fabrics (Stokes, 2003). The EU's much heralded everything-but-arms initiative of 2001, which gave free access to non-military imports from developing countries, specifically excluded rice, sugar and bananas, items of importance to many countries (which are subject to other special protocols).

The rich countries should simply allow developing countries to compete on more equal terms in their own markets with their own producers. It is also market sense to lower tariffs and end agricultural subsidies. Keeping cheaper goods out of the market, and heavily subsidizing American cotton producers and European and Japanese farmers is artificially increasing the costs of living for all their consumers.

The rich countries are also demanding quid pro quo reductions in the import tariffs raised by developing countries. There have already been large reductions in rates during successive trade rounds. But because of huge differentials in economic strength, completely free trade would seriously disadvantage the weaker partners. Some protection is needed to help the poorer developing countries diversify their economies and develop new products for export. History has taught that from colonial times right into the era of the Asian tigers, the now well-to-do countries helped to build up their economic strength through trade by keeping out cheaper imports.[4] No trade regimes are going to be 'fair', therefore, if they do not allow the still weak trading partners to also use some protective measures – albeit on a transitional basis – against the stronger.

The rich countries should allow this – for example, through the 'special and differential treatment' provisions of the ongoing global trade negotiations – and they should permit transitional arrangements to facilitate an orderly process of export capacity building in the weaker developing countries.

Proposal: A better trade market requires fairer rules and conditions. It means phasing out completely the wasteful and inefficient farm subsidies that many rich countries provide. It means opening their own markets unconditionally to imports of the goods and services that developing countries can produce more cheaply. And it means allowing developing countries selective transitional protection of their own markets to facilitate the emergence of sustainable export capacity.

A better financial market

The World Bank has always been one of the largest donors in financial terms. On its own it has lent almost US$500 billion since its creation in 1944. Back then, it was one of the few sources of development finance, whereas today it represents only 0.5 per cent of the global total (Lerrick, 2005b). But its policy influence is considerably larger than its diminished financial heft.

In the past, the Bank played an important role in supplementing the resources of some of the faster-growing developing countries on their way to graduation to full commercial financing. By the 1980s, however, these countries were weighing the diminishing interest rate subsidy of the Bank negatively against commercial loans that were free of conditionality. Funds are now returning in spades. From a positive flow until five years ago, repayments from Latin American clients to the Bank in 2002–2004 were US$15 billion, presaging a possible end to the era of development financing to that continent. But, in order to remain in China (foreign exchange reserves are US$800 billion, incoming foreign direct investment is US$60 billion per year), the Bank's loans are now being additionally subsidized by the UK Treasury. This subsidy represents a huge market distortion. In 2000, the authoritative Meltzer Report to the US Congress recommended that World Bank lending to countries with more than US$4000 annual incomes per capita should cease, and be phased out to countries with more than US$2500 (Meltzer, 2000).

Today, 70 per cent of World Bank loans by value go to just 12 mostly middle-income countries, all with ready access to commercial capital markets. Persisting with these borrowers allows the Bank to continue being a bank in the orthodox sense, generating a healthy income. But the Bank's real potential value is to the poorest and neediest countries, and it is precisely to this category where it has been least productive and where results have even been perverse because of the development costs of failed programmes. Unpayable debt should be recognized as such, using realistic development criteria and not just elaborate financial formulae, and the debt should be dropped. More Bank programmes to the poorest countries should be in the form of grants rather than loans. Part of the IDA (about 20 per cent) has now been earmarked for this purpose. It should be made 100 per cent for the poorest and most fragile states, through more IDA grants, which should be more equitably identified and managed by a more inclusive World Bank.

The IMF is also a much-changed institution. It had once been envisaged as a world central bank, designed to defend fixed exchange rates among currencies by rebalancing trade surpluses and deficits. All that changed fundamentally in the early 1970s when first the dollar, then the other major currencies were allowed to float freely. Foreign exchange transactions were effectively privatized and there was no longer a global monetary system worthy of the name. After the change, the rich countries soon stopped coming to the IMF for financing.

The Fund was then reinvented and its articles changed to 'exercising firm surveillance' over exchange rate policies. Rather than surveillance, in practice it became an exclusive policing body for developing countries in financial stress, exercising a monopolistic position of bankruptcy judge, lender, adviser and plan designer (Sachs, 1994). Being an exclusive banker of last resort is justified where the results are successful and where there are clearly no alternatives. But that is not the case. During the Asian financial crisis, Malaysia was one of the few countries that did not go to the IMF and that came through relatively unscathed. Argentina overcame its 2001 crisis after eschewing further IMF assistance.[5] At the end of 2005, it repaid all outstanding loans to the IMF (almost US$10 billion) ahead of schedule. There are many other instances of IMF failure and non-IMF success, as this book has tried to illustrate. So while the IMF can help, it may also hinder where other solutions are clearly available but not entertained.

As long as the IMF continues its exclusive status, there will be calls to increase its resources. But liquidity is not in short supply in East Asia where there is much more than a trillion dollars in foreign exchange reserves. These surpluses help to finance the huge trade deficit of the world's largest economy, but the mediation occurs through bond markets quite independent of the IMF. If it is to be restored as a global instrument of short-term financial facilitation and stabilization, the IMF should withdraw from its role as exclusive lender of last (and in practice often first) resort. It should again become an effective intermediary that connects countries to a choice of funding sources, without the kind of heavy-handed policy advice that has often proved counterproductive in the past. It should provide a forum for settling financial problems, but without having to be the bankruptcy court, and without having to provide all the temporary financing.

As far as bilateral financing is concerned, some small progress has been made to dilute donor control by untying aid. In 2001, the OECD/DAC agreed to untie 'to the largest extent possible' aid to the least developed countries. The agreement specifies loans and grants for capital equipment, sector assistance and import support, but excludes technical assistance and food aid (OECD/DAC, 2001b). Procurement will be open to international competition and no longer reserved for suppliers in the donor country. The OECD itself estimates that tied aid costs much more than if goods and services are procured competitively. The sums are not large. Total bilateral aid to the LDCs is less than 20 per cent of total ODA and the recommendation unties part of that total: about US$5 billion.

In the last few years, donors have also agreed to pool the funds they provide to recipient countries, mainly in Africa, through sector-wide approaches (SWAps) and direct budget support. The purpose is to vest aid with more local ownership, enhance coordination and ensure that donors are aligned to national development priorities. In these aims, they have been partially successful. But the preponderance of donor policy is still visible: 'the content of sector strategies tends to show a remarkable degree of consistency between countries, which again makes it hard to detect whether strategies being endorsed are 'owned' by Government, or are echoes of known donor policy positions' (Brown et al, 2001).[6]

Proposal: A better financial market requires that subsidized lending arrangements through the public sector – multilateral (World Bank, regional development banks) and bilateral – cease for the middle-income countries, which are able to borrow on commercial markets. For the low-income countries, and especially the most fragile among them, outstanding debts should be cancelled and replaced either by grants or by concessional loans that are untied, and not bound by special conditions imposed by the lenders. Any 'conditionality' should be based on developmental – rather than sterile financial – criteria linked to human development goals. The IMF's monopoly as a full-service agency for the insolvent countries should end and its role enhanced as an intermediary between borrowing countries and a choice of lending institutions.

A market for technical assistance

Besides a fairer market for trade and finance, a market is also needed for technical assistance – the expertise-and-policy-advice tail that wags the development aid dog. Under pure market conditions, the rich countries would stop prepaying their expertise and advice, and the developing countries would start paying for what they need.

It is an enticing scenario. Technical aid would become truly 'demand-driven' and 'country-owned', as countries – their governments, private, civil and academic institutions – independently seek out the best providers to meet their needs. They would not have to accept – nor would they be able to easily afford – a lot of additional policy baggage if they did not want it. Governments would not have to put in place a whole public department to attempt to coordinate the many (solicited and unsolicited) programmes of technical assistance. They would not have to learn a complex range of different donor procedures for writing proposals, hiring staff and procuring goods. These 'consumers' would have their own procedures. They would not be engaged in the hosting of large numbers of donor missions that they did not invite, nor putting their names to myriad reports required by donors (for the donors' accountability). There would be little duplication and more competition among development agencies.

These are all the things that donors say that developing countries deserve. But it would also threaten the existence of some agencies. Among all the providers – agencies, universities, research centres, consultancy firms and non-governmental entities – the stronger and most reasonably priced would survive, but the weaker, less relevant and more expensive sources (including multilateral agencies) would diminish in number and eventually disappear entirely. At the same time, many new sources would emerge from the developing countries themselves. Countries like Brazil, China, India, Israel, Singapore, South Africa and Taiwan would be among the main beneficiaries – even without the inducements of aid that they themselves provide as donors from the South. The consequences would be far-reaching, but bringing more efficiency and downward accountability to the aid industry should be considered a global benefit.

BUT WOULD IT HAPPEN?

Not yet for the poorest and more fragile states. Aid for them will still be needed, although not on the traditional terms of conditioned patronage. As we discussed in Chapter 5, turning political wills will need benign soft-power engagement. And building local capacity will require smart and discriminating development assistance, combined with targeted humanitarian aid that does no harm. For the conflict-prone states, a peace-building commission is in the making. For the chronically weak and incapacitated, there is no alternative to multilateral channels for aid, able to iron out the distracting bilateral influences. Meeting fragility will be for both the UN and the OECD/DAC – and for some of the regional organizations – their most critical set of tasks by far. Success will also depend in part on the amenability of the superpower.

But yes, it can begin to happen for the more robust states and those of middle-income status. The donors will not simply agree to stop offering aid, but developing countries can start to take more control.

In 2003, India – enjoying rapid growth and flush with foreign exchange earnings of more than US$80 billion – asked 22 of its bilateral donors, providing about one-third of total ODA to the country, to close down their official aid programmes at the end of their current cycles. (The same donors could continue to provide aid to non-governmental bodies.) Although it has since allowed some of those donors back, India has not wavered from its intention to graduate from aid dependence. The country harbours more of the world's poorest people than any other, but the government said 'no', partly because of reduced need, partly because of its desire to build an image as a regional power, and partly because it no longer wanted to be preached at by donors.

Symptomatic of this growing sense of independence was the reaction to the Tsunami disaster of December 2004. India chose not to become part of the humanitarian appeal, and made a significant contribution in cash and kind to the recovery in Sri Lanka and Maldives. Thailand also declined to take part in the Tsunami appeal (although it has not refused subsequent offers of assistance), in keeping with its long-standing decision to decline development aid selectively. From the early 1980s, Thailand was already turning down offers of assistance from bilateral donors, and reducing its dependence on World Bank loans in order to avoid the conditions they carried. From the early 1990s on, other countries like Botswana and Costa Rica have significantly reduced their dependence on externally-funded technical assistance.

More countries are also ready to pay their way in training. In order to boost their levels of expertise, for example, the governments of South Korea, Indonesia and Malaysia have, for many years, been sponsoring large numbers of their graduates to undertake further specialized studies abroad on government scholarships. These sponsored students are then expected to return home and work in the public sector for a specified period.

A clearing house

Under OECD/DAC auspices, there have been many proposals for the reform of technical assistance, designed to give the recipients more independent discretion in their choice of partner. But the reforms have been mostly piecemeal. An exception is the Paris Declaration of March 2005, mainly driven by the donors, but with developing country representatives participating in the launch. It is quite wide-ranging, designed to promote better aid practice. It retains many features of the central-planning technique, with the North agreeing to try to meet certain goals and targets in the provision and management of its aid. The recipient South ('partner countries') will agree in return to budget soundly, procure cleanly and govern wisely.[7]

The Paris Declaration has indicators as incentives for meeting the goals. But there is none for the untying of technical assistance. Some donors – including Australia, The Netherlands and the UK – have begun to loosen the bonds to home sources and TA pooling has been tried – again mostly in Africa – but the results have been mixed. The major part of TA still remains tied to its sources and it mostly comes in kind, rather than cash.

If a true market is to be encouraged, then these top-down reforms will not be sufficient. A common global pooling system, which donors might agree to fund from part of their aid budgets, has already been proposed (Easterly, 2002). Parties in developing countries would apply for funds from the pool and use them to procure development services from the sources of their choice. Alternatively, the pool could issue vouchers to be distributed to poor communities in developing countries, for encashing with preferred partners. These proposals take untying a step further, but they still depend on pre-financed aid from traditional sources and carry with them the continuing preoccupation of donors that their money is going to the countries and the purposes that they consider the more deserving.

And realistically, there is only so much reform that donors can countenance. Donors provide aid because it promises to deliver results of interest to them. But if the aid ties are loosened, and control is lost over its use, the less likely it is to be forthcoming.

To promote a real market, a strong consumer council of developing countries is needed – a southern Development Assistance Committee. Developing countries have long had their interest groups, notably the G77 and the Non-Aligned Group. But the 'Southern DAC' should be run more along the lines of the Northern version, not simply as a debating counterweight to the donors in international forums, but as an independent inter-governmental organization with an agenda to help its members find and negotiate the best sources of assistance. (A possible example is given by the South Centre, a body comprising 49 developing countries that provide it with financial support. Membership has to be approved by the respective parliaments. Its principal role is to discuss common concerns in international negotiations, particularly in the trade field, although it aspires to much broader functions.[8])

A Southern DAC would help what has been described as a 'bottom-up approach to aid reform' (de Renzio and Rogerson, 2005), posing conditions for donors in a kind of inverted Paris process. But its most useful role could be in providing a clearing house or forum of information on all potential sources of assistance, from the traditional donors, but more especially from the huge number of other companies and organizations from every country of the world. It would not be difficult to do. Once a virtual (online) forum is created, suppliers of technical assistance will be motivated to post their presence there.

The forum could also be designed to help developing countries – governments or civil society organizations – find finance to assist in the purchase of technical assistance. The sources are many and growing in number. For example, a recent Google search for 'donating development aid online' yielded over 13 million entries!

Proposal: A real technical assistance market is something that developing countries are ready for and have made the first steps towards. For passive recipient countries to become active consumers of products and services, countries will take their demands to a global marketplace, facilitated by a Southern DAC to act as a consumer interest group, and an online clearing house of information on sources of technical assistance and independent funding.

A CRITICAL ROLE FOR ODA: GLOBAL PUBLIC GOODS

There is still an unqualified need for pre-financed aid (ODA), and that is to pay for the global public goods and services that are fundamental to the fair and effective working of an increasingly interconnected global cooperative system. They facilitate development processes and they can substitute profitably for traditional forms of targeted bilateral aid, which is open to the distortions of influence. Putting more ODA into global public goods is justified on several grounds. First, the private corporate sector cannot be counted on to invest sufficiently in public goods that are primarily of social benefit. Second, many developing countries themselves lack the resources and the incentives to invest in goods of much broader than national benefit (de Velde, 2002).

Global public goods[9] (GPGs) can take the form of negotiated agreements or goods and services. Negotiable global public goods include international environmental agreements and conventions on human rights, gender equality and corruption. One of the most successful conventions to date has been the Montreal Protocol. It was drawn up in 1987, ratified by more than 160 countries, and it specified for all countries steep reductions in the emissions of chloro-fluorocarbons (CFCs), which were steadily eroding the earth's protective ozone layer. It has been successfully implemented and it has been a planet-saver. (To save the planet again, environmentally speaking, will require reductions in global warming, but for the time being there is not the political will to negotiate a successful Kyoto Protocol.)

Many universal conventions on human rights, discrimination against women and against corruption have also received multiple ratifications, but the majority remain unimplemented. A critical complement to international conventions is the promulgation and enforcement of national laws and the mobilization and education of public opinion. Nowhere is this more important than in the control of corruption, on which the effective provision of many other public goods depends.[10] Aid can help here too, if it is allowed to.

Global goods can also be purchased. A good example is provided by vaccines and drugs to treat communicable diseases that are widespread in the developing countries, like childhood infections (among them measles, yellow fever, Haemophilus influenza, hepatitis B) and HIV/AIDS. The Global Alliance for Vaccines and Immunization (GAVI) is designed to improve vaccination rates in developing countries and accelerate the development of new vaccines against common childhood diseases.[11] It could help to save every year the lives of up to 3 million children under 5. Another major health initiative is the Global Fund for AIDS, Tuberculosis and Malaria, 3 diseases which alone kill more than 6 million people every year. Since its founding in 2002, GFATM has raised nearly US$5 billion from public and private sector sources for disbursement as grants to individual countries. The Clinton Foundation has also helped to secure very low-price antiretroviral drug treatments for AIDS sufferers from manufacturers in India and South Africa by guaranteeing a substantial volume of purchases. To be fully beneficial, these GPGs need to be complemented by local capacity to spend funds and manage national programmes effectively. The responsibility for developing and utilizing such capacity will largely rest with the countries concerned.

Collective public initiative can also help to eliminate the global 'bads' that hinder development progress. In Chapter 5, we saw how many developing countries are still held back by conflict and violence, but also how beneficial the establishment and enforcement of peace by the international community can be. In monetary terms this translated into a small ounce of prevention for a very large pound of cure (Collier and Hoeffler, 2004). International efforts can also help address problems of trafficking of people, drugs, landmines and small arms. But these efforts also need to be universal. The Ottawa Convention (1997) to ban landmines has been ratified by 145 countries, but these do not include the largest producers and users of mines.

FINAL WORD

Because of the way aid is currently financed and managed, it is linked inexorably to influence. All manner of aid reforms have been proposed. But donors are as influential as ever, in spite of commitments to improve the relevance and quality of aid through: demand-driven development, country ownership, consultation and participation, fairer trade and finance, debt cancellation, global public goods, simplification and harmonization, SWAps, untying, pooling and budget support... among other things.

In its tortuous way, aid to individual developing countries may help more than it hinders the development process. But that largely depends on the target country. Almost invariably aid-supported development will entail a few backwards and sideways steps along with any forward motion. And along with helping-aid come the hindrances of protectionism of product, service and intellectual property, Damoclean debt, and the many prescriptions of how the richer countries want to make the poorer countries to be more like them.

Aid is still poorly matched to need. For fragile and failing states, hectoring aid will not work. Aid will need to be applied differently and coupled with more enlightened forms of engagement. For all other developing countries, it is the firm contention of this book that they could make faster and more sustainable progress if they behaved more like consumers than recipients, and if their development needs could be met through the more efficient working of markets for trade, finance and technical assistance. Markets are more likely to promote efficiency and competition, and provide developing countries with what they really want. The countries that can follow their own instincts and steadily divest themselves of 'free' aid, are those that will progress furthest and fastest. History is the best witness.

Notes

CHAPTER 1

1   The book was called *Aid and Influence: The Case of Bangladesh* (1981). The authors were Just Faaland, Jack Parkinson and Nurul Islam; the latter was the first Deputy Chairman of the Bangladesh Planning Commission.

2   The HDI is a composite index, developed by the UN Development Programme (UNDP) and computed annually, from data representing longevity, education and income levels. The index ranges from 0 to 1. Low levels of human development are below 0.5, and medium levels are between 0.5 and 0.8. The developed countries are mostly over 0.9.

CHAPTER 2

1   This was the energetic Fiorello La Guardia – it would be hard to envision a similar career transition today.

2   Later the Center for American Relief Everywhere.

3   Three years later, negotiations resumed in Havana to draw up a constitution for an International Trade Organization, but the US Congress opposed it. Almost half a century was to pass before the World Trade Organization came into being, this time with US urging.

4   In 1966, the General Assembly established the UN's own small capital grant facility, the UN Capital Development Fund (UNCDF). Funding of the UNCDF has always been at very modest levels, however, and it is now in danger of being wound up.

5   The Economist's long-term price index for traded commodities (excluding oil and precious metals) in 2005 was less than half its level in 1950 in real US dollar terms.

6   As long ago as 1812, the US had provided humanitarian assistance under the Act for the Relief of the Citizens of Venezuela (Hjertholm and White, 2000). Also, under its 'Good Neighbor Policy', the US had given financial assistance to Latin America in the 1930s. A British precedent was the Colonial Development Act in 1929, through which the UK began extending patronage to its colonies. The Colonial Development and Welfare Acts followed in 1940 and 1945, and the Colonial (later Commonwealth) Development Corporation was established in 1948.

7   It proved to be an ill-judged strategy. It would have needed more than a Marshall Plan to achieve this aim, and a series of foreign exchange crises, followed by more borrowing on near-commercial terms, increased rather than diminished a cumulative dependence on foreign aid.

CHAPTER 3

1   Easterly (2001) is one of the more recent books based on this assumption.

2   See, for example, Harrod (1939).

3   World Bank's annual reviews of project performance audit results (Operations Evaluation Department).

4   Studies pointing to a weak correlation include: Mosley (1987); Boone (1996); Burnside and Dollar (1997). However, a paper by Hansen and Tarp (2000) on aid and growth regressions claims to show a positive correlation between aid and growth.

5   Quoted in Raffer and Singer (1996).

6   Jepma (1996); Morrissey (1993). A study by CIDA in 2001 estimated the additional costs of aid tying at between 15 and 30 per cent.

7   Browne (1990). The proportion has declined over time, however.

8   In more equal (but less typical) societies, however, like South Korea, the benefits of growth were more widespread.

9   Robert S. McNamara, 'Address to the Board of Governors' 25 September 1972.

10   In fact, even the most draconian birth control campaigns had limited effectiveness. (The most significant and sustainable impact on fertility is made by girls' education.) During the Emergency in India in the mid-1970s, people were forced to undergo sterilizations and vasectomies, with very little impact on fertility. A 'one-child' policy was adopted by China in 1979, yet a significant fertility drop had already occurred between 1970 and 1979 when live births fell from 34 to 18 per 1,000 people. Since the introduction of the one-child policy, there has been no significant further fall in fertility. The governments of many other developing countries were largely unconcerned about curbing population growth and some, such as Iran, were intent on accelerating it.

11   Debt cancellation was not permitted by their statutes, and would have compromised their Triple A credit rating on financial markets.

12   For example, Please (1984): 'unpropitious external circumstances were intensified further by the widespread failure of developing countries to take effective steps to assure their ability to meet the debt-service obligations on the large flows of funds obtained from commercial banks during the second half of the 1970s'.

13   The human consequences of structural adjustment raised concerns in other multilateral agencies, including UNICEF. See Cornea et al (1987).

14   Among many other sources on the role of NGOs are Korten (1990) and Clark (1991).

15   Change in Eastern Europe had been spurred by the yearnings for democracy and more open markets, but the break-up of the Soviet Union had been mainly precipitated by a failure of leadership in Moscow. This failure stoked the separatist fires in some (but by no means all) of the Soviet republics and the resulting revolutions were initially of statehood, rather than of democracy or economic reform.

16   UNDP's first national human development report from the region spoke of 'PhDs in the potato plots' of Ukraine.

17   The author knows of at least one instance when the technical assistance coordinator of the government of a former Soviet Union country was invited to Brussels to observe the approval process of the European Commission's programme of assistance to his country, on condition that he did not speak during the deliberations.

18 Article III of its Articles of Agreement specifies that loans are to be made 'with due attention to considerations of economy and efficiency and without regard to political or other non-economic influences or considerations'.

19 There are also problems of defining democracy. Robert Pinkney (2003) has identified five versions – radical, guided, liberal, socialist and 'consociational' – distinguished by such factors as forms of collective or individual representation, degree of state paternalism and respect for individual rights. Moreover, each can degenerate into more perverted types, from totalitarianism (as an extreme form of guided democracy) to immobilism (consociational). Given this range, most developing countries could – and do – claim some democratic credentials.

20 www.globalcorruptionreport.org/gcr2005/download/english/corruption_ research_%20I.pdf

21 A comparison between the two developing giants, undemocratic China and democratic India, is instructive. Adult female literacy in China is almost twice as high: 87 per cent against 45 per cent. On the economic front, federal government tax receipts are 19 per cent of GDP and rising, in India the ratio is 9 per cent. China invests over 40 per cent of its GDP, India 23 per cent. China receives US$50 per head of foreign investment annually, India US$5. China's growth has averaged 9.7 per cent from 1991 to 2003, India's has been 5.8 per cent. It can also be argued that China's labour market is freer and its system of enforcing rights and contracts is more effective (India has a freer judicial system but a nightmarish backlog). It is also quicker and easier to register a new business in China.

22 There were sharp drops in aid from some donors at mid-decade (for example, Japan and Australia, for different reasons), but the total picked up again after 1997.

23 A recent example is Nepal.

CHAPTER 4

1 In his 2004 article, Morrissey is more nuanced, stating that policy-based aid can play a positive role in helping developing countries 'not by dictating choice but by informing and supporting the policy process'. The author agrees. Advice should be free – or it could even be paid for by recipients when they are ready. The most damaging part of conditionality has been its link to coercive lending programmes, a high proportion of which are failures.

2 At the urging of its donor partners, Ukraine embarked on a privatization programme soon after independence in 1991. Many different formulae were advocated, but privatization in all forms remained a highly controversial subject lacking a political consensus. In early 2005, the new government has begun to undo some earlier privatization deals on the grounds that they were based on political favouritism.

3 When working in Rwanda, the author was often solicited by visiting IMF missions for information on the country's defence spending, which was not made explicit in the national accounts. Needless to say, my information was little better than the IMF's.

4 http://www.saprin.org/SAPRI_Findings.pdf

5 The UNDP has an office in Yangon, but is constrained by US Congressional fiat from working directly with the government. However, the UNDP and other UN agencies also work – unrestricted – in North Korea, where the UN has had a major development and humanitarian aid programme for many years.

6   The human costs of the sanctions prompted two UN coordinators in succession to resign (in 1998 and 2000). From 2000, the consensus began to come apart.

7   The countries selected are: Armenia, Benin, Bolivia, Cape Verde, Georgia, Ghana, Honduras, Lesotho, Madagascar, Mali, Mongolia, Mozambique, Nicaragua, Senegal, Sri Lanka, Vanuatu. Morocco has been added.

8   When it became clear that their original timetable would never be met, the World Bank came up with the Interim PRSP (I-PRSP) as a staging post for debt forgiveness and new lending.

9   There have been some notable exceptions, however, as in Cambodia, where – in parallel with the World Bank's three-year PRSP – the Asian Development Bank has supported the country's five-year socio-economic development plan, which has some of the same objectives.

10   This point is raised by, among others, Jim Levinsohn (2003).

11   The government chose Geneva as a venue for the round table. Interestingly, some donors claimed it should have been held in Mali!

12   The author actually witnessed the World Bank president reprimanding his own staff over it.

CHAPTER 5

1   The HDI is a composite index that purports to measure average achievement along three dimensions of 'human development': longevity, knowledge and standard of living. For these it uses proxies: life expectancy for longevity; a combination of adult literacy and gross combined enrolment rates for knowledge; and a normalized calculation of GDP per head for standard of living. The HDI is measured from zero to 0.100 and a level below 0.500 is determined to be 'low human development'.

2   UNDP was actually expelled from Oman because of an observation in a *Human Development Report* comparing the country unfavourably with Costa Rica.

3   The term 'Millennium Development Goal' was first used in a country progress report on Tanzania, developed by the author in February 2001 (Browne, 2001).

4   Even though it was an obvious quid pro quo for monitoring developing country performance, the idea of Goal 8 was strongly opposed by some of the donors at first. One of the most vocal opponents was the UK Secretary of State at the time, although subsequently the British government became more supportive.

5   See discussion in Robert Pinkney (2003).

6   In our table of fragile states, only two – Bangladesh and Liberia – are headed by women.

7   See also Centre for the Future State (2005) Signposts to *More Effective States: Responding to Governance Challenges in Developing Countries*, Institute of Development Studies, Brighton, Sussex:

> Many countries in the South today have formal institutions of representation, accountability and administration built on models transferred from OECD countries, but they often work very differently. They lack legitimacy and effectiveness because they were not forged through a political process of state/society negotiation, and are not supported by socio-economic structures that encourage organisation around broader, common interests. In particular, organisation around ethnic identity rather than economic interests

> *can be problematic because the former is less likely to provide a*
> *basis for compromise, and for identifying positive sum outcomes.*

8 Each year, Burma is visited by about 200,000 people, Thailand by 50 times that number – 10 million.

9 Botswana today has one of the highest levels of per capita income in Africa. But its success has not been entirely unalloyed: it suffers from chronic inequality, a very high rate of HIV/AIDS incidence and one of the lowest life expectancies in the world.

10 Dynasties may petrify or they may evolve. At the time of writing, the daughter of the South Korea dictator Park Ching-Hee (1963–79) is leader of the opposition in a democratic state, and has a reasonable prospect of becoming the country's next president.

11 During the 1990s, an estimated 6 million people were killed in violent conflict, most of them poor and civilian. Some 40 million people were internally displaced or became refugees, 80 per cent of them women and children.

12 The diagram is inspired in part by the analysis in USAID (2005).

13 Also referred to as Myanmar by the regime.

14 In reality, there have been periods during her house arrest when prospects for change were quite positive, and periods during her freedom when matters were worsening.

15 An official report on the Millennium Development Goals produced by the Government of Myanmar, Yangon, in April 2005 claims average annual real growth above 10 per cent between 2001 and 2004, an adult literacy rate of 93 per cent and steadily improving health statistics.

16 According to James Morris, head of the World Food Programme, who visited Burma in August 2005.

17 Hard facts have always been hard to come by. In the early 1980s, the author was the Burma correspondent for a country intelligence service and had to rely extensively on secondary sources.

18 'Sanctions, ostracism and tough talking have clearly all failed to make the slightest dent in the regime's behaviour', said *The Economist* on 23rd July 2005 ('How to save Myanmar').

19 Representatives of donors in Yangon (in 2005) all advocated more engagement, and in some cases expressed frustration with the policies of their capitals – an all too frequent pattern in the aid business

20 The massacres in Cambodia in the late 1970s were even more deadly, but they were not ethnically-based.

21 There is a large and passionate literature documenting the Rwandan genocide, including Melvern (2000); Gourevitch (1998); Keane (1995); Prunier (1995). Most of these sources apportion a large part of the blame for the genocide to the international community.

22 For example, Dallaire (2003); des Forges (1999).

23 OXFAM, Global Campaign for Education.

24 This phenomenon has been appropriately described (by *The New York Times*) as the second global superpower.

25 Except the few that recognize Taiwan. Chinese aid can therefore be seen as a means of buying loyalty.

26 The territory includes two self-proclaimed mini-states in the north: Somaliland and Puntland.

27 GTZ (2001): DfID (2002); UNDP (2003b); The Netherlands Ministry of Foreign Affairs (2005); World Bank (2005).

28 The study found that an 8th mission to Congo (1960–64) had been a failure.

29 In an operation that was the subject of the 2001 film, *Black Hawk Down*.

30 The transition is often difficult. In the course of major humanitarian interventions, many well-resourced international NGOs are present and are inclined to stay on as long as possible, leading to their subsequent expulsion by governments (for example, Rwanda in 1995, Indonesia – post-Tsunami Aceh – in 2005).

31 A very early model for such an arrangement was the Organisation for European Economic Cooperation – later the OECD itself – established by the recipients of Marshall Aid in 1948.

32 Following a one-year extension until 2006 to complete the handover to the new government, the mission was renamed UNOTIL.

33 These institutional arrangements are normally headed by a 'Special Representative of the Secretary General', the experience and qualities of whom are usually critical to the success of the enterprise. Unfortunately, the process of appointment is rather subjective. Knowledge of the country – even the region – and prior experience are often not considered in the selection and in some cases no briefing at all is provided, outside some casual encounters with relevant desk officers.

34 The OECD/DAC Working Party on Aid Effectiveness and Donor Practices set up in May 2003 coordinates donor efforts at harmonization and alignment. See www.oecd.org/dac/effectiveness

35 'Fragile states as a group have not only been under-aided but aid flows have also been twice as volatile as those to other low-income countries, even when changes such as the onset or cessation of conflict and large performance changes are taken into account. Within the fragile state group, flows received by the under-aided countries are the most volatile' (McGillivray, 2005).

36 See Carnegie Foundation for International Peace (2005) *Foreign Policy*, September/October, Washington DC. See also Chapter 6.

37 One of the most glaring examples is provided by the US cotton subsidies, which amounted to US$4.5 billion in 2004. OXFAM has calculated that the economies of the West African countries Benin, Burkina Faso and Mali lose between 1 and 2 per cent of their GDP as a direct result of these subsidies (OXFAM, 2005).

38 Another useful contribution to the debate on donor engagement can be found in Jones et al (2005).

CHAPTER 6

1 http://www.military.com, http://www.globalsecurity.org

2 The rest of the world holds US financial assets of more than US$3 trillion (3 x 10^{12}). This is a potential source of vulnerability, but also means that many countries have a vested interest in the continuing strength of the US economy.

3 US aid was almost 2 per cent of GNI in the late 1940s and above 0.7 per cent in the early 1960s, before the target was invented.

4 Reuters (27 June 2005) 'US defends aid policy', http://go.reuters.com

5 http://www.usaid.gov/about_usaid/usaidhist.html

6 OECD/DAC data (see www.oecd.org/dac/stats/dac/reftables).

7 The secretary of state in the 1950s, John Foster Dulles, called them 'vital to our welfare' (Ferguson, 2004).

8   China in particular was perceived as the greatest long-range threat (Bobbit, 2004). By 2002, however, perceptions had changed and China's president was a guest on Bush's Texan ranch.

9   A phrase coined by Charles Krauthammer.

10 It has been argued that 'had terrorists not attacked America on September 11, Iraq would likely have remained a secondary issue in American foreign policy' (Daalder and Lindsay, 2003).

11 In fact, there were four countries that passed the indicators test, but were not chosen: Bhutan, Guyana, Mauritania and Vietnam and four countries that did not pass the test but were chosen: Bolivia, Georgia, Morocco and Mozambique. The adjustments were probably due to other considerations. Those that were dropped may have been considered insufficiently democratic, while there were special political factors that favoured the four additions (see Lucas and Radelet, 2004).

12 Albania, Burkina Faso, Guyana, Kenya, Malawi, Paraguay, Philippines, Sao Tome, Tanzania, Timor-Leste, Uganda, Yemen, Zambia.

13 Randall Tobias of Eli Lilly, who in 2006 became head of USAID.

14 'The US Government is opposed to prostitution and related activities, which are inherently harmful and dehumanizing, and contribute to the phenomenon of trafficking in persons. None of the funds made available under this agreement may be used to promote or advocate the legalization or practice of prostitution or sex trafficking'.

15 There are other controversies surrounding PEPFAR. In August 2005, it was being alleged that in Uganda, the US programme had been discouraging even the use of condoms in the anti-AIDS campaign. The UN's special envoy for HIV/AIDS in Africa, Stephen Lewis, put it quite bluntly: 'there is no question that the condom crisis in Uganda is being driven and exacerbated by PEPFAR and by the extreme policies that the administration in the United States is now pursuing' (*New York Times*, 30 August 2005, 'US blamed for condom shortage in fighting AIDS in Uganda').

16 http://mepi.state.gov/

17 http://www.whitehouse.gov/omb/budget/fy2004/state.html

18 Despite the fact that the Defense Secretary Rumsfeld has reportedly stated that 'we lack metrics to know if we are winning or losing the global war on terror' (internal Pentagon memo dated 22 October 2003, reported in Fox News).

19 'If we are an arrogant nation, [foreigners] will view us that way, but if we're a humble nation, they'll respect us'.

20 'The army's top brass has no interest in provoking the terrorist mayhem and increased extremism that would certainly follow if bin Laden is caught or killed on Pakistani soil', (*International Herald Tribune*, 12 July 2005, 'Little incentive to nab bin Laden').

21 *The Economist* (3 September 2005) 'An awkward friend for America'.

22 *International Herald Tribune* (20 August 2005) 'US finds few Latin allies in push to limit court'.

23 *International Herald Tribune* (13 October 2005) 'Food aid for Africa languishes in Congress'.

24 http://www.opensecrets.org/industries/indus.asp?Ind=H04. In 2004, an election year, the major pharmaceutical companies contributed a total of US$20 million to the Republican and Democrat parties.

25 For a loan to be considered as 'aid' it must have a 'grant element' of at least 25 per cent. An example would be a loan carrying an interest rate of 5 per cent, repayable over 15 years, with no grace period.

26   Gibson Consulting online, http://www.gravmag.com/oil.html
27   Energy Information Administration, http://www.eia.doe.gov/emeu/aer/txt/ptb0504.html
28   As Fareed Zakaria (2003) describes it: 'the government is efficient in only one area: squashing dissent and strangling civil society'. A rigged presidential election in 2005 does not herald significant change.
29   'In December 1981, when Israel decided to alter the status of the Golan Heights by bringing the area under its own law, jurisdiction and administration, the United States supported a UN resolution condemning this action' (Ferguson, 2004). By 1982 'in their responses to external threats, the Israelis felt under no obligation to consult the United States' (Ferguson, 2004). In modern times, the US has held limited sway over Israel's policy on Palestine. In September 2005, for example, Prime Minister Sharon declared his intention to continue building new Israeli settlements in the West Bank, in spite of US opposition.
30   The Basel Convention has been ratified by all signatory countries except Afghanistan, Haiti and the US, the Biodiversity Convention has been ratified by 190 countries, only excluding the US.
31   Newt Gingrich (13 September 2005) 'A limited UN is best for America', *International Herald Tribune*.
32   US programmes also give the nod to multilateral influence in other ways. Although it chose a bilateral approach to promoting democracy in the Middle East, the MEPI did use the framework of the UNDP's Arab Human Development Report, which identifies four key pillars of development progress: economic, political, educational and women's empowerment.

CHAPTER 7

1   Since 2000, when a pro-independence president (Chen) was elected in Taipei, some recipients got cold feet and Taiwan has subsequently 'lost' five aid clients: Dominica, Grenada, Liberia, Macedonia and Vanuatu. There are now 25 recipients of Taiwanese aid (May 2006).
2   Poland, Hungary, Czech and Slovak Republics met in Visegrad in 1991 and decided to coordinate their entry into the European Union. They all joined in 2004. They are also members of OECD and they have observer status in the DAC.
3   The United Arab Emirates is a constitutional federation of seven emirates: Abu Dhabi, Dubai, Sharjah, Ajman, Umm al-Qaiwain, Ras al-Khaimah and Fujairah. Much aid is determined at the level of the individual emirate and by its ruler.
4   The combined country of Czechoslovakia provided aid – mostly as loans – to 124 countries during the 1980s (Andersen, 2002).
5   Polish Government policy is to increase ODA substantially to over US$200 million in 2006.
6   Albania, Bosnia-Herzegovina, Bulgaria, Croatia, Former Yugoslav Republic of Macedonia, Moldova, Romania, and Serbia and Montenegro.
7   *Zakah*, from the Arabic verb 'to purify', is one of the five pillars of Islam and requires a person to make an annual alms payment of 2.5 per cent of his/her excess wealth, accumulated over one year (from the Islamic Relief UK website).

CHAPTER 8

1 The AAA rating of the World Bank on financial markets permits it to borrow at exceptionally favourable rates of interest, which it can pass on in its lending programmes. Statutory obligations preclude the Bank from ever compromising this rating, so that it can never allow delinquent debts.

2 Over the five-year period 2000–2004, more than US$24 billion of ODA has been in the form of debt relief. The amounts will increase sharply in 2005 and 2006 because of debt cancellation for two of the world's largest oil producers: Iraq and Nigeria.

3 The term itself conveys the inherent bias in development finance.

4 'The numerous success stories among developing countries over the last 50 years, from the Republic of Korea and Taiwan to more recent examples in China, India and Viet Nam, show that, while some trade liberalization may be necessary and beneficial, infant industry protection is vital in the early stages, and trade should be liberalized gradually, in line with the economy's ability to upgrade its capabilities. Success stories such as the Japanese and Korean auto industries, or Korean steel conform to the historical pattern established by almost all successful industrial countries from 18th century Britain onwards' (Chang, 2005).

5 Between 1980 and 2001, Argentina received 33 structural adjustment loans from the IMF and World Bank. These did not prevent the renewed crisis at the end of 2001 and in a subsequent report, the IMF criticized its own policies, saying they had exacerbated the problems.

6 Direct budget support can also be a mechanism of strong donor leverage, as the following example attests. The UK is one of the strongest proponents of direct support and aid pooling, and is the largest bilateral donor to Uganda. In December 2004, the UK agreed to provide a grant of £145 million to Uganda in direct budget support over three years. By the end of 2005, £35 million (out of £40 million) had been disbursed, £5 million being held back because of UK concerns over the halting political transition. A further £15 million was reduced from the next year's allocation because of further UK doubts about the democracy and governance (statement by Hilary Benn, Secretary of State for International Development, to House of Commons, 20 December 2005).

7 For example, 'Partner countries commit to: intensify efforts to mobilise domestic resources, strengthen fiscal sustainability, and create an enabling environment for public and private investments. Publish timely, transparent and reliable reporting on budget execution. Take leadership of the public financial management reform process.'

Donors commit to: provide reliable indicative commitments of aid over a multi-year framework and disburse aid in a timely and predictable fashion according to agreed schedules. Rely to the maximum extent possible on transparent partner government budget and accounting mechanisms' (Paragraphs 25–26, http://www.oecd.org/dataoecd/11/41/34428351.pdf).

8 It 'promotes South solidarity, South consciousness and mutual knowledge and understanding among the countries and the peoples of the South; promotes South–South cooperation and action, South–South links, networking and information exchange; contributes to coordinated participation by developing countries in international forums; fosters convergent approaches among countries of the South with respect to global economic, political and strategic issues; contributes to better

mutual understanding and cooperation between the South and the North and to the democratization and strengthening of the United Nations and its family of organizations' http://www.southcentre.org

9   Public goods are defined by at least two sets of qualities: they are 'non-excludable' (meaning that no party can be barred from consuming them) and 'non-rivalrous' (they are not depleted by consumption) (Kaul, Grunberg and Stern, 1999).

10 'Ultimately, the global public good of corruption control will be provided and durable only if the public demands it and is vigilant and empowered. Central to the process are attractive measures that are difficult to reverse, such as improving education, deepening democracy, and increasing transparency and access to information' (Eigen and Eigen-Zucchi, 2003).

11 More than half of GAVI's funding so far (US$750 million) has been provided by the private Gates Foundation in one of the more spectacular examples of individual philanthropy.

References

ActionAid International (2005) *Real Aid: An Agenda for Making Aid Work*, ActionAid International, Johannesburg

Andersen, L. (2002) 'Changing from recipients to donors of technical cooperation – Central Europe and the Baltic States', unpublished report, UNDP, New York

Andersen, M. (1999) *Do No Harm: How Aid Can Support Peace or War*, Lynne Rienner, Boulder CO

Berg, E. (1993) *Rethinking Technical Cooperation: Reforms for Capacity Building Africa*, UNDP, New York

Bobbitt, P. (2004) 'Better than empire', *Financial Times*, 13 March

Boone, P. (1996) 'Politics and the effectiveness of foreign aid', *European Economic Review*, vol 40, no 2, February, pp289–329

Boyce, J. and Leonce, N. (2001) 'Is Africa a net creditor?', *Journal of Development Studies*, vol 38, no 2, December, pp27–56

Brainard, L. and Driscoll, A. (2003) *Making the MCA Work for Africa*, Brookings Institution, Washington, DC

Bratton, N. and van de Walle, N. (1997) *Democratic Experiments in Africa*, Cambridge University Press, Cambridge

Brown, A. Foster, M. Naschold, F. and Norton, A. (2001) 'The status of sector-wide approaches', Working Paper 142, ODI, London

Browne, S. (1990) *Foreign Aid In Practice*, Pinter and New York University Press, London and New York

Browne, S. (1999) *Beyond Aid: From Patronage to Partnership*, Ashgate, Aldershot

Browne, S. (2001) 'Waiving *and* Drowning? Debt and the MDGs', WIDER Discussion Paper number 2001/111, World Institute for Development Economics Research, Helsinki

Browne, S. (ed.) (2002) *Developing Capacity through Technical Cooperation: Country Experiences*, Earthscan, London

Buira, A. (2003) 'An analysis of IMF conditionality' in Buira, A. (ed.), *Challenges to the World Bank and IMF*, Anthem Press, London

Burke, E. (1793) 'Remarks on the policy of the allies with respect to France', reprinted in *Works of Edmund Burke Part 4* (2004), Kessinger Publishing, Whitefish, MT

Burnside, C. and Dollar, D. (1997) *Aid, Policies and Growth*, World Bank Policy Research Working Paper 1777, World Bank, Washington DC

Burnside, C. and Dollar, D. (2000) 'Aid, policies and growth', *American Economic Review*, vol 90, no 4, pp847–868

Carlsson, J., Chibbamullilo, P., Orjuela, C. and Saasa, O. (2000) Poverty and European aid in Zambia: A study of the poverty orientation of European aid to Zambia, Working Paper 138, ODI, London

Cassen, R. and Associates (1986) *Does Aid Work?*, Oxford University Press, Oxford

Chang, H. J. (2005) 'Why developing countries need tariffs', South Centre and OXFAM, Geneva

Chauvet, L. and Collier, P. (2005) 'Policy turnarounds in failing states', Centre for the Study of African Economies, Oxford (mimeo)

Chenery, H., Ahluwalia, M., Bell, C., Duloy, J. and Jolly, R. (1974) *Redistribution with Growth*, Oxford University Press, Oxford

Chenery H. and Strout, A. (1966) 'Foreign assistance and economic development', *American Economic Review*, vol 56

Clark, J. (1991) *Democratizing Development: The Role of Voluntary Organisations*, Kumarian Press, Hartford

Clay, E. J., Riley, B. and Urey, I. (2005) 'The Development Effectiveness of Food Aid: Does Tying Matter?', OECD, Paris

Collier, P. (1999) 'Learning from failure: The international financial institutions as agencies of restraint in Africa', in Schedler, A., Diamond, L. and Plattner, M. (eds) *The Self-Restraining State: Power and Accountability in New Democracies*, Lynne Rienner, Boulder and London

Collier, P., Elliott, V. L., Hegre, H., Hoeffler, A., Reynal-Queroll, M. and Sambanis, N. (2003) *Breaking the Conflict Trap: Civil War and Development Policy*, World Bank, Washington, DC

Collier, P. and Hoeffler, A. (2004) 'The Challenge of Reducing the Global Incidence of Civil War', Copenhagen Consensus Challenge Paper, Oxford University, Oxford

Cornea, A. G., Jolly, R. and Stewart, F. (1987) *Adjustment with Human Face: Protecting the Vulnerable and Promoting Growth*, Clarendon Press, Oxford

Cortright, D. and Lopez, G. A. (2000) *The Sanctions Decade*, Lynne Rienner, Boulder CO

Cortright, D. and Lopez, G. A. (2002) *Sanctions and the Search for Security: Challenges to UN Action*, Lynne Rienner, Boulder CO

Cotterrell, L. and Harmer, A. (2005a) 'Diversity in donorship: The changing landscape of official humanitarian aid. Aid donorship in the Asia', ODI, Humanitarian Policy Group, London

Cotterrell, L. and Harmer, A. (2005b) 'Diversity in donorship: The changing landscape of official humanitarian aid. Aid donorship in the Gulf States', ODI, Humanitarian Policy Group, London

Cukrowski, J. (2002) 'The Kyrgyz Republic: Developing new capacities in a post-transition country', in Browne, S. (ed.) (2002) *Developing Capacity through Technical Cooperation: Country Experiences*, Earthscan, London

Daalder, I. and Lindsay, J. (2003) *America Unbound: The Bush Revolution in Foreign Policy*, Brookings Institution, Washington DC

Dallaire, R. (2003) *Shake Hands with the Devil: The Failure of Humanity in Rwanda*, Caroll and Graf, New York

Debiel, T. and Klein (ed) (2002) *Fragile Peace: State Failure, Violence and Development in Crisis Regions*, Zed Books, London

de Renzio, P. and Rogerson, A. (2005) 'Power to Consumers? A Bottom-up Approach to Aid Reform', ODI, London

des Forges, A. (1999) 'Leave None to Tell the Story: Genocide in Rwanda', Human Rights Watch, available at www.hrw.org/reports/1999/rwanda/

de Silva, L. (1984) *Development Aid: A Guide to Facts and Issues*, UN-NGLS and Third World Forum, Geneva

de Velde, D. W. (2002) 'Aid Financing for International Public Goods', ODI, London

DfID (2002) Conducting Conflict Assessments: Guidance Notes, http://www.dfid.gov.uk/pubs/files/conflict-assess-guidance.pdf

Dobbins, J., McGinn, J. G., Crane, K., Jones, S. G., Lal, R., Rathmell, A., Swanger, R. M. and Timilsina, A. (2003) *The UN's Role in Nation-Building: From Germany to Iraq*, Rand Corporation, Santa Monica, CA

Dobbins, J., Jones, S. G., Crane, K., Rathmell, A., Steele, B., Teltschik, R. and Timilsina, A. (2005) *The UN's Role in Nation-Building: From the Congo to Iraq*, Rand Corporation, Santa Monica, CA

Easterly, W. (2001) *The Elusive Quest for Growth: Economists' Adventures and Misadventures in the Tropics*, MIT Press, Cambridge MA

Easterly, W. (2002) 'The Cartel of Good Intentions', *Foreign Policy*, July/August, Carnegie Endowment for International Peace, Washington DC

Eigen, P. and Eigen-Zucchi, C. (2003) 'Corruption and global public goods', in Kaul, I. (ed) *Providing Global Public Goods: Managing Globalization*, Oxford University Press, New York

Faaland, J., Islam, N. and Parkinson, J. (1981) *Aid and Influence: The Case of Bangladesh*, Macmillan Press, London

Ferguson, N. (2004) *Colossus: The Price of America's Empire*, Penguin, New York

Fukuyama, F. (2004) *State-Building: Governance and World Order in the 21st Century*, Cornell University Press, New York

Galtung, J. (1969) 'Violence, peace and peace research', *Journal of Peace Research*, vol 6, no 3, pp167–191

Gourevitch, P. (1998) *We Wish to Inform You that Tomorrow We Will Be Killed with Our Families*, Picador, New York

Griffin, K. and Enos, J. L. (1970) 'Foreign assistance: Objectives and consequences', *Economic Development and Cultural Change*, vol 18

GTZ (2001) *Conflict Analysis for Project Planning and Management*, http://www2.gtz.de/dokumente/bib/04-5230.pdf (in German)

Haass, R. N. (2002) 'From reluctant to resolute: American foreign policy after September 11', remarks to the Chicago Council on Foreign Relations, Chicago, IL, 26 June, available at www.cfr.org/publication/4758/richard_n_haass_director_policy_planning_staff.html

Hall, D. and de la Motte, R. (2004) *Dogmatic Development: Privatisation and Conditionalities in Six Countries*, War on Want, http://www.waronwant.org and http://www.psiru.org

Hanspach, D. (2004) 'Visegrad 4 countries and development cooperation: (Re)emerging donors', unpublished report, UNDP, New York

Hansen, H. and Tarp, F. (2000) *CREDIT Research Paper*, University of Nottingham, Nottingham

Harrod, R. F. (1939) 'An essay in dynamic theory', *Economic Journal*, vol 49

Hjertholm, P. and White, H. (2000) 'Foreign aid in historical perspective', in Tarp, F. (ed) *Foreign Aid and Development*, Routledge, London and New York

Hunter, S. (1984) *OPEC and the Third World*, Croom Helm, London

Huntington, S. (1991–92) 'How countries democratise', *Political Science Quarterly*, vol 106, no 4, winter, pp579–616

Ignatieff, M. (2003) *Empire Lite: Nation-building in Bosnia, Kosovo and Afghanistan*, Vintage, London

ILO (1977) 'Employment, Growth and Basic Needs: a One World Problem', International Labour Office, Praeger, New York

IMF (2001) *Conditionality in Fund-Supported Programs*, International Monetary Fund, Washington DC http://www.imf.org/external/np/pdr/cond/2001/eng/overview

InterAction (2003) *Foreign Assistance in Focus*, http://www.interaction.org/cgi-bin/texis/webinator/iasearch?query=Foreign+Assistance+in+Focus&search=ia&x=1 3&y=15

Jepma, C. (1996) 'The case for aid untying in OECD countries', in Stokke, O. (ed) *Foreign Aid Towards the Year 2000: Experiences and Challenges*, Frank Cass, London

Jones, S., Riddell, R. and Kotoglou, K. (2005) 'Aid allocation criteria: Managing for development results and difficult partnerships', Oxford Policy Management for OECD/DAC Learning and Advisory Process on Difficult Partnerships, Paris, http://www.opml.co.uk/docs/jlam_Published_OECD_Report.pdf

Kanbur, R. (2000) 'Aid, conditionality and debt in Africa', in Tarp, F. (ed) *Foreign Aid and Development*, Routledge, London

Kanbur, R. (2003) 'The economics of international aid', http://www.arts.cornell.edu/poverty/kanbur/HandbookAid.pdf

Kaufmann, D. A. K. and Mastruzzi, M. (2005) 'Governance Matters IV: Governance Indicators for 1996–2004', World Bank Policy Research Working Paper 3237, Washington DC, http://worldbank.org/wbi/governance/pubs/govmatters4.html

Kaul, I., Grunberg, I. and Stern, M. (1999) *Global Public Goods: International Cooperation in the 21st Century*, Oxford University Press, New York

Keane, F. (1995) *Season of Blood: A Rwandan Journey*, Viking, London

Killick, T. (1997) *Donors as Paper Tigers: Why Aid With Strings Attached Won't Work*, http://www.id21.org

Knack, S. (2004) '*Does foreign aid promote democracy?*', International Studies Quarterly, vol 48, no 1, March, pp251–266

Korten, D. (1990) *Getting to the 21st Century: Voluntary Action and the Global Agenda*, Kumarian Press, Hartford

Kuznets, S. (1954) 'Underdeveloped countries and the pre-industrial phase in the advanced countries', in *Proceedings of the World Population Conference*, United Nations, New York

Lal, D. (1983) *The Poverty of Development Economics*, Institute of Economic Affairs, London

Layne, C. (2003) 'America as European hegemon', *National Interest*, vol 72, summer

Lederer, W. J. and Burdick, E. (1958) *The Ugly American*, Norton, New York

Lerrick, A. (2005a) 'The debt of the poorest nations: A gold-mine for development aid', International Economics Report, Carnegie-Mellon University, Pittsburgh, PA

Lerrick, A. (2005b) 'Why is the World Bank still lending?, American Enterprise Institute, Washington, DC

Levinsohn, J. (2003) 'The Poverty Reduction Strategy Paper approach: Good marketing or good policy?', in Buira, A. (ed) *Challenges to the World Bank and IMF*, Anthem Press, London

Lucas, S. and Radelet, S. (2004) *An MCA Scorecard*, Center for Global Development, Washington DC

Macrae, J., Shepherd, A., Morrissey, O., Harmer, A., Anderson, E., Piron, L. H., McKay, A., Cammack, D. and Kyegombe, N. (2004) 'Aid to "poorly performing" countries', ODI, London

Mahbubani, K. (2005) *Beyond the Age of Innocence: Rebuilding Trust Between America and the World*, Public Affairs, New York

Mallaby, S. (2004) *The World's Banker*, Yale University Press, New Haven NJ

McGillivray, M. (2005) 'Aid Allocation and Fragile States', World Institute for Development Economics Research, Helsinki, http://www.oecd.org/dataoecd/32/43/34256890.pdf

McNamara, R. S. (1972) 'Address to the Board of Governors', World Bank, Washington DC

Meltzer, A. H. et al. (2000) 'Report to the US Congress of the International Financial Advisory Commission', available at www.house.gov/jec/imf/meltzer.htm#_ftnref28

Melvern, L. (2000) *A People Betrayed: The Role of the West in Rwanda's Genocide*, Zed Books, London

Morgan, P. (2002) 'Technical assistance: Correcting the precedents', *Development Policy Journal*, vol 2

Morrissey, O. (1993) 'The mixing of aid and trade policies', *The World Economy*, vol 16, no 1

Morrissey, O. (1998) *Promises, Promises. Can Aid with Policy Reform Strings Attached Ever Work?*, http://www.id21.org

Morrissey, O. (2004) 'Conditionality and aid effectiveness re-evaluated', *The World Economy*, Volume 27, February, pp153–172

Mosely, P., Harrington, J. and Toye, J. (1991) *Aid and Power: The World Bank and Policy-based Lending*, Routledge, London

Mosely, P. (1987) *Overseas Aid: Its Defence and Reform*, Wheatsheaf Books, London

Netherlands Ministry of Foreign Affairs (2005) Stability Assessment Framework http://www.clingendael.nl/publications/2005/20050200_cru_paper_stability.pdf

Neumayer, E. (2003) 'What factors determine the allocation of aid by Arab countries and multilateral agencies?', *Journal of Development Studies*, vol 39, no 4, pp134–147

Neumayer, E. (2004) 'Arab-related bilateral and multilateral sources of development finance: issues, trends and the way forward', *World Economy*, vol 27, no 2, pp281–300

Nye, J. (2002) *The Paradox of American Power*, Oxford University Press, New York

Nye, J. (2003) *US Power and Strategy after Iraq*, Foreign Affairs, Council of Foreign Relations, New York

OECD (1978) *From Marshall Plan to Global Interdependence*, OECD, Paris

OECD (2004) *OECD Agricultural Policies 2004 at a Glance*, OECD, Paris

OECD/DAC (2001a) 'Poor performers: Basic approaches for supporting development in difficult partnerships', OECD, Paris

OECD/DAC (2001b) 'DAC recommendation on untying ODA to the Least Developed Countries', OECD/DAC, (2001)12/FINAL, Paris

OECD/DAC (2003) 'Synthesis of lessons learned from donor practices in fighting corruption, DCD/DAC/GOVNET(2003)1, Paris

OECD/DAC (2005) 'Survey on harmonisation and alignment', OECD, Paris

Oxfam (2005) *Cultivating Poverty: The Impact of US Cotton Subsidies on Africa*, Oxfam, Oxford

Pinkney, R. (2003) *Democracy in the Third World*, Lynne Rienner, Boulder CO

Please, S. (1984) 'The World Bank: Lending for structural adjustment', in Feinberg, R. and Kalab, V. (eds) *Adjustment Crisis in the Third World*, Overseas Development Council, Washington, DC

Powell, C. (2005) 'No country left behind', *Foreign Policy Magazine*, January–February 2005, Carnegie Endowment for International Peace, Washington DC

Prunier, G. (1995) *The Rwanda Crisis 1959–1994: History of a Genocide*, Hurst, London

Raffer, K. and Singer, H. (1996) *The Foreign Aid Business*, Edward Elgar, Cheltenham

Radelet, S. (2004) 'US Foreign Assistance after September 11th', Testimony for the House Committee on International Relations, Washington DC

Rand Corporation (2005) *The UN's Role in Nation-Building*, Rand Corporation, Santa Monica, CA

Rist, G. (1997) *The History of Development*, Zed Books, London and New York

Rogerson, A. (2005) 'What if aid harmonisation and alignment occurred exactly as intended?', ODI, London, mimeo

Rostow, W. W. (1956) 'The take-off into self-sustained growth', *Economic Journal*

Rostow, W. W. (1960) *The Stages of Economic Growth*, Cambridge University Press, Cambridge

Rosenstein-Rodan, P. N. (1961) 'International aid for underdeveloped countries', Review of Economics and Statistics, vol 63, no2

Sachs, J. (1994) 'IMF, reform thyself', *Public Policy Inquiry*, Palo Alto, Hoover Institution, Stanford University, New York

Santiso, C. (2001) 'Good governance and aid effectiveness: The World Bank and conditionality', *The Georgetown Public Policy Review*, vol 7, no 1

Schultz, T. W. (1960) 'Value of US farm surpluses to underdeveloped countries', *Journal of Farm Economics*, vol 42

Singer, H. (1982) 'Terms of trade controversy and the evolution of soft financing: early years in the UN, 1947–51', IDS Discussion Paper, Brighton

Stiglitz, J. E. (2002) *Globalization and its Discontents*, Norton, New York

Stokes, B. (2003) 'Foreign aid: Heal thyself', Council for Foreign Relations, New York, available at www.cfr.org/publication/5633/foreign_aid.html?breadcrumb=default

SAPRI (Structural Adjustment Participatory Review International Network) (2004) *Structural Adjustment: The Policy Roots of Economic Crisis, Poverty and Inequality*, Zed Books, London

UN Panel (2005) 'A more secure world: Our shared responsibility', UN High-Level Panel on Threats, Challenges and Change, New York

UN (2005) 'In larger freedom: Towards development security and human rights for all', Report of the Secretary General, A/59/2005, New York

UNDP (United Nations Development Programme) (2002) *Human Development Report 2002: Deepening Democracy in a Fragmented World*, Oxford University Press, New York and Oxford

UNDP (2003a) *Human Development Report 2003*, Oxford University Press, New York and Oxford

UNDP (2003b) 'Conflict-related Development Analysis (CDA)', UNDP,
available at www.undp.org/bcpr/conflict_prevention/ca_note%20_2_.pdf

UNDP (2004) *Democracy in Latin America*, UNDP, New York

USAID (2005) 'Service delivery in fragile states: An issues paper', USAID, Washington DC

Uvin, P. (1998) *Aiding Violence: The Development Enterprise in Rwanda*, Kumarian Press, Bloomfield CT

Uvin, P. (2001) 'Difficult choices in the new post-conflict agenda: The international community in Rwanda after the genocide', *Third World Quarterly*, vol 22, no 2, pp177–189

Uvin, P. (2004) *Human Rights and Development*, Kumarian Press, Bloomfield CT

von Weizsäcker, E., Young, O., Finger, M. and Levett, R. (2005) *Limits to Privatization: How to Avoid Too Much of a Good Thing*, Earthscan, London

Weber, M. (1946) *From Max Weber*, translated and edited by Gerth, H. H. and Wright Mills, C., Galaxy, New York

Weisskopf, T. E. (1972) 'The impact of foreign capital inflow on domestic savings in less developed countries', *Journal of International Economics*, vol 2, no 1, February, pp25–38

White, H. (2002) 'Long-run Trends and Recent Developments in Official Assistance from Donor Countries', Discussion Paper 2002/106, IDS, Brighton

Williamson, J. (1990) 'What Washington means by policy reform', in Williamson, J. (ed) *Latin American Adjustment: How Much Has Happened?*, Washington, DC

Wittes, T. C. and Yerkes, S. E. (2004) 'The Middle East Partnership Initiative: Progress, Problems, and Prospects', Saban Center Middle East Memo no 5, Saban Center, Brookings Institution, Washington, DC

World Bank (1992) 'Governance and Development', World Bank, Washington DC

World Bank (1997) *World Development Report 1997: The State in a Changing World*, Oxford University Press, New York

World Bank (1998) *Assessing Aid: What Works, What Doesn't, and Why*, Oxford University Press, New York

World Bank (2005) 'Conflict Analysis Framework (CAF)',

http://lnweb18.worldbank.org/ESSD/sdvext.nsf/67ByDocName/ConflictAnalysis

World Development Movement (2004) 'Zambia: Condemned to debt', www.wdm.org.uk/campaigns/cambriefs/debt/zambia/zambia.pdf

Zakaria, F. (2003) *The Future of Freedom*, Norton, New York

Zhang, H. (2005) 'China's aid to Southeast Asia', Institute of Southeast Asian Studies, mimeo, Singapore

About the Author

Stephen Browne is Director of Operations for the International Trade Centre in Geneva and has worked in development assistance for 30 years, mostly in developing countries. He was the United Nations Coordinator of Development and Humanitarian Assistance in Rwanda and Ukraine and has also lived and worked in Thailand and Somalia. In New York, he was a Director in the United Nations Development Programme and produced the first country progress report on the Millennium Development Goals, coining the term for the first time. He holds economics degrees from Cambridge and Paris (Sorbonne) universities, and is the author of *Foreign Aid in Practice* (1990), *Beyond Aid: From Patronage to Partnership* (1999) and *Capacity Development through Technical Cooperation* (2002), among other publications.

Index